Redefining a Period Style

"Renaissance," Mannerist" and "Baroque" in Literature

John M. Steadman

DUQUESNE UNIVERSITY PRESS
Pittsburgh, Pennsylvania

Published in the United States of America
by Duquesne University Press
600 Forbes Avenue
Pittsburgh, Pennsylvania 15282

Library of Congress Cataloging-in-Publication Data

Steadman, John M.
    Redefining a period style : "Renaissance," "Mannerism," and
"Baroque" in literature / John M. Steadman.
        p.   cm. — (Duquesne studies. Language and literature series;
    v. 10)
    Includes bibliographical references.
    ISBN 0–8207–0221–8
    1. European literature—Renaissance, 1450–1600—History and
criticism.   2. Baroque literature—History and criticism.
3. Mannerism (Literature)   4. Style, literary.   I. Title
II. Series.
PN721.S82   1990
809'.031—dc20   90–2925
                                                                CIP

REDEFINING A PERIOD STYLE

Contents

Introduction

This study questions current assumptions concerning the inter-relationships between our concepts of historical periods and the criteria we commonly employ to define and differentiate varieties of literary style. Of particular concern is the application (or, frequently, misapplication) of terms and values derived from the visual arts to the arts of discourse. Such terms as renaissance, mannerism and baroque are often used so broadly, so loosely, and so inconsistently that they become meaningless; and even when applied to specific literary works, their significance frequently varies widely with individual critics. When applied to such elusive concepts as the "spirit of an age" (or *Zeitgeist*), these terms are apt to prove especially misleading. It behooves us therefore to be on guard against using such terms *in vacuo*, against oversimplifying notions of period style and positing stylistic influences across the boundaries between the visual and verbal arts.

In reexamining the traditional classifications of style and the problem of their applicability to both verbal and visual modes of representation and expression, I shall consider the value as well as the limitations of current classifications of historical periods and period styles and the relationship of style to "world-view" (*Weltanschauung*) and intellectual history (*Geistesgeschichte*). I shall also discuss some contemporary stereotypes of Secentismo: the differentiation of mannerism and baroque, their relationship to Renaissance styles, and their links with *concettismo* and metaphysical poetry. The first chapter centers on the classification of historical periods and their function as categories of sensibility and style; some of the interrelationships between the Renaissance and the Middle Ages are reconsidered. The second chapter explores interconnections between the conventional *genera dicendi* and period styles as categories of perception or expression. The third and fourth chapters discuss supposedly "classical" and "anticlassical" trends in the verbal and visual arts, and the influence of humanist education on Renaissance attitudes toward antiquity and on our

1

own conceptions of Renaissance classicism. The last four chapters analyze recent interpretations of mannerism, the baroque, and metaphysical poetry as period phenomena: categories of style and reflections of the sensibility of the age.

In interpreting stylistic categories as historical phenomena — associating them with the intellectual and spiritual preoccupations of particular epochs, regarding them as modes of perception and expression, reflections of the "world-view" and the sensibility of the age — literary scholarship has often underestimated their continuity with the styles of earlier and later periods. The following chapters are devoted primarily to problems of continuity and discontinuity, tradition and innovation, imitation and reaction in Renaissance literature and art; to analogies between visual and verbal modes of expression; and to the shifting relationships of both poetry and painting to the changing intellectual and social patterns of the sixteenth and seventeenth centuries. How far, if at all, did the literary styles of this period exhibit clearly defined "Renaissance," "mannerist" or "baroque" phases? To what extent are these styles explicable as specifically historical phenomena? To what degree were they *consciously* shaped by traditional theoretical concepts (such as unity and variety in form and content, decorum in style and genre, correlation of *genera dicendi* with levels of subject matter, and the imperatives of reconciling verisimilitude with marvel, and instruction with delight)? To what extent did contemporary poets and painters share the same theoretical and critical heritage: a common legacy of principles concerning the nature and end of their respective arts? In what respects did they significantly differ in theory, and to what extent were they actually aware of these differences? What could poetry and painting borrow from each other, either in theory or in practice? To what degree did theory influence the actual practice of the writer or artist? To what extent can theory aid, or mislead, a twentieth century critic or scholar in interpreting a poem or painting of the sixteenth or seventeenth century?

There would appear to be few simple answers to these questions. The differences between Renaissance and modern conceptions of style are profound, and the apparent resemblances are sometimes misleading. To impose our own categories on the sixteenth and seventeenth centuries is anachronistic, but to accept their critical theories as a framework for interpreting their literature and art also has distinct disadvantages. The rhetorical and poetic theories of the period still centered largely on concepts originally applicable to Greek literature, subsequently transferred to Roman poetry and prose, and ultimately reimposed (with major or minor qualifications, accidental or deliberate revisions) on Neo-Latin and vernacular authors of the Renaissance. The latter might honor the authority of their predecessors, but might differ radically in interpreting their alleged precepts and following their example; and in *practice* they might imitate, alter or disregard them altogether.

Seventeenth century notions of style might be both narrower and more general than our own. "Style" could on occasion refer to the manner of discourse characteristic of a particular author or work, and it could reflect the idea of style as an expression of the character and personality of the writer. "Style" could also denote the practice of a group of writers at a particular period; it could be associated with ideas of cultural as well as specifically linguistic perfection or decadence, but it was far from implying modern conceptions of a period style. Most commonly, "style" denoted levels of discourse correlative with speaker, audience, subject matter and the characters and actions represented. In both rhetorical and poetic theory, style was sometimes equated with speech (*lexis* or *elocutio*) and distinguished from both argument and disposition — though it must, of course, be accommodated to both of these. Although some rhetoricians might have preoccupied themselves almost exclusively with diction and ornament, many of the more influential and authoritative treatises subordinated these considerations to logical and formal coherence. For Aristotle, plot was the most important element in a tragedy, logically as well as chronologically, prior to *lexis* or style. For Ramus, writers had first to turn to logic or dialectics for the choice and arrangement of their arguments, and only subsequently to rhetoric for style and delivery.

For most of our own contemporaries, style would comprise far more than this. In analyzing the style of a particular author or artist, formal disposition or structure might seem the most significant, indeed the essential element, in style — far more important than either rhetorical colors or those of the pallette, than brush techniques or verbal expression.

Similarly, for our own contemporaries, the principle of decorum has lost the commanding position that it once held in Renaissance theory and often in practice. In the sixteenth and seventeenth centuries, the nomenclature of styles depended largely on the level of diction and degree of ornamentation; these *genera dicendi* were closely linked with literary genre and with social hierarchy. Style was likened to a garment; and, like any self-respecting tailor, the poet had to accommodate style to the dimensions of the persons being clothed. The poet had to show due regard for "the fitted stile, of lofty, mean, or lowly" — although perhaps discreetly proposing a loose-fitting garment instead of a tight one, and perhaps skillfully varying or even flouting these principles in the spirit of a carnival ball.

However rusty it may seem today, the notion of decorum is still a key to understanding sixteenth and seventeenth styles; but it is not the only one. Notions of the *genus grande* or *genus humile*, of Attic and Asiatic styles, of Senecan and Ciceronian models; ideas of aureate or plain diction, harsh or smooth cadences, clarity or obscurity, copiousness or succinctness, symmetry or conscious asymmetry; and varying attitudes toward the exploitation of schemes and tropes help to establish a general framework that may enable twentieth century readers to recognize those traits that sixteenth or seventeenth century authors shared with their predecessors and contemporaries. These stylistic concepts are apt to be less effective, however, in defining and evaluating the more individual characteristics of each author's style. Not only our stylistic categories but our notions of style itself often differ from those held by the very poets, painters and theorists whose works we are interpreting.

Aside from these differences between twentieth century and seventeenth century concepts of style, there are also other significant points of divergence: discrepancies between the views of the theorists and the actual practices of the poet or painter, between the stylistic problems encountered in the verbal and visual arts, and between the stylistic categories applicable to different works in the same medium or even in the same genre. The notion of a period style tends at times to blur distinctions between the arts of discourse and those of design, or between these and intellectual or political history. All too frequently it reduces the various styles current during the period in a variety of art forms to a single formula: a monolithic image of the sensibility of the age (even though, to be sure, the critic may define this as a "divided sensibility"). Recognizing the same underlying principles in the history, art and literature of a society, this notion tends to define the period by the style, or contrariwise the style by the period. The same terms and boundary markers suffice to define chronological frontiers and frontiers of sensibility. The idols of the political historian become those of the literary critic, and vice versa.

Though it would be rash to try to dissociate the analysis of poetry and painting from political and intellectual contexts, or to attempt to understand the intellectual history of a society entirely apart from its art, the mixture of disciplines may sometimes become highly misleading; we should be cautious in adapting the concepts of the political historian and investing them with aesthetic significance.

Among students of literary history or the history of art, a bias toward exaggerating the importance of period styles is perhaps unavoidable. By the very nature of these disciplines, one can hardly avoid the stereotypes of political or intellectual history: interpreting stylistic phenomena in terms of the historical process itself, emphasizing patterns of continuity or discontinuity and development or reaction. One encounters linear or cyclical models for the history of styles, comparable to the patterns that earlier generations of historiographers have imposed upon the "world-process." The very attempt to define historical periods or to differentiate one style from its predecessors or successors may result in overstressing the differences rather than the similarities between them. (Arnold Hauser, for instance, noted that Heinrich Wölfflin interpreted the evolution of the "classic" style of the Renaissance toward the baroque as a movement between contraries. In this way, he underestimated the degree to which some of the principal features of baroque style had been anticipated by Renaissance artists. Other critics have raised similar objections to recent analyses of the relationship of mannerism to Renaissance style, and of baroque to mannerism.) All too often, categories of style are interpreted primarily in terms of the historical process, and history itself is conceived largely in terms of dialectics.

The attempt to make the history of art and literature appear more logical than it is — and the history of society logically inevitable — frequently results in imposing a pattern of dichotomies and contraries on the historical process. The intellectual framework that we sometimes apply not only to the history of styles but to history in general has been, all too often, a dialectical schema of statement and counterstatement, action and reaction, influence and counterinfluence: an interaction between logical opposites. This is essentially the familiar pattern of the debate or disputation, with its proofs and counterproofs, its confirmations and refutations, transferred to the evolution of culture. Ciceronian and anti-Ciceronian, Petrarchism and anti-Petrarchism, mannerist and antimannerist — these belong to the same category as "classicism and anticlassicism." In a somewhat different intellectual

context, one encounters the same dialectical schema in the oppositions between Reformation and Counter-Reformation, Renaissance and Counter-Renaissance — or, for that matter, Aristotelian
and anti-Aristotelian currents in Western thought.

Such an approach to literary history — a kind of aesthetic
Manicheism — possesses the merits of clarity and the demerits of
oversimplification. It is altogether too easy to reduce a complex,
and in some respects baffling, system of influences to a formula of
sic et non, and some of these formulas have been comparatively
short-lived. It was once fashionable to polarize literary history in
terms of a continuous dialogue between romanticism and classicism, or tradition and the individual talent, or convention and
revolt. It is still not uncommon to find the development of early
seventeenth century prose represented as a conflict between Senecan and Ciceronian models of style, and the poetry of the age
neatly classified in terms of the rival traditions of Jonson and
Donne (with the Spenserian tradition still just strong enough to
convert an apparent dichotomy into a trichotomy).

In studies of the civilizations of the late Middle Ages and the
Renaissance, this kind of schema is practically unavoidable, especially in view of the prominence of dialectics and/or rhetoric in the
intellectual traditions of both periods.[1] Accustomed to thinking
and writing in terms of contraries — to organizing their thoughts
on a wide variety of subjects in terms of clear-cut propositions that
could be debated pro and con and affirmed or denied, and developing arguments that could be advanced to prove or disprove and
to persuade or dissuade — learned men of the period did in fact
tend to view the course of history polemically — as a strife between
contraries — and to express their opinions on aesthetic as well as
theological problems in terms of dichotomies and opposites. The
schema of the *disputatio* survives in sectarian nomenclature ("Re-
monstrant," "Protestant"), and the influence of the rhetoric of
invective is still apparent in the term "Anti-Ciceronian." Writers
and painters of the sixteenth and seventeenth centuries were apt to
polarize concepts of style — to compare or contrast ancients and
moderns, to correlate or oppose the "rules" of art with the
individual's native genius and freedom of invention, to treat the
example of classical poets as universally valid, scarcely less binding
for the moderns than for the Greeks and Romans of antiquity, or as
dispensable anachronisms, ill-suited for the tastes of a contemporary audience.

The same Renaissance writers were also inclined to interpret the
course of civilization — the arts and sciences, as well as arms and

religion — in terms of clearly-defined geographical and chronographical schemas (frames of reference partly conditioned by presuppositions derived from astrology). The four cardinal directions, the early tripartite division of continents (complicated by the discovery of America), the four ages or four monarchies, the analogy between the days of the week and the ages of the world, could be regarded as historical determinants, affecting the minds and temperaments as well as the destinies of human beings. Excellence or decadence in arms and letters could be regarded as coeval. The arts and sciences, the course of wars and empires, and the progress of sin and religion alike moved from east to west. These are schemas that we can no longer regard as valid, and we might likewise question the validity of the contrasts and antitheses that writers of the sixteenth and seventeenth century used in differentiating their own period from its immediate or remote precursors and their own literary and artistic styles from those of their contemporaries or those of earlier centuries.

The problem of nomenclature can be a source of embarrassment not only for critics of the arts of discourse and design but also for the cultural historian. For the names of styles are transferred to historical epochs, and vice versa. The evolution and transformation of the styles of medieval, Renaissance and post-Renaissance Europe are frequently explained in terms of changing developments in intellectual and social history, and the styles themselves are identified by the name of a period or of a century. Conversely, both the name and the interpretation of an era may be derived from literary or art history. One speaks of the "age of the baroque" as though it were a distinct era, endowed with a distinctive sensibility which found spontaneous and distinctive expression in baroque art. In this instance, a term originally applied to the visual arts and to music and subsequently transferred to literature and to social history has become not merely the name of a "period style" common to art and literature and music alike, but the name of a historical period, applicable to the political and intellectual movements of the time.

The term "mannerism" is somewhat less embarrassing for the historian, for one is less apt to use it as a period term. One is less likely, for instance, to speak of "the age of mannerism," as one is accustomed to speaking of "the age of the Renaissance" or "the age of the baroque." Critics are still disputing the question as to whether a specifically "mannerist" period ever existed and, if so,

precisely when it began and ended. Yet even those who restrict
this term almost entirely to style are accustomed to explaining it
partly in terms of intellectual and political history. The style, then,
was an expression of "mannerist sensibility," an international
malaise, a symptom of a spiritual disease scarcely less pervasive
and alarming than the *morbus gallicus*. Its essential origins and
explanations were apparently to be found in the political and
spiritual crises that befell Renaissance society in the early sixteenth
century and that continued to divide Europe well into the "age of
the baroque." The mannerist style (it has been argued) represented
the disintegration of the classical style of the High Renaissance,
just as the European society in which this new style flourished
represented the decadence and disintegration of Renaissance
society.

In reexamining these and similar concepts, one must take account not only of their ambiguity, but of the tendency of historians
to employ them alternately as stylistic categories, as the names of
historical epochs, and even as psychohistorical designations —
diagnoses of conditions of mind. One writer may be called mannerist because of a "mannerist uncertainty" and *Weltschmerz*, or
baroque because of a subordination of inner doubts to affirmations
of triumphant certitude. Another will be called baroque because of
the uneasy marriage between the sensual and the spiritual in the
writer's poetry. Another will seem baroque or mannerist, propor-
tionately, as the writer resolves or leaves unresolved the inherent
tensions in the work, or because of the way in which the writer
employs antitheses, paradoxes and *contrapposti*. Another will be
labelled baroque not so much on the grounds of style or sensibility,
as on grounds of chronology: because this writer chanced to live in
"the age of the baroque."

Attempts by cultural historians to find a single comprehensive
formula for an age — a single value or cluster of values implicit in
its thought, its science, its political and economic life, its literary
and artistic styles — appear to be in large part a legacy of the
Hegelian *Zeitgeist*. Though this would still be a valid concept
within the framework of Hegelian dialectic, the myth of "the spirit
of the age" has outlived Hegel and his philosophy of history and
survives today primarily among metahistorians and philosophies
of civilization. Although few historical scholars still assume the
existence of a *Zeitgeist*, this assumption has nevertheless conditioned modern theories of historical epochs and stylistic analogies

among the visual and verbal arts and parallels between the arts and sciences.

But perhaps the "ghost of the age" need haunt us no longer. Not a few modern historiographers have consigned the *Zeitgeist*[2] to the outer limbo of vanities where Milton banished Empedocles, and Aristotle the Platonic archetypes. The analogies between literature and art, and between artistic styles and modes of thought, are more substantial. Though some of these parallels may be little more than eidola — apparitions and empty forms of air — others are based on facts or probabilities. These confront the Renaissance scholar with the task of ascertaining their specific gravity, separating intrinsic analogies from superficial resemblances, and weighing valid evidence against windy conjecture, "solid pudding" against critical "pie in the sky." The probability of such analogies depends primarily on the interdependence of the arts, in theory and in practice, rather than on a hypothetical "time-spirit."

Differentiating historical periods and cultures by styles is as common to students of modern European history as to archaeologists and prehistorians. We, too, trace the evolution and diffusion and decline of a society by its artifacts. Instead of gray Minyan ware or al-Ubaid pottery, we examine ogival vaulting, Corinthian capitals, techniques of rendering drapery in stone or bronze or pigments, epic propositions and invocations and epithets, the formal composition of prose sentences and verses or the organization of palace facades and church interiors, the structure of dramatic plots or the arrangement of human figures in painting and statuary. We isolate certain decades as the "age" of Chaucer or Spenser or Milton, contrast the societies and worldviews of Dante and Shakespeare and Dryden, or define the psychology of mannerism and the politics of the baroque era.

We should, however, be skeptical of chronological divisions. They appear to be methodological conveniences and expedients rather than objective realities. The static patterns that we impose on cultural movements — vertical distinctions between epochs, graphs and arcs describing the evolution and decline of ideologies and styles — are all too often our own abstractions and working hypotheses, neither more nor less real than the crystal shells and epicycles that an earlier generation of astronomers projected upon the face of the heavens. Efforts to define intellectual history by military and political events (such as the fall of Constantinople or the sixteenth century sack of Rome) can be no less misleading than attempts to distinguish historical epochs by literary and artistic styles — neoclassical or mannerist or baroque.

It is easy to exaggerate the social and psychological significance of styles and their symptomatic value. As a rule, styles are less spontaneous and more premeditated — less expressive of either individual or collective personality — than the critic or historian sometimes assumes. Like other vogues and modes, changing aesthetic tastes and shifting fashions in literature and art are objectively as well as subjectively conditioned. They are as much imitation as expression. Even though these styles may be more or less appropriate to a particular intellectual or emotional content, better or worse suited to the expression of specific cultural or psychological values, they are not always or entirely conditioned by the latter. In western Europe especially, where the influence of Renaissance Italian modes was frequently retarded and sporadic, attempts to interpret particular styles as the conscious or unconscious expression of indigenous spiritual or social tensions — mirrors to trap the elusive "spirit of the age" — are apt to be misleading. As Roy Strong has observed, the painters and architects of the early Tudor court managed to compress within a single decade, 1530 to 1540, "the artistic development of . . . many decades," moving out "of a late lingering medievalism, on through a transitory moment of renaissance classicism" into "mannerism at its most bizarre."[3] In this instance, the sequence of styles is not the expression of different epochs or of radical changes in sensibility, but primarily an indication of "cultural lag."

The literary historian, like the art historian, can scarcely afford to equate stylistic with social or psychological developments or to interpret changes in manner of expression as an index of basic changes in the attitudes of a society or in the mind of an individual poet or painter. The critic cannot, on the basis of style alone, posit essential spiritual differences between late medieval and early Renaissance artists or writers; between High Renaissance and mannerist, baroque and neoclassical painters or architects; between metaphysical and neoclassical authors; or between British poets who followed French or Italian, Flemish or Spanish fashions, or the indigenous Chaucerian tradition. Still less can the critic afford to overstress the subjective significance of different styles in the works of the same artist.

In many instances, the different "expressive" or subjective content is primarily an illusion effected by the style itself. The author's variations in manner are much more likely to reflect a personal, conscious response to the nature of the subject and audience, the challenge of contemporary fashions, or the traditional literary or cultural associations of a particular style, rather than an unconscious intention of the author. During their apprentice years, poets or painters may experiment with several styles, learning their craft by imitating more eminent contemporaries or predecessors; accordingly, literary critics and art historians must be equally cautious in drawing inferences about the artist's personality, the author's sensibility, or the "spirit" of that age, from the characteristics of the artist's style alone. Milton learned his craft by imitating a wide variety of poets — classical, English and Italian — following Latin models in his Neo-Latin elegies and epigrams, emulating Italian exemplars in his sonnets and in several of his early songs, and combining the motifs of Greek and Latin pastoral with adaptations of the Italian *canzone-stanza* in *Lycidas*. His earlier exercises in English include a close translation of Horace, which attempted to retain (as far as possible) the movement and pattern of the original; lyrics in the Spenserian and Jonsonian tradition; and epitaphs in the fashionable conceited or "metaphysical" style; and a Jonsonian masque. Many of these were apprentice works, and though they reveal a maturing personality as well as developing craftsmanship, one would be reluctant to associate these changes in style with major changes in Milton's own sensibility or in that of his society.

Attempts to define a period style[4] or a personal style may be essential to the literary historian or the art dealer in endeavoring to ascribe authorship and date to an anonymous composition. They are of less value, however, to the practicing critic. The *differentiae* of style, the features which assist one in identifying a particular author or school or period, are sometimes of minor importance for the total design. The general features of style — those abstract principles which one may derive through analyzing particular works — may be indispensable for literary or art theory, but they are not always equally valuable in analyzing and interpreting a specific poem. For the latter, an analysis of the particular treatises and models utilized by the writer and a detailed examination of that writer's selective borrowings and innovations might possess considerably greater exegetical value.

Like other "ideas" of style — such as the diverse categories proposed by Cicero, Demetrius, Hermogenes and their posterity — these paradigms of period styles are often confused with universals. Like other class terms or general ideas, they have been abstracted from particulars, and they may have little reality outside the mind of the individual critic. One cannot theorize about historical periods or large groups of specific works without paradigms of period styles; but (like the older classifications of rhetorical style) they are often too rigid, too stereotyped, too "idealized" to be of unqualified merit in practical criticism.

ONE

Renaissance Boundaries: Frontiers of Sensibility?

In this section I shall consider the diversity of the Renaissance tradition, as opposed to a monolithic and oversimplified conception of the period. I shall discuss the Renaissance poet's ambiguous relation to the ancients, the frequent overemphasis on allegedly "pagan" aspects of Renaissance culture and its secularization of art and learning, the stereotype of Renaissance individualism, and the relations between the Renaissance movement and the forces of the Reformation and Counter-Reformation. Both of these religious movements profoundly modified the literature of the period, but they resulted rather in the transformation of the Renaissance movement than in its disintegration or decline. Many of the salient features that we now associate with late Renaissance (or post-Renaissance) styles like mannerism and baroque have their roots in the culture of the High Renaissance, or earlier, and it would be misleading to regard them as symptoms of a new sensibility or *differentiae* of a new age. Not only is it difficult to set chronological limits to the Renaissance, but it is dangerous to treat even tentative chronological boundaries as frontiers of sensibility.

Like the majority of political frontiers, the divisions between historical epochs are arbitrary but convenient fictions. Artificial rather than natural boundaries, they belong to historiography rather than to the historical process. Wisely patrolled by border guards who are not overly vigilant and customs officials who are not overly strict, these imaginary borders may prove useful to the literary or social historian — deterring medievalists from invading Renaissance territory, and Elizabethan specialists from encroaching on medieval terrain; preventing a specialized understanding of one style or period ("Gothic" or "mannerist" or "neoclassical" or "baroque") from prejudicing the interpretation of another period style. Yet too rigid an insistence on historical specialization can be as discouraging to critical enterprise as a sealed frontier.

Historical divisions are, in fact, more arbitrary than either geographical or chronological divisions; for in the latter there is occasionally some real dividing line: a mountain range, a river, a sea; high noon or sunrise or sunset. For an earlier age, nurtured on theories of correspondences between human beings and the world and believing that the revolutions of kingdoms no less than the cycles of the year were divinely ordained, it was comparatively easy to posit a similar formula underlying the historical process and that of nature. The same patterns were apparent in the history of a kingdom and the life of a fly, the course of a millennium and the course of a day; the difference was primarily one of scale. It seemed natural, accordingly, to impose the same temporal divisions — the four seasons of the year or the seven days of the week — on the life of humanity and the history of the world.

Though these schemes of classification have long since become obsolescent, they still linger on the fringes of cultural history. In neo-Hegelian circles, it is still fashionable to compare the life span of a culture with that of a physical organism. Civilizations (it has been argued) follow the cycles of human generations: birth and death, growth and decline. Longer-lived but no less mortal than men and women, these too are born and give birth, beget and are begotten, displaying the same patterns of affiliation and espousal and attracting the same prognostications from astrologers. They are also endowed with full legal rights as testators and inheritors, receiving "legacies" and miscellaneous heirlooms from the past and bequeathing them, augmented or severely diminished, to their own posterity.

The historical process, like biological processes, resists the attempt to differentiate categorically between its stages of development. Its phases merge imperceptibly into each other; the metamorphosis is gradual and perceptible only over long periods of time. It is only in fiction — Virginia Woolf's *Orlando* and the syllabuses of graduate courses — that historical epochs can shift perceptibly; that one age may end, and another begin, precisely at the turn of the century, while the bells are tolling midnight.

1.

The adolescence of a culture is no less indefinable than that of an individual. "Not yet old enough for a man, nor young enough for a boy, as a squash is before 'tis a peascod, or a codling when 'tis almost an apple. 'Tis with him in standing water, between boy and man." Malvolio's description of Viola-Cesario may, perhaps, exemplify the difficulty of defining and delimiting the Renaissance with any degree of exactitude. An "age of transition" (for the cliché is justified) is as hard to define as the "middle style." Insofar as it is truly transitional, its character and personality result, in large part, less from the emergence of completely new or different qualities than from changing patterns of emphasis or from shifting combinations of qualities that it shares with the preceding or following ages.

The period between the fourteenth and seventeenth centuries has usually resisted attempts to reduce it to a formula — a Cartesian "clear and distinct idea" — or to assign it a definite beginning, middle and end, like an Aristotelian tragedy. In the absence of viable definitions, literary scholars have usually found metaphorical description more attractive — biological images of rebirth and adolescence or maturity, chronological images of dawn or spring or return to a Golden Age, physiological images like reawakening after long sleep, or (pejoratively) metaphysical images like the descent of the mind from the goods and evils of the afterlife to those of this life, and from the glories and torments of the Otherworld to the delights and pains of this world — from *caelestia* to *terrena*.

The transformations in European society between the fourteenth and seventeenth centuries — artistic and intellectual, political and religious — were too complex, and the forces that produced them too closely interrelated, to be reduced to a set of convenient formulas. Clear-cut dichotomies or facile antitheses like "medieval" and "Renaissance" may be useful in limited contexts as learning aids (clarifying and underlining certain facets of the age by radical simplification) or as mnemonic devices (providing an easy schema for classifying and arranging literary and historical data), but they are apt to disrupt the pattern and order of history. While bringing certain tensions of a complex era into sharper focus, these categorical distinctions may blur others that are equally important.

Renaissance authors might hail the rebirth of learning in their own centuries, but they did not usually employ it as a specific or definitive label for their own age. They might, on occasion, exploit it as a topic of encomium in extolling the achievements of their contemporaries, just as (in other contexts) they might deplore with equal eloquence the degeneration of a sound learning in their own day, the neglect of the arts, and the ignorance and barbarism of their times. Complaints of the Muses against the corruption of the arts, and of St. Peter against the corruption of the church, tended to argue from the standpoint of the decay rather than the rebirth of secular and religious learning. The early humanists looked to a future age for the perfection of their classical studies and the diffusion of their pedagogical disciplines — just as Francis Bacon would look to posterity for the instauration of learning and the fulfillment of his program for the interpretation and conquest of nature, and just as the Reformers would look to the instauration and renovation of the church in the immediate or distant future. Cultural rebirth and spiritual regeneration, the renovation of learning and the reformation of church and state, were disparate but analogous concepts. The metaphor of returning to a golden age paralleled the image of a recovered paradise and prophecies of a millennium. The ideal of recovering the original purity — in the human soul, in ecclesiastical doctrine and organization and liturgy, in the laws and principles of the poetic genres, or in the recovery and interpretation of ancient texts — underlies a wide variety of separate, but sometimes interrelated, disciplines. People looked for a restoration or *instauratio* of ideal and universally valid patterns in natural as in humanistic learning, in spiritual as in secular society, in theology and physics as in grammar and rhetoric and poetics. The instauration of the secular arts corresponded to that of theology, and the recovery of the literary or political or ethical standards of the past was analogous to the renovation of the individual believer and the general restoration of humankind.

The metaphors of rebirth and renovation[1] functioned as rhetorical arguments, and the writer's exploitation of these commonplaces might vary with individual polemical intent. Similarly, in different rhetorical contexts, comparison with the ancients could serve as a topic for exhortation or dehortation, and for praise or blame. The argument from comparatives had long been a traditional instrument of demonstrative and deliberative rhetoric. When Renaissance poets compare their patrons to Hercules or Scipio, we do not normally take these statements at face value. We should observe similar caution in evaluating Renaissance comparisons between ancient and modern authors.

Relationships between the humanistic currents of the Renaissance and the forces of the Reformation and Counter-Reformation are too complex to be reduced to a schema of cultural reaction. Erasmus applied the same metaphors — "renewal" and "restoration" — to literature and piety. Francis Bacon stressed the relationship between humanistic philology and Reformation exegesis and controversy, erroneously tracing the origins of Renaissance Ciceronianism to the philological studies of the Reformers:[2]

> Martin Luther . . . was enforced to awake all antiquity, and to call former times to his succors to make a party against the present time; so that the ancient authors, both in divinity and in humanity, which had long time slept in libraries, began generally to be read and revolved. This by consequence did draw on a necessity of a more exquisite travail in the languages original wherein those authors did write, for the better understanding of those authors and the better advantage of pressing and applying their words. And thereof grew again a delight in their manner of style and phrase, and an admiration of that kind of writing. . . . So that these four causes concurring, the admiration of ancient authors, the hate of the schoolmen, the exact study of languages, and the efficacy of preaching, did bring in an affectionate study of eloquence and copie of speech, which then began to flourish.

John Milton, in turn, coupled the rebirth of learning with the discovery of the "true faith," applying to the Reformation one of the principal commonplaces of the Renaissance — the recovery of ancient truth from medieval darkness:[3] "I call to mind at last, after so many dark ages . . . how the bright and blissful Reformation . . . struck through the black and settled night of ignorance and anti-Christian tyranny. . . . Then was the sacred Bible sought out of the dusty corners where profane falsehood and neglect had thrown it, the schools opened, divine and human learning raked out of the embers of forgotten tongues." In "divine" learning, Milton perceived the same rebirth and restoration that the humanists had achieved in "human learning." The same philological techniques they had employed to restore classical texts were now being applied to the Greek and Hebrew scriptures. In both fields, secular and religious, the age was restoring (he believed) the pristine verity of the ancients which the "dark ages" had corrupted. Humanistic philology was, in his opinion, the ally of the Reformation, serving as an instrument for establishing a more reliable text of the Scriptures and ascertaining its literal meaning. Accordingly, in his theological treatise, the *De Doctrina Christiana*, and in many of his polemical works, he relied heavily on philological techniques, attempting to fix the meaning of a particular expression by comparing its usage in several different passages, distinguishing its shades of meaning, and applying his findings to the elucidation of ambiguous proof-texts.

2.

Reformers and Counter-Reformers alike drew on the resources of humanistic philology in the cause of sacred eloquence, adapting the principles of classical oratory and the classical poetic genres to the ideals of the orthodox faith. A critical attitude toward the ethical and religious values of antiquity was by no means incompatible with a love of classical poetry and rhetoric or admiration for the political and military virtues of the ancients. In his *Genealogy of the Gods*, Boccaccio went out of his way to denounce the superstitions of the Gentiles even while extolling the moral doctrines hidden under the veil of myth and allegory. Throughout the period, veneration of the classical arts and sciences coexisted with condemnation of the pagan fables or with attempts to reinterpret them as shadows of Christian truth. Erasmus feared a revival of paganism. Milton delighted in the pagan Muses, yet dismissed them as an empty dream. Similarly, the mid-seventeenth century poet Abraham Cowley could protest that

> Still the old *Heathen Gods* in Numbers dwell,
> The *Heav'nliest* thing on Earth still keeps up *Hell*.
> Nor have we yet quite purg'd the *Christian Land*;
> Still *Idols* here, like *Calves* at *Bethel* stand.[4]

The Renaissance ideal of "divine" poetry, which attracted Neo-Latin and vernacular authors alike, was almost as heavily indebted to the humanist reorientation of learning as the "pagan" poetry of the period, richly embroidered with the loves and vendettas of the ancient gods.

Though it was once fashionable to speak of the "pagan" Renaissance, this element in the culture of the period has been exaggerated. Here again we must not mistake a convenient rhetorical *topos* for historical truth. When Renaissance moralists accuse their contemporaries of paganism, they may in fact merely be condemning the secular and erotic content of these contemporary poems and paintings, or reproaching these artists for portraying empty fables and seductive fantasies instead of solid and useful truths, or — more rarely — attacking a superstitious belief in astrology. Similar tensions between the literary cult of the Gentile gods and the worship of the one true God are apparent in medieval literature. Dante condemns the "false and lying gods," but continues to invoke them. Chaucer exploits the pagan marvellous as epic machinery, but inveighs against the pagan deities and their accursed rites. In medieval and Renaissance literature alike, the essential factor underlying such apparently contradictory attitudes toward classical mythography is the opposition between sacred and profane imagery and subject matter, rather than an antithesis between orthodoxy and paganism. In both periods, moreover, the pagan pantheon and its associated mythography, heavily overladen with allegorical interpretations, had become a sort of poetic shorthand — an armory of symbols and *exempla* for ethical and scientific doctrines. The pagan symbols were the vehicles of moral and physical ideas, furnishing *topoi* for poet, rhetorician and artist, and providing a concrete language in which these commonplaces could be expressed. Finally, the attack on pagan elements in Renaissance poetry was frequently based on literary as well as religious grounds. Was it not inconsistent with decorum to depict a Christian ruler as a pagan god, eulogizing him as Jove or Mercury or Neptune? Did it not violate verisimilitude and probability to utilize the pagan divinities as epic machinery? It is not on religious grounds, but on literary taste, that Carew commends Donne for banishing "the goodly exil'd traine Of gods and goddesses" and for having silenc'd the "tales o'th'Metamorphoses. . . ."[5]

Both in the late Middle Ages and in the Renaissance, the "revival of learning" had been conditioned by social, economic and political factors to an extent that neither scholastic nor humanist writers fully recognized or cared to admit. Both medieval and Renaissance learning were shaped by — and in turn helped to reshape — their social milieu, as well as the character and demands of the political, ecclesiastical and educational institutions with which they were associated. The apparent contradictions and inconsistencies in Renaissance learning resulted in part from conflicts between different institutions and social forces; conversely, institutional and social conflicts were partly stimulated by tensions within and between different learned disciplines. Though some fortunate individuals might be free to pursue knowledge or art for its own sake, the majority of late medieval and Renaissance scholars and artists were compelled, either by their own convictions or by economic and social pressures, to regard their respective disciplines as instruments of church or state and to reflect the values of the social classes and institutions who patronized them.

In view of the political rivalries of the period — between popes and emperors, princely states and bourgeois "republics," between family and civic loyalties, national and regional sentiments, secular and spiritual allegiances, and the rivalries among the learned disciplines themselves, it would seem ill-advised to look for much consistency in the Renaissance movement or to overstress its relationship to one discipline or one social institution at the expense of the others. By overemphasizing the worldly character of the Renaissance and its relationship to the state, cultural historians have tended at times to interpret its religious aspects and its relation to the church as anti-Renaissance phenomena. Renaissance civilization had developed, however, in a social context that included ecclesiastical as well as civic pressures. It could no more evade the demands of the church than those of the state. Though these religious demands were undoubtedly repressive at times, they were also on occasion a stimulus to creativity.

The same institutions that sometimes thwarted the creative artist also extended patronage. The political and ecclesiastical interference that appeared to be (and sometimes was) a major obstacle to humane and scientific learning was ostensibly directed toward the reorientation of art and knowledge, and their evolution along lines favorable to the ecclesiastical or secular "establishment." Alternately extending the carrot and the stick, church and state alike exerted a moderating role on the development of Renaissance civilization, attempting to convert it to their own ends. Subjected to this variety of conflicting pressures, Renaissance art and learning proved, on the whole, remarkably flexible, adapting themselves to the interests of Reformation and Counter-Reformation, to the papal Curia as well as to municipal governments and princely courts, to the spiritual exercises of religious orders and the philological exercises of aristocratic academies. The metamorphosis of Renaissance civilization at the hands of Reformers and Counter-Reformers may have been more drastic than the various national and cultural transformations it underwent during its passage from southern to northern and western Europe; but, like these changes, it is a metamorphosis *within* the Renaissance tradition.

That Renaissance learning should have been subjected to ecclesiastical as well as state supervision was, on the whole, quite consistent with contemporary beliefs concerning the final causes of the arts and sciences. Theoretically, all the learned disciplines were oriented toward the common good of humanity and the felicity or peace of church and state. For Aristotle, the master discipline, controlling the subordinate arts and sciences, had been politics; for the schoolmen, it had been the divine science, theology. Humanistic learning was no exception — and in emphasizing the value of humane studies for moral philosophy and the service of the state, or alternatively stressing the merits of poetry as a form of theology, the humanists had implicitly or explicitly acknowledged the hierarchy of the arts and sciences. Though exponents of different disciplines might disagree on the internal organization of this hierarchy, few challenged the supremacy of politics and theology. In the polemics of the period, the defense of the various arts and sciences had frequently been based, in large part, on their civil and religious value. In theory, at least, they served both secular and spiritual ends and the interests of secular and spiritual authority. That they should receive punishment as well as reward from the very authorities they professed to serve may strike the modern observer as ironic, but it is not incompatible with Renaissance ideas of government and the relationship of the arts and sciences to church and state.

Just as overstressing the allegedly pagan aspects of the Renaissance has frequently led to misunderstanding, an overemphasis on its secularization of art and learning (though partly justified) can also be misleading. Renaissance humanists had frequently exalted poetry as a form of theology; and, especially in northern Europe, humanistic methods had been associated with the ideal of a "learned piety."[6] Though more than a few philosophers had proclaimed the independence of their discipline from theology, many others had consciously endeavored to reconcile rational and revealed truth; some had discovered the outlines of the true religion even in the myths of the Gentiles. Rivalry among the various learned disciplines was no less characteristic of the Renaissance than of the Middle Ages, though it might on occasion appear under different forms. Tensions between theology and other arts and sciences persisted throughout the Renaissance. Like the tensions between logic and rhetoric, these were often an inheritance from late medieval academic conflicts. It would be rash, therefore, to interpret their manifestations during the Reformation and Counter-Reformation as a specifically "anti-Renaissance" phenomenon.

Throughout the Renaissance, the intense rivalry among the learned disciplines, as well as among individuals and schools within the same discipline, contributed significantly to the dynamics of the period, to the force of the movement that (for many persons of the time) seemed to underlie developments in all of the arts. The rival claims of Latin and the vernacular, of eloquence and philosophy, of classicism and theology, are all significant aspects of the Renaissance movement, and to all of them contemporary writers applied the same metaphor of rebirth.

3.

Like the contrasts between the secular and spiritual literature of the period or between High Renaissance and "baroque" styles, the differences between medieval and Renaissance sensibility have frequently been exaggerated. Like other cultural antitheses, this opposition achieves logical clarity at the expense of historical accuracy, oversimplifying and distorting the character of both periods. Nineteenth century critics, influenced by political theories of the relationship of the individual to the nation-state and by romantic theories of art as the expression of personal emotion and the creative artist as a natural genius, tended to interpret the Renaissance in terms of these ideas. The Renaissance had, in their opinion, fostered the rise of the individual and the evolution of the state as a work of art. The Renaissance "spirit" (for indeed many of these critics believed so strongly in the *Zeitgeist* that historiography sometimes became a form of retrospective conjuring or literary necromancy) had manifested itself in the emancipation of the natural human nature from otherworldly obsessions. This spirit appeared (they believed) unmistakably in the frank recognition of the needs of the body and the claims of the world, in the uninhibited delight in sensuous beauty, in the unabashed pursuit of secular glory and fame, in the development of personality and the free expression of personal emotion. Like anthropologists digging for skullbones of the first *homo sapiens*, these historiographers displayed the cranium of Petrarch, proudly identifying it as a fossil of the "first modern man." Had he not frankly avowed his own ignorance? Had he not openly confessed his love and his longing for fame? But Petrarch was merely a precursor, a person of the dawn. In the artists of the High Renaissance, they recognized the species in its maturity. Michelangelo, Leonardo and Cellini represented the *uomo universale* in his perfection. Creative spirits endowed not only with versatility, but with original genius and more than a touch of the heroic frenzies, they were, above all else, strong and forceful personalities. If *sprezzatura* was the mark of a Renaissance gentleman, *terribiltá* was that of the Renaissance artist. The more extraordinary the individual, apparently, the more faithfully he exemplified the "type" of Renaissance man.

Modern scholars are more skeptical of this stereotype of the period. For some of them, these alleged manifestations of the Renaissance spirit are no less a myth than the notion of the pagan Renaissance.[7] Human beings have always craved power and fame and the delights of the senses. The gifts of fortune and the goods of the body were no less attractive in the Middle Ages than in the Renaissance; and in both periods the craving for them was often condemned as vicious. Though the educational program of the humanists was directed towards the perfection of the individual, its emphasis was ethical, and it was usually oriented also towards the good of society. The poet or schoolmaster who endeavored to form the character and train the mind of a gentleman was not only equipping him for a life "according to virtue" in a private sphere, but indirectly training him for public service as well. Milton's educational scheme, for instance, aimed at training his pupils to perform all duties, both public and private, in peace and war.

Whatever innovations in curriculum and methodology the schoolmaster might introduce, the orientation of his course of studies remained essentially idealistic, moralistic and conservative. Cicero's *Orator* had emphasized the moral and intellectual perfection and public duty of the ideal speaker, as well as a mastery of rhetorical techniques. Renaissance treatises on poetics and the visual arts demanded a similar combination of personal and professional excellence on the part of poet and painter; Milton would insist that the poet himself must be a pattern of the virtues he sought to exemplify in others. The accomplishments of Castiglione's ideal courtier are not ends in themselves; they are means to the more effective service of his prince. Manuals for the education of princes and governors reiterate the commonplace that the ruler must first learn to master himself. Only a few political theorists and historians were sufficiently revolutionary to emphasize not how princes ought *ideally* to achieve success, but how they actually *did* achieve it. The overt vilification of Machiavelli — and subsequently of Hobbes — may serve as an index of the strength and weakness of the idealistic tradition in politics. The strength of Marlowe's tragedies results in part from their exploitation (perhaps more than three parts unconscious) of the tension between the ideal public order and a pseudo-heroic defiance of this order by an ambitious and extraordinarily gifted individual. Like Milton's Satan and Shakespeare's Richard III, Marlowe's tragic heroes are heroic outlaws.

An emphasis on order and degree in microcosm and macrocosm alike is, on the whole, scarcely less common in the Renaissance than in the Middle Ages. In both periods the revolt against such order — whether as passion against reason, or as individual against the constituted authority of church or state — is usually condemned as evil. According to its object, it is heresy, treason, or some species of moral vice.

The Renaissance ethic was no more permissive than that of the Middle Ages; in theory at least, passion had to be moderated by reason. Actual practice was, of course, a different matter altogether. Nevertheless, one suspects that poets and their audiences were just as "simple, sensuous and passionate" in one age as in the other. One doubts that Renaissance princes were more promiscuous than those of the Middle Ages or that medieval courtiers found less delight in the poetry of passion than their great-grandchildren.

Similarly, the personalities of medieval individuals must have been just as forceful and as strongly marked as those of the Renaissance. If they seem less individualized to us, more like institutionalized types than clearly defined personalities, it is because we know less about them. The defect lies in our own ignorance, the comparative scarcity of specific data, and (in some instances at least) the limitations of medieval historiography.

And even in the literature of the Renaissance, the individual is often obscured and overshadowed by the universal. For both medieval and Renaissance writers, the concrete example functioned as a form of inductive inference, from particulars to general concepts. Its instructive and persuasive force resided in its relation to a universal idea. In relating the deeds of individual men and women, poet and historian alike tended to focus their attention on abstract norms of conduct, patterns of virtue and vice for emulation or avoidance. Both history and poetry provided useful exemplars of contrasting ethical and political types — the unjust tyrant and the just king, the temperate ruler and the magistrate enslaved by his own passions, the ambitious rebel and the contented sage obedient to the will of Providence. In epic heroes they detected paradigms of wisdom or patience, charity or martial valor. Poetry is more philosophical than history (sixteenth century critics had learned from Aristotle) precisely because it can depict universals.

Though medieval and Renaissance poets might present a fairly wide range of character types, these remained, on the whole, typical rather than individualized. From rhetorical and poetic theory, they had inherited the ideal of decorum — not only in style but in characterization — according to clearly differentiated personal attributes: social rank and occupation, age and sex, nationality, passions, dominant interest (*studium*) and the like. Classical and medieval theory distinguished at least eleven major classes of these *attributa personarum*,[8] and most of them were taken over intact by early Renaissance critics like Badius Ascensius. Similar considerations of decorum underlie the characterization of social types in Renaissance comedy (including the Jonsonian comedy of humors), the vogue of the Theophrastan characters in seventeenth century England, and the assortment of miscellaneous yet characteristic objects with which Flemish portrait painters surrounded their merchants and money lenders, burgomasters and cavaliers. Though some of these writers and artists undoubtedly were interested in emphasizing personal uniqueness, many of them were largely concerned with achieving the appropriate decorum for particular social or moral types and physical or psychological temperaments. What may appear at first glance to be individualized portraiture may prove, upon closer examination, to be merely a traditional but highly specialized form of characterization according to type. The actual focal point of the writer's vision may be centered less on the individual as a unique personality than on the individual as a social stereotype, as a representative of a particular subspecies of that contemporary society.

Like classical antiquity and the Middle Ages, the Renaissance usually attached a universal rather than a particular significance to the injunction *nosce teipsum*. Self-knowledge meant not so much the discovery of the individual as recognition and acceptance of the paradoxical nature and condition of humankind, its dignity and its misery, and its intermediate position on the scale of beings between god and beast. The primary emphasis falls, traditionally, not on awareness of one's unique personality, but on one's participation in the general nature and common lot of humanity. The awareness of self in the narrower sense can, as a rule, be taken for granted; it must be transcended in genuine self-knowledge. Indeed, much of the strength and power we find in Renaissance treatments of this *topos* results directly from the tension between these two kinds of selfhood, from the struggle between the imperatives of the individual ego and those of the human condition.

On the Renaissance stage, as in Greek drama, the tragedy frequently springs from a violation of the demands of human nature and the limitations of the *condition humaine*. In their pursuit of infinites — infinite knowledge, infinite power, infinite wealth — Marlowe's tragic heroes strive to be more than human; indeed, they almost convince us that they have succeeded, until death exposes their mortality. Milton's Samson struts like a petty god; in his humiliation he becomes a mirror of our "fickle state." Lear wrests self-knowledge from adversity by realizing his mortality and learning the misery of the human condition. In *Paradise Lost*, Adam first acquires a knowledge of the dignity and limitations of his position in the scale of being and subsequently a more painful insight into the wretchedness of his fallen condition. In all three of the latter instances, the process of self-knowledge involves a tension between personal and generic consciousness. The former, however, is essentially an awareness of personal guilt; this guilt arises in part from violation of the larger and more comprehensive mode of self-knowledge, from transgression against the nature and condition of humankind.

Though the tradition of self-knowledge tends to subordinate the sense of personal identity to recognition of the general nature and universal condition of humankind, it does on occasion emphasize the role of the individual will. Thus for Pico della Mirandola, the essential dignity of the human being lies in the power of rational decision; by personal free choice, the individual may either sink to the level of brutes through vice or assimilate the self to the gods through virtue.

4.

Similarly, though the taste of authors and their audiences inevitably conditioned the style and content of their poetry and their sensitivity to classical or contemporary influences, this alone cannot account for the principal differences between medieval and Renaissance literature. If pressed too rigorously, this explanation appears to end in a circle or to beg the question; it leaves the grounds for the shift in taste largely unexplained. Moreover, there is substantial continuity in the literary tastes of courtly society between the late Middle Ages and the Renaissance. The mixture of erotic sentiment and chivalric adventure, the introduction of magicians and fairies along with legendary knights and ladies, the techniques of interlacing the various strands of the narrative, the *mise en scène* in castle and forest, the exaggerated emphasis on courtly behavior and the condemnation of churlish manners — these recur alike in medieval and Renaissance romance. Ovidian fables, with their mixture of sensuality and marvel, are fashionable in both periods. There is also substantial continuity in the erotic lyrics of the periods; medieval French forms like the ballade remain popular in western Europe until well into the sixteenth century, when they are gradually replaced by forms that have long been fashionable in Italy, the sonnet and the madrigal and the *canzone*. With the exception of blank verse, the principal verse forms employed in Renaissance narrative poetry are medieval or early Renaissance in origin: the heroic couplet, *ottava rima* and rhyme royal. The Spenserian stanza, in turn, like rhyme royal, has been regarded as a development from English adaptations of the French ballade stanza. Both of these English stanzas were also comparable in length and structure to *ottava rima* and were frequently used for the same kinds of extended narrative poetry, epic and romance.

Just as there are marked similarities in taste between twelfth and fifteenth century humanists and between medieval and Renaissance admirers of Terence and Seneca, there is likewise a decided resemblance between the kinds of secular literature favored by aristocratic circles in the late Middle Ages and in the Renaissance. One should not, however, overlook the significant differences which spring from greater familiarity with the classics. Renaissance romance becomes increasingly subject to the influence of Alexandrian and Byzantine prototypes, and to Renaissance conceptions of epic, pastoral and tragicomedy. With notable exceptions, medieval elements are replaced by elements reminiscent of antiquity or the continental Renaissance — classical or Italian names and settings, pagan oracles and divinities. A court audience capable of appreciating the mythological symbolism of a Valois fête or a Jacobean masque would experience little difficulty in following the pseudo-classical story of a fashionable romance or in decoding the classical allusions in a contemporary lyric.

Within limits, then, the tastes and education of a medieval or Renaissance audience could affect the poet's treatment of classical themes and conventions. Close imitation of the ancients would have had little meaning or value for an audience unfamiliar with classical literature. To some readers it would have seemed merely a pedantic refinement, and in many instances it would probably have run counter to the tastes and expectations of the author's patrons. Perhaps one reason for the success of the humanist movement in Renaissance Italy was that it had effectively trained successive generations of aristocrats and gentlemen in the aesthetic and moral values of classical literature, thereby creating a potential audience and patronage for the writings of the humanists themselves. The education of taste and the mastery of classical style, the cultivation of the audience and the refinement of poetry and oratory proceeded, on the whole, *pari passu*.

5.

In the age of the anti-hero, we can afford to cast doubt on the reality of an earlier and more heroic age. Paradoxically, our doubts may bring us closer to the actual sensibility of the Renaissance. For this was scarcely a "unified sensibility." It was, in some respects, the sensibility of an adolescent age, marked by extremes of confidence and doubt. Alternating between pride and misgivings about its own achievements, between confidence and distrust in its own powers, it was capable on occasion of almost paranoid extremes of ambition and despair. The status of the artist ranged between public honor and insignificance, acceptance as a gentleman and menial rank. The position of the patrons on whom he depended — whether princely autocracies or republican commonwealths — was often unstable. The judges of literary and artistic tribunals were frequently biased or divided; the author or painter could expect the same work to be simultaneously lauded and condemned.

The poet's relation to the ancients was usually ambiguous — and therefore controversial.[9] If the poet disregarded classical models and precepts altogether, in accordance perhaps with personal tastes or those of the audience, then critical censure could result — though the hazards would undoubtedly vary with time and place. French or English writers of the sixteenth century would run fewer risks, for instance, than their contemporaries in Italy or their own compatriots a century later. Their potential challengers — novices in the techniques of the neo-Aristotelian *duello* — would be fewer and less deadly; and their blades heavier and blunter, tipped with less powerful venoms.

The writer who attempted to conform strictly to ancient models would be subject to criticism on literary grounds as well as by moral and religious standards. Close imitation of the ancients in language and style or content could provoke accusations of paganism or Gentilism, charges of pedantry and lack of originality, or censure for violating probability and verisimilitude as well as the ethical and spiritual ends of poetry. If the major writers of antiquity had lived in the sixteenth century (critics could, and did, argue), they would have held very different views concerning the principles and models for poetic imitation. They would have followed the literary tastes and the moral and religious beliefs of the moderns, celebrating the truths of the Christian faith instead of Gentile myths, and exploiting the resources of nonclassical genres like tragicomedy and romance. On the other hand, a Renaissance poet who displayed greater freedom in following classical models could be criticized for failing to observe the rules of poetry.

Whether attempting to imitate the ancients closely or loosely, the poet usually had to face the problems resulting from the historical discontinuity between the civilizations of antiquity and modern Europe — problems of interpreting and evaluating the classical texts, reconciling apparent discrepancies and contradictions, and adapting their form and content, their manner and matter, to the demands of the contemporary language and the tastes and values of Renaissance society.

Spiritually and aesthetically, the Renaissance poet belonged to divided worlds. If literary authority belonged to the ancients, political authority rested with the state and spiritual authority with the church. As the poet's classical models were, for the most part, pagans, their ethical and religious values were potentially suspect; they must be judged and revalued in the light of orthodox doctrine. On this controversial issue, Renaissance moralists were again divided; some attempted to reconcile classical and Christian thought, while others stressed the opposition between them. If Renaissance poets seriously sought to imitate the ancients, they had to take into account not only the aesthetic differences between classical models and classical theories, but also the spiritual differences between classical antiquity and the Christian Europe.

Spiritually and aesthetically, the Renaissance poet was confronted with diverse and sometimes contradictory authorities. To harmonize them without violating the principle of authority — without clearly exalting one authority at the expense of the others, or without substituting individual judgment and taste as the supreme arbiter — was virtually impossible. The poet or critic could reconcile the claims of Renaissance church and state with those of classical poetics — or resolve the conflicts within classical poetics itself — only by explaining away their apparent discrepancies. The variety and inconsistency of Renaissance criticism and the diversity of Renaissance poetry even within the same genre are hardly surprising. Though modern readers may raise their eyebrows at finding Homer and Virgil praised or censured by precepts drawn from Aristotle and Horace, or a modern logician smile at the attempts of Renaissance theorists to force Aristotle into Plato's mold or vice versa, these dialectical shifts were not entirely disingenuous. Despite their unconscious sophistry, they represented a serious attempt to face the problems inherent in the Renaissance crisis of authority — problems that could not be solved effectively within the Renaissance frame of reference.

The uneasiness, the ambiguities, the conflicting values and

irreconcilable tensions that some of us perceive in the baroque are also present in the art and literature of the High Renaissance. These cannot be satisfactorily explained by so volatile and evasive a concept as the "spirit of the age" (which is scarcely an explanation at all) or by clichés almost as nebulous: *Weltanschauung* and sensibility, "optimism" or "pessimism," "worldliness" or "otherworldliness." Cultural historians who contrast Renaissance optimism with baroque pessimism usually ignore the continuity of the *contemptus mundi* themes in Renaissance literature and the extent to which the quality and expression of sensibility in art or literature have been conditioned by the formal and material requirements of subject and genre. The underlying tensions apparent in much of the art and literature of the Renaissance spring in part from aesthetic and moral contradictions — conflicts between the personal tastes of the author and audience, between well-established native traditions and neoclassical aesthetic theory, or between the moral or political values of contemporary societies and those of antiquity.

For a Renaissance work of art was not an expression of nature, but (in theory at least) an imitation of nature composed according to formal principles and "rules." Far from representing a spontaneous overflow of powerful feelings or an unmediated vision of reality, a poem was usually regarded as a conscious artifact; it was literally a "thing made."[10] Fashioned in accordance with the laws of poetics and rhetoric, and conditioned by the formal requirements of style and genre, it was a construct — in the idiom of the modern scientist, a "model" or "paradigm." Imitating an actual person or event — portraying action, passion or character — a poem was also committed, in theory, to imitating abstract ideas and the works of standard authors. A heroic poem, for instance, would not only imitate a heroic action; it would also imitate, in varying degrees, the heroic epics of antiquity and perhaps the more outstanding epics or romances of the moderns. The poet's task, then, was to focus simultaneously on the idea or form of the epic and on the idea of heroic virtue. In the protagonist of the poem — Scipio or Godfrey or Lancelot — the Renaissance poet had to portray not only the traditional character of this historical or legendary hero, but also the idea of magnanimity or temperance or fortitude. In the same figure, moreover, the poet might imitate the traits of other epic heroes or actual contemporary persons.

The variety of objects of imitation available to the poet — living and dead worthies, literary heroes, abstract ideas — gave the poet ample scope for exercising originality and ingenuity, not only in the invention of a subject and the disposition of the plot, but also in the exploitation of allusions — direct or oblique — to earlier works. Sensitive to the complexity of classical and modern traditions, the Renaissance poet successfully combined details derived from multiple (and sometimes discordant) sources into a new and original image, all the more striking because of the inherent tensions among the contrary elements out of which the image itself (like the walls of Cusanus's paradise) had been constructed. On the other hand, instead of fusing or combining such elements — pagan or Christian, ancient or modern, tragic or satiric, heroic or comic — the poet might exaggerate the differences or analogies between them through the method of polarity, bringing their opposition into focus through contrary and antithetical images, like the divine and infernal heroisms in *Paradise Lost* manifested in Messiah and Satan. By thus combining or contrasting elements reminiscent of several overlapping traditions, a skillful writer could not only evoke several different or related traditions, but could also use these allusions to play the traditions themselves against each other, and thus suggest comparison and contrast. Allusions to different traditions could reinforce or undercut each other, providing a basis for ethical as well as literary criticism.

Such innovations were facilitated by the diversity of the Renaissance tradition. Its complexity gave the poet an opportunity to invest each work with equal complexity. Its variety left the poet free to combine conventional elements in new and startling forms, or to invest conventional forms with fresh significance. Its inconsistencies enabled the poet to achieve *maraviglia* or surprise through innovations, while retaining the authority and persuasive force of tradition. Despite whatever restrictions literary theory or contemporary taste tended to impose on the Renaissance poet or painter — particularly at the beginning and the close of the period, when critical standards and tastes were in a stage of transition — these artists possessed comparative freedom to enliven old forms with new materials, or to combine traditional materials in new and original forms. Tradition and innovation could serve as foils for each other. The conventional materials or forms gave additional emphasis to the originality and ingenuity of the poet's own inventions and the wit the poet could display in a particular treatment of commonplaces. Conversely, these innovations helped to "set off" the traditions the poet was consciously evoking.

6.

Critics have sometimes associated this harmony of contraries with late Renaissance styles — *concettismo* and the "pointed" or "aculeate" style in literature, and mannerism and baroque in plastic art. Nevertheless, it is characteristic of the entire period — of early and late Renaissance alike, and of science and theology no less than art and literature. The tensions reflected in Renaissance art are inherent in the age itself and in the very notion of a "rebirth" of antique learning or beauty or piety. Resulting from the imposition of anachronistic standards — aesthetic or moral, religious or political — on contemporary society, these tensions are inherent in the framework and foundations of Renaissance culture. The inevitable conflict between ancient and modern traditions, sacred and profane authorities is apparent in the attempt to reform contemporary literature and society by the standards of the ancient pagans or the ancient church, in the appeal to irreconcilable authorities — Biblical or classical — and in the inevitable revaluation and questioning of these authorities in the process of interpreting and explaining them.

Insofar as the literature of the period mirrors its culture, it exhibits analogous tensions, deriving an unstable equilibrium from the struggle of warring elements and the siege of contraries.

7.

Though it is perhaps true that in literature (as in art) these late Renaissance styles (mannerist, metaphysical, baroque, "conceited" — whatever the historian chooses to call them) were characterized by a greater emphasis on contradictory values and modes of perception or representation, this was in large part the result of the deliberate application of conventionally recognized devices of rhetoric: *contrapposti*, antitheses, paradoxes, the juxtaposition of contraries. These stylistic features could easily be adapted to contemporary Renaissance conflicts, religious or political or metaphysical; but they were not, on the whole, an automatic or instinctive response to such conflicts. The tensions of the late sixteenth and seventeenth centuries may have been different in many respects from those of the earlier Renaissance; but they were not altogether more alarming, more distressing, or more tragic. Nor can one seek the origins of these styles in the epistemological crisis of the late Renaissance and in a divided sensibility.

Writers of the period did intend to portray such conflicts (how could they have avoided doing so?), adapting the supernatural machinery of heroic poetry to the struggle of truth and falsehood, the wars of religion, and national or factional struggles. Yet this was scarcely new; Virgil had done so long before in the *Aeneid*, applying the Homeric motif of rival divinities to the rivalry between Rome and Carthage. The technique of dramatizing contrary concepts by bringing them into direct confrontation — often through personification-allegory — had been traditional in literary and visual psychomachias and battles of virtues and vices. The *Eclogue of Theodolus* had brought the Christian marvelous into direct confrontation with pagan myth through the dialogue of Truth and Falsehood, Alithia and Pseustis. The medieval debate tradition had served as a vehicle for juxtaposing contraries. The schemas of moral opposition underlie the structure of Dante's *Commedia* and the spiritual geography of Purgatory, Heaven and Hell.

In the Middle Ages and in the earlier Renaissance alike, such structural and stylistic antitheses had served to bring spiritual and political tensions and conflicts into sharper focus. In these late Renaissance writers, however, as in the visual arts of the period, there is a more exaggerated use of counterpoint and antitheses, a more obsessive interest in paradox, and a tendency (largely influenced by the cult of wit) to enlist paradox in the service of poetic imagery, and vice versa. The image and the idea or object that it illustrates sometimes belong to such patently disparate categories or planes of being that one is left not only with a sense of the writer's ingenuity (as Samuel Johnson observed of the metaphysicals), but with a strong impression of the discordance rather than the consonance between the figure and its referent, or between tenor and vehicle.

TWO

Categories of Perception or Expression? Levels of Discourse and Period Styles

In this chapter I shall reexamine the relevance of Renaissance conceptions of the *levels* of style as well as the specialized vocabulary of recent art criticism to the complex problems of literary style. For many classical and Renaissance theorists, style (*lexis* or *hermeneia* or *elocutio*) was one of the qualitative parts of rhetoric and poetics, and the primary principle governing its use or abuse was fitness or decorum. Words were the images of thoughts and ideas, just as thoughts were the images of things; the mode of expression (*verba*) should be appropriate to the matter (*res*) that they expressed or imitated.[1]

Like the imagery of cookery and cosmetics, the metaphor of discourse as the garment of thought is of venerable antiquity. Though it has long ago worn threadbare, it still possesses a certain evidential value as a commonplace. In different contexts, this metaphor has been applied favorably or pejoratively, to the use or abuse of rhetorical art, for or against a bare expository style or a figured and sensuous embellishment of naked truth.[2]

So conceived as the garment of thought, styles were differentiated according to the character and level of subject matter, the kinds of oratory (deliberate, demonstrative, forensic) or the poetic genres, the end or purpose of the orator (to teach, to delight, to move), the nature and character of the speaker and the audience. Usually theorists distinguished three kinds of style (high, middle, low), which were sometimes correlated with three different func-

34

tions (to move, to delight, to instruct);[3] but there were also subdivisions of these *genera dicendi*, as well as alternative classifications: the fourfold division of Demetrius and the sevenfold "characters" or "ideas" of Hermogenes.[4] Theoretically, *elocutio* was subsequent to the invention and disposition of arguments or subject matter,[5] and the exploitation of schemes and tropes was regarded primarily as extrinsic and applied ornament. Plain or ornate discourse invited comparison with modesty or ostentation in dress, the garments of the chaste matron or the sumptuously arrayed harlot.

1.

Classical antiquity recognized distinctions in the styles of various authors and regional schools and the superiority of certain periods over others. More significantly, it also possessed an evolutionary theory of styles. A fully developed or clearly articulated conception of period styles in the modern sense, however, had not been achieved. This deficiency inevitably complicated the task of the Renaissance critic, who was confronted on the one hand with a comparatively rigid schema of styles inherited from classical theory and on the other hand with changing contemporary tastes and modes, new developments that could not easily be accommodated to a classical frame of reference. The embarrassment that the critic sometimes felt in dealing with the phenomena that we should normally classify as "period styles" may also become a source of embarrassment for modern critics, insofar as they endeavor to interpret the actual practice of Renaissance poets against the background of Renaissance theory. For the period styles could not as a rule coincide with the traditional threefold or fourfold divisions; indeed, they frequently cut squarely across the conventional distinctions according to subject matter and genre.

These difficulties are compounded for modern critics by the cyclical theory of the evolution and progression of period styles — a notion alien to the majority of Renaissance theorists.[6] The latter could not, and did not, isolate and define mannerist and baroque and impressionistic phases as certain modern historians have done. They could not regard style as the reflection of a worldview,[7] even though they often tended to regard principles of order and harmony and symmetry as fundamental both to the structure of the cosmos (and the various animate and inanimate species that it contained) as well as to the composition of a poem or painting. Many theorists, though, justified variety and multiplicity in the

work of art or literature by the argument that these were characteristic of the universe, and a few writers (like Montaigne) drew an
analogy between a fluid and changing manner or style and universal flux. The majority of sixteenth and seventeenth century theorists continued to think in terms of the traditional levels of style, to
regard these as universally binding laws, and to explain departures
from this schema and the phenomenon of what we would term
"period styles" in terms of decadence, as a reflection of degenerate
or barbarian tastes. Other critics (and these were, it would seem, a
minority) sometimes endeavored to defend such departures as
reflections of the natural genius or *ingenium* of individuals, whose
native talent was superior to the rules of art, or as legitimate
responses to contemporary taste.

Like twentieth century scholars, Renaissance literary theorists
emphasized the expressive qualities and functions of style — its
instrumentality in the expression and imitation of thought and
feeling as well as in adorning them. They possessed, however, a
rhetorical and logical tradition in which the possible means of
argument, the varieties of passion, the kinds of character or personality, and the range of syntactical patterns and figurative language had been methodically organized and defined. Though this
system usually made allowances for individual temperament, natural genius and the force of inspiration, it did not as a rule regard
style as an intuitive projection of an individual or collective
unconscious, as an expression of a culture or the spirit of an age or
of hidden tensions within an individual or society. Emotional or
ideological conflicts were recognized by Renaissance artists and
theorists, but they tended to rationalize and externalize these
conflicts through conventional rhetorical devices such as dialogis-
mus (the inner debate of a character in soliloquy or monologue) or
through external debate. This is not to deny that there could have
been deeper tensions of which a particular poet was largely
unaware and that these may have found unconscious expression
in the poet's art. On the whole, however, Renaissance poets were
acutely conscious of precisely what ideas or emotions they were
attempting to express and of the available means for expression,
and they were equally aware that expression was posterior — not
prior — to invention and disposition, the choice of matter and the
imposition of structural form. Without making due allowance for
the role of deliberate artistry in selection of content, in structure
and in choice of style, the modern critic may easily mistake the
results of conscious craftsmanship for a spontaneous expression of
psychological or historical forces.

Like literary critics, Renaissance theorists of art thought in terms of traditional rhetorical principles — the topics of invention, the principles of composition, the observance of decorum in style and (on occasion) distinctions in genre and stylistic levels. These common theoretical principles must have made it easier for poets to borrow from artists and vice versa, and for practitioners of one art to exploit fresh developments in the sister arts.

2.

In theory, the majority of Renaissance poets approached the problem of style (as did Milton) in terms of "the fitted style of lofty, mean or lowly," the laws of the several poetic species, and the principle of decorum, "the grand masterpiece to observe" (*Of Education*). They were frequently aware, however, of other schemas. Dionysius of Halicarnassus had differentiated the three principal stylistic modes as "the austere or severe; the smooth, polished, or florid; and the harmoniously blended." Demetrius had defined four simple styles — the elevated, the elegant, the forcible and the plain — as several composite types.[8] Hermogenes had isolated seven major "characters" of style: clarity, grandeur, beauty, rapidity, ethos (i.e. moral character), truth and gravity.[9]

In addition to these major categories, Renaissance writers were also familiar with the concept of individual or personal styles and of schools of style. They recognized legitimate variations within a given style and within a particular literary genre. They contrasted the vices or extremes of style — its excesses and defects — with the proper mean or "rule." And they acknowledged the styles of particular authors or periods as superior, and therefore more worthy of study and imitation, than those of other writers and epochs. Humanist pedagogical emphasis on the judicious and selective imitation of major authors, together with Quintilian's warning against limiting their study and imitation to a single writer, sometimes tended to allow writers to employ a more flexible and subjective approach to problems of style and to mitigate and relax the Draconic code or Procrustean framework of theory.

Theoretically, most of these personal and "period" variations in style could be rationalized in terms of the principal stylistic categories and their respective vices; but in practice, these academic distinctions were often a handicap. Renaissance writers imitated, and frequently parodied, a wide range of styles for which the classical categories offered no exact parallel and which could be fitted into the classical schema only with considerable ingenuity and difficulty. Theories of style sometimes stood in the way of immediate response to nuances of style and to echoes (sometimes ironic) of particular works and fashions. In the drama especially, and often in nondramatic poetry, the style of discourse often functioned as a personal attribute. It differentiated various categories of society or temperament, and personal *ethos* or emotion. In the theater, the response of the audience would be strongly influenced by its familiarity with ancient or modern conventions of appropriate style, rather than by the principal *genera dicendi*. Though the individual poet could have found guidance in rhetorical and poetic manuals, it was easier to imitate or adapt the manner and style associated with a particular type of character in contemporary and in classical literature. The ideal of imitation, the pressure of contemporary stylistic modes and conventions, and the demands of parody made it easier in practice to underplay, though not altogether to bypass, theoretical discussions of the principal levels of style.

In an age when language was closely correlated with decorum in character and in genre, any audience would be expected to react spontaneously to the style of a dramatic character — the varied and changeable styles of the moody lover, the manner of the malcontent or satirist, the fashion of a braggart soldier or flattering courtier, the style of an irascible old man or a severe magistrate or a stoic sage — and to react to significant variations in pathos and *ethos* without thinking abstractly in terms of the established *genera dicendi*.

Like the ideal of imitation, the principles of decorum occasionally undercut the rigid classifications of style with which they had been traditionally associated — even though the theorists themselves were not always aware of this potentiality. The "fitted" styles of "lofty, mean or lowly" were usually defined in such general terms (for indeed they were "genera" dicendi) that they resembled ready-made clothing from some mail order house rather than the styling of a custom tailor. Categories of style that originated in the criticism of oratory and had subsequently been imposed upon the poetic genres could not, without considerable qualification and refinement, be applied to the diverse objects of imitation or subjects of expression in Renaissance literature: to moral and scientific concepts of varying degrees of certitude, to a wide range of characters and actions and passions, and to a multiplicity of rhetorical stances, even within the same work. The matter or content of Renaissance poetry and prose was often too varied to be fitted into a threefold or fourfold schema; if writers seriously attempted to mirror this variety in their modes of discourse, they had to achieve a comparable range and variety in their style.

Conversely, just as the traditional schema was too narrow for the representational and expressive functions of style, the effects and affects conventionally associated with the three major styles — lofty, mean, lowly — could scarcely do justice to the range of emotions and attitudes, the variety of actions and passions, doubts or convictions that the writer sought to induce. Instruction, delight, admiration — sometimes regarded as the separate effects of the three major styles, but also regarded as applicable to most modes of poetic and rhetorical discourse — were, on the whole, too broad to be useful; the theorists themselves were frequently compelled to analyze the kinds of instruction or passion or delight appropriate to the different poetic species.

3.

In addition to the frequent discrepancy between theory and practice in Renaissance literature and art and the questionable relevance of concepts borrowed from literary doctrine for the historical development of Renaissance art, there are significant differences between Renaissance concepts of style and the terminology of the modern literary or art historian. Not only is the term *style* notoriously ambiguous,[10] but the same ambiguity often surrounds stylistic designations that were actually current in the Renaissance,[11] as well as other designations that were unknown to individuals of the period but have since become part of the technical vocabulary of the student of Renaissance styles. Literary scholars are still debating the precise meaning and the varieties of the grand, plain and middle styles and their relation to alternative designations: Attic, African, Asiatic; Gorgian, Isocratic, Ciceronian and anti-Ciceronian; Senecan and Stoic. Though current in sixteenth and seventeenth century criticism, these last two terms are themselves ambiguous; and to apply them effectively to the literature of the period, recent scholars have been compelled to redefine them. George Williamson, for instance, found it necessary to distinguish "the Stoic (or Attic)" style from the "Senecan style," separating for analysis what was "not distinguished in fact. . . ."[12] Other literary historians have been forced to rely on an anachronis-

tic nomenclature — "libertine" prose, "metaphysical" style, mannerism and baroque — and the precise definitions of these terms and their relevance to particular authors and works still remains controversial.

An additional problem for the literary critic who is concerned with relationships between visual and verbal modes is the specialized vocabulary of art criticism. In adapting art historical terminology,[13] the critic must not only bear in mind the variety of senses of "style" and the ambiguity of our nomenclature for period styles, but must also recognize the diverse schemas or "models" for the progression of styles current in nineteenth and twentieth century art history. The relationship between "classic" and "baroque" phases and the explanation for their development will usually vary according to the historian's schema: the simplified "cyclic" theory, the Wölfflinian model, the views of Alois Riegl[14] and others. The literary historian cannot arbitrarily transfer these terms to literature without examining the merits and demerits of these various art historical "models" and establishing their actual relevance to changes in literary style.

On the whole, recent art historical (and, to a considerable extent, literary historical) concepts of style bear little relationship to the standard levels of style that dominated Renaissance literary theory. In current usage, designations for period styles in the visual arts usually refer to the handling of line, space, form and the like, and are often employed in some modification of Heinrich Wölfflin's schema; personal or individual styles, on the other hand, are normally conceived in terms of the peculiarities of technique that distinguish the work of particular artists from that of their contemporaries (all of which may belong to the same period style) or differentiate various phases of an artist's own development. As a rule, both period styles and individual variants are regarded as largely independent of subject matter and themes. Finally, in recent years the tendency to interpret stylistic qualities (in art and literature alike) as expressions of large-scale social and intellectual movements or attitudes, as reflections of the psychology or epistemology or metaphysics of an age — its sensibility and feeling, its "way of seeing," or its worldview — is more pronounced on the part of cultural and literary historians than among students of art history.

A further difficulty is the relationship between formal structure and verbal expression. Most Renaissance literary theorists distinguished between *elocutio* (or style) and *dispositio* (or formal organization), though they acknowledged the interdependence of these concepts. In twentieth century literary theory, on the other hand, structural composition has frequently been regarded as one of the most significant and revelatory aspects of style. The influence of *Gestalt* psychology and depth psychology, along with the techniques of structural linguistics and structural anthropology, has, in turn, increased the gap between our own critical approaches and those of the Renaissance. For the majority of Renaissance theorists, the formal structure of a literary work was not an intuitive projection on the part of the individual poet or of the collective unconscious of that age, but an integral part of a highly rationalized poetic or rhetorical art. In poetry, it was an essential factor in mimesis, a means of imitating an action and investing this imitation with organic unity. In rhetoric, the formal structure was a means of achieving real or apparent probability, and of persuading most effectively. It was not a spontaneous projection, not a way of seeing or knowing, but a way of making an audience see and know. It served primarily as a frame of reference for communication rather than as a mode of cognition for the individual poet. The formal structure of a dramatic plot or of an oration was a consciously achieved construction or artifact, and the secondary structures — tensions between imagistic modes (similes, metaphors, allegories) and their conceptual referents, or tensions between contrary ideas (virtues and vices, nature and grace, fortune and providence, etc.) were often the result of deliberate artistry, traditional rhetorical means of clarifying and defining a concept either by analogy and comparison or by contrast and opposition.

4.

Though the *genera dicendi* had been primarily correlated with different literary kinds, they were also applicable to the visual arts. Stylistic considerations based on the social rank of characters or audience and levels of subject matter concerned the painter as well as the poet, especially when the painter found occasion to portray the same historical or legendary events or to celebrate the same patron. In literary theory, distinctions in style and genre had their correlatives in flora and fauna (as in the medieval "wheel of Virgil") or in dramatic settings and scene designs (the Vitruvian décor of tragedy, comedy and satyr-play). The rhetoric of encomium and the resources of the grand style appeared in triumphal arches, painted apotheoses, and monumental tombs no less than in demonstrative oratory and poetic eulogies. In portraying heroic virtue, the painter — no less than the poet — was committed to an idealized conception of art. Insofar as style itself was the garment of thought — whether words and rhetorical figures or lines and colors were the medium for communicating subject matter — stylistic decorum acquired epistemological significance. Like an imperfect mirror, an inappropriate style produced a false image, distorting and obscuring the true and essential nature of its subject.

Like other stylistic categories, the *genera dicendi* provide too narrow a frame of reference and too arbitrary a canon for literary criticism; they are no less awkward, and certainly far more restrictive, for the art historian. Frequently these categories appear too rigid and insensitive to inform critical analysis of works composed under their influence, and they are partly responsible for the saline flats and sterile deserts that the modern reader encounters in sixteenth and seventeenth century criticism of particular authors and individual works.

Nevertheless, though one cannot rely on the *genera dicendi* absolutely, any more than one can depend uncritically on Renaissance stereotypes of tragedy or epic or pastoral, one cannot ignore these stylistic distinctions. They conditioned (though they did not determine) differences between "ideal," "naturalistic" and "realistic" art; and, though the latter stylistic modes cannot be reduced to so simple a formula as that posited by the *genera dicendi*, these modes did not develop in isolation from traditional categories of stylistic level and decorum. The differences between a Dutch landscape or kitchen scene and some Italian baroque apotheosis or heroic combat are not altogether explicable in terms of national traditions or period styles. They are partly attributable to the notion of decorum, and the accommodation of style to subject and class.[15] The contrast between bourgeois or agrarian realism and courtly or romantic idealism is inherent in medieval and Renaissance distinctions between comic or satiric modes on the one hand and tragic or heroic on the other. As the author of *Don Quixote* recognized, windmills and barbers' basins and peasant girls are out of place in a chivalric romance, and only a madman would confound plebeian reality with romantic fantasy.

A meticulous observance of decorum in personal attributes (*attributa personarum*) according to age and sex and profession occurs not only in literature and oratory but also in pictorial art — sometimes cluttering up the foreground with minute but significant detail. In certain respects, this painstakingly "verisimilar" mode of imitation parallels the methods of bourgeois comedy and the Theophrastan character sketch. It fosters the illusion of individuality through a scrupulous delineation of conventional class-attributes, building up an appropriate verbal or visual portrait through the accumulation of details associated with recognized categories of character. Using traditional social and emotional categories as well as personal idiosyncrasies as a point of departure, this method often turns out to be no less "idealistic" than "realistic." The norms of the class form a basis for judging the individual — whether favorably or unfavorably — as in the verbal portraiture of Chaucer's pilgrims. On the other hand, the heroic mode, in art and literature alike, requires a less particularized style, a conscious departure from the ordinary and familiar. Minute imitation of detail, in art and literature alike, could therefore lower and depress the elevated style. Caravaggio's critics deplored his realism as "low" and "vulgar"; it converted the heroes of the faith and the saintly personages of Scripture into Neapolitan peasants.

Though it would be unwise to press the analogy between literary and plastic styles too far (since, in large part, major innovations and developments in style have been conditioned by technical problems peculiar to verbal or visual presentation), one should bear in mind the strongly "idealistic" emphasis underlying pictorial as well as poetic conceptions of the grand style, the heroic or tragic subjects with which this style was associated, and its characteristic "affects" of pity or fear or admiration. Torquato Tasso endeavored to reconcile the demand for admiration with the requirements of probability and verisimilitude through the Christian marvelous. A later generation of art critics faced a similar problem, insisting on the dual imperative of fidelity to the abstract idea and truth to nature, censuring their mannerist predecessors, who had distorted nature in the interests of artistic technique and sacrificed verisimilitude to marvel. Whereas the work of the "mannerists" seemed fantastic, capricious and bizarre, the artists of the high baroque sought magnificence without violating decorum, combining admiration with studied gravity, exploiting reason to imitate passion, exploiting the devices of art to stimulate ecstasy, achieving elevation largely through the understanding rather than by fancy.

5.

In the late Renaissance, one encounters a conscious effort on the part of poets to heighten the grand style by increasing its artificiality and reforming the traditional genres, in the interests of greater dignity and structural unity. This is apparent in Della Casa's tightly integrated sonnets, with their Latinate inversions of normal word order and their deliberate creation of tensions between syntactical units and verse-patterns, in Tasso's heroic sonnets and his blank verse epic on the creation of the world, and in the poetry of Milton, who had been strongly influenced by both poets.[16] Adapting the fourfold categories of Demetrius's treatise *On Style* to the requirements of the poet, Tasso had distinguished between the grave or forceful style of tragedy, the magnificent or rugged (*aspro*) style of heroic poetry, the ornate or graceful style suitable for romantic or lyric passages and the themes of love and beauty, and the plain or familiar style. The first was associated with the effect of passion, the second with wonder, the third with delight, and the fourth with instruction.[17]

In Tasso's adaptation of Demetrius's scheme, the "decorated" style is not the *genus grande* of epic and tragedy, but a style more appropriate for descriptions of gardens, nightingales and flowers, and the dalliance of lovers. Within a particular genre, poets might vary their style according to their subject matter, but these subsidiary or secondary modes had to be accommodated to the primary style. The "tragic" style would exhibit different characteristics in epic or comedy or tragedy, and the graceful style would not be identical in lyric and heroic poetry. For Armida's bower and the exploits of the battlefield, for the revolt of the angels and the delights of Eden, a heroic poet would not employ precisely the same style. One might expect similar variations on the part of painters. Though it is difficult to trace the influence of Demetrius's and Tasso's conceptions of style on the visual arts, some painters must have read their treatises and recognized the distinction between *asprezza* as the basis of the magnificent style and a source of marvel, and the decorative ornament of the graceful style. In addition to the "grace" that the fifteenth century painter Alberti had sought as a source of delight, a later generation of artists would look specifically for the qualities that suggested grandeur and aroused wonder.

Longinus's treatise *De sublimitate* was first published in 1554. Though its influence on sixteenth century and early seventeenth century critical thought is sometimes difficult to trace with precision, it contained doctrines that would eventually lead to further modifications in the concept of the grand style. Of the five sources of sublimity in style, the two most important — "a firm grasp of ideas" and "vigorous and inspired emotion" — are primarily natural gifts, while the others belong to art. "Excellence of style is the concomitant of a great soul," and sometimes, "without a word being uttered, a bare conception amazes us because of the nobility of soul it expresses. . . ." Longinus is concerned specifically with the qualities of style that produce admiration. "Genius does not merely persuade an audience but lifts it to ecstasy. The astonishing is always of greater force than the persuasive or the pleasing. . . ."

Though this concern for the marvelous can also be found in the so-called "mannerist" poets and painters, Longinus's emphasis on nature and his attacks on stylistic affectations and the quest for novelty anticipate the criticism that neoclassical critics would level against mannerist art or metaphysical poetry. Condemning "pseudo-tragic" bombast and ill-timed pathos, he censures the puns of Plato and Herodotus as frigid and "cheap ornaments" and criticizes extravagant metaphors like calling water a "sober god." Though he regards the unusual and exceptional as a source of wonder, he condemns the "craze for novelty" responsible for so many "gaudy weeds . . . in literary style. . . ."[18] He recommends the "imitation and emulation of the great prose writers and poets of antiquity," and stresses the force of "imaginative pictures" (or "poetic images") in "producing massiveness, grandeur and energy." He associates imagination with emotional excitement and vividness: "In your enthusiasm and strong feeling you seem to see what you speak of and put it before the eyes of your audience; in poetry it strives to strike the hearer with a sudden shock, but in oratory it seeks vividness." He praises Demosthenes for "nervous energy" and "intense and violent feeling"; he "may be likened to a tornado or a thunderbolt because of the way he burns and scatters everything with his vehemence, speed, power and energy," whereas Cicero's "inexhaustible fire" burns with a steady flame.[19]

Though there are evidences of Longinus's direct influence on seventeenth century literary criticism, his impact on the theory of art can be traced more easily in eighteenth century treatises. Many of his ideas — the ecstasy of the poet or painter, the emphasis on *energeia* (energy) and *enargeia* (vividness), the imaginative expression of passion, the vehemence of the orator, the imitation of the classics, the stress on admiration, and the superiority of natural genius to the principles of art — can be paralleled in Seicento treatises on art or in baroque painting. Nevertheless, these ideas were, on the whole, commonplaces of classical — and Renaissance — rhetorical or poetic theory. Longinus's treatise simply brought them into focus. Though these principles may seem to have been

exemplified in Milton's epic poetry and in baroque art, there is
little conclusive evidence for the direct influence of the *De sublimitate* in either case.

The subsequent history of the grand style, and the elevation of
the sublime from a synonym for the *stilus altus* or *genus grande* into
a separate aesthetic category applicable to nature as well as art,
need not concern us here. That the grand style should provide a
basis for enthusiasm in poetry, for the veneration of original
genius, and for the natural expression of passion is not surprising.
The most striking development was the eventual elevation of
landscape painting and locodescriptive poetry from their comparatively humble rank as associates of the lowly pastoral into vehicles
of the sublime — media for celebrating the grandeur and magnificence of nature, for arousing terror and admiration and awe — and
the Wordsworthian exaltation of pastoral and rural subjects as
being closer to nature and to the natural expression of natural
passions. These developments remained for the future, though
foreshadowed in the heroic landscapes of seventeenth century
painters and the powerful but homely realism of Caravaggio.
(Caravaggio's subsequent influence in the Netherlands is particularly interesting in view of Spanish influence in Naples, and the
influence of Flemish and Burgundian art at the Spanish court.)

6.

The problems of discussing style during the Renaissance were
accentuated not only by an ambiguous relationship to antiquity
and to the Renaissance tradition itself, but also by polemical or
apologetic strategy. Innovations in manner or reactions against
prevailing styles could be defended in a variety of ways: on the
authority of the ancients themselves, as original inventions of the
moderns, or on the authority of venerated writers or artists of the
early Renaissance or the late Middle Ages. In reacting against
excessive emphasis on verbal ornament at the expense of substance — the exaltation of manner over matter, and words (*verba*)
over things (*res*)[20] — "anti-Ciceronians" could appeal to the example of Pliny or Seneca, Caesar or Tacitus, or to discussions of the
Attic style in Quintilian or in Cicero himself. Similarly, artists could
find justification for apparently "unclassical" styles in histories of
antique art, and claim the same right to free invention that the
ancients themselves had exercised.

Thomas Carew could simultaneously praise Ben Jonson's "la-

bour'd workes" and his "rich spoyles . . . torne/ From conquered
Authors" and extol John Donne for not imitating the ancients too
closely — for purging the "Muses garden" of "Pedantique
weedes," for planting "fresh invention" instead of "servile imitation," for avoiding the "Licentious thefts" of poets who must be
inspired "with Anacreons Extasie,/ Or Pindars, not their owne,"
and for surpassing "all the ancient Brood/ Our superstitious fooles
admire. . . ." Now that Donne is dead, Carew foresees that poets
will revert to the old and hackneyed conventions of the classical
style, calling back "the goodly exil'd traine/ Of gods and goddesses,"
and adoring "those old Idolls . . . with new apostasie. . . ."[21]

Clearly, stylistic categories are often far too general and abstract
to serve as reliable instruments or standards for the criticism of
particular works. They tend to become stereotypes — too rigid and
inflexible to do justice to the subtleties of even a comparatively
simple picture or poem. Stylistic categories belong primarily to
theory, and are apt to prove clumsy in practice. In the criticism of
Renaissance art and literature, they have been an embarrassing but
inevitable necessity. Efforts to discriminate Ciceronian and anti-
Ciceronian, Senecan or libertine, Petrarchan and anti-Petrarchan
styles in literature have raised just as many problems as they have
resolved. Further, architectural and pictorial categories — such as
mannerism and baroque — cannot be systematically applied to
literature without distorting their original denotation. Their original sense is frequently ambiguous, and to transfer them to literary
criticism is to introduce further equivocation.

The conventional classifications of styles according to their elevation and ornament (high, middle, low; magnificent or austere,
graceful or plain; aureate or plain, Asiatic or Attic, etc.) and
according to genre (heroic, tragic, comic, pastoral, satiric, etc.) and
the medieval "wheel of Virgil" are likewise too broad and too
ambiguous to provide a reliable critical vocabulary. Cicero's own
style varied far more widely, in different works and at different
periods, than his Renaissance disciples usually cared to acknowl-
edge. If decorum required different styles for different subjects and
genres, it could also require variations in style within a particular
genre in accordance with the character, emotion or situation of the
speaker. Comedy could raise her voice, according to Horace, for
the expression of passion, and tragedy might sink to the language
of prose for complaint in adversity. As both Scaliger and Tasso
recognized, Virgil not only accommodated his style to different
genres but also varied it within each genre, sinking at times in the
Aeneid, as in his description of the epic games, and occasionally

rising above the prevailing style of the *Georgics* or the *Eclogues* to treat a loftier theme.[22] Even so, in lowering his pitch, he could still manage to maintain heroic dignity and epic decorum. As Addison (and Pope's "Scriblerus") observed of the *Georgics*, Virgil could toss dung with "an air of Majesty."[23]

Alternative classifications of style — threefold, fourfold, sevenfold — complicated the problem for the poet or orator and for the critic. Roughness and obscurity could heighten the grand style, but they also belonged to satire. Plainness pertained traditionally to the low style, but it was sometimes associated with the passionate and the sublime. Elaborate ornament has been commonly associated with the grand style, but it could also be associated with the middle or graceful style. For different critics or in different genres the grand style might be ornate or harsh, magnificent or severe, perspicuous or obscure; the plain style elegant or vulgar; the middle style less ornamented than the *stilo alto*, or more lavishly decorated.

In many instances, moreover, these terms are anachronistic. Some of them are the inventions of modern critics (such as "libertine prose"), while others ("mannerist" and "baroque") are importations from art history and their value is at best merely metaphorical. Most of the remaining categories are anachronistic in a different sense. They belonged to the actual vocabulary of Renaissance criticism, but for the most part they represented an attempt to impose classical labels on the vernacular tradition, and Renaissance authors sometimes employed them very loosely indeed. Few of them could have understood "Attic" and "Asiatic" in the sense in which Greek and Latin rhetoricians — or twentieth century scholars — have understood these terms. There were strict and lax "Ciceronians" and "Senecans." Not all prose writers follow the example of the ancients — Cicero or Seneca, Livy or Pliny, Tacitus or Velleius Paterculus — with the same fidelity, and there are notable divergences in the style of works by the same author. Sir Thomas Browne's *Christian Morals* may be regarded as "Senecan," but the label is hardly applicable to *Hydriotaphia* or *The Garden of Cyrus*. Similarly, no single category of style can do justice to Francis Bacon's rhetorical variety, his distinctions between the styles appropriate for persuasion and for the discovery and elucidation of scientific knowledge, and his condemnation of Senecan terseness as well as the orotundity of Ciceronian stylists like Osorio. It is significant that in revising his essays he attempted to eliminate many of their "Senecan" mannerisms.

Like the "Petrarchan" and "Ovidian" traditions, the "Ciceronian" and "Senecan" styles tend to resist precise definition. Authors adapted and assimilated Cicero and Seneca just as they adapted Ovid and Petrarch, picking and choosing in accordance with their own judgment, the demands of their subject, or the tastes of their audiences; and deriving their ideas of style from English or Continental authors as well as from the original classical "models" of style. In the vernacular tradition, an author's style would usually be as strongly molded by personal taste and by the example of other Renaissance writers as by classical models. In practice, if not always in theory, the actual influence of Cicero or Seneca or of other classical stylists frequently became obscured by the tradition itself. As such an influence became assimilated, it often lost its distinctive character; and the attempt to isolate it in the works of particular authors — labelling one writer Senecan or another Ciceronian — may easily result in obscuring the primary qualities of the author's *personal* style, imposing classical or twentieth century stereotypes on the literature of the sixteenth and seventeenth centuries. With a few notable exceptions, the scholar's primary consideration is not the classification of authors according to "Ciceronian" or "anti-Ciceronian" labels, but the distinctive features of their respective styles — their innovations on stylistic traditions rather than the traditions themselves.

Literary criticism dealing with "mannerism" and "baroque," in turn, has frequently overstressed their significance as period styles, exaggerating their spontaneity and their homogeneity, and underestimating their dependence on conventional stylistic categories and on the constants of poetic and pictorial tradition. In emphasizing the expressive value of mannerism or baroque as manifestations of the "spirit of the age" — reflections of its sensibility or projections of its inner tensions and conflicts — scholarship has sometimes understressed their continuity with the styles of earlier and later periods. Also, scholars have often failed to examine the extent to which the style of both verbal and visual arts has been consciously conditioned by traditional theoretical distinctions — levels of subject matter, decorum in genre (in poetry) or in place or occasion or function (in the visual arts). Rhetorical distinctions between particular styles in terms of contrasting qualities (magnificence and simplicity, ornamentation and nakedness, obscurity and plainness, severity and grace or charm) or functions (instruction, delight, passion, admiration) could condition plastic styles as well as poetry. The painter or architect who differentiated tragic, comic and "satyric" sets for the theater could be scrupulous in distinguishing between the décor for a private bath and an audience chamber, a grotto and a hall of state, a garden casino and a cathedral — adapting the style (as poets themselves had done) to scenes of pleasure or regal pomp, or religious devotion, or to private and public functions. In decorating a royal retreat or a merchant-prince's banquet hall, the architect and painter would have ampler scope for the lighter effects of the "graceful style" than in designing a throneroom. Even in ecclesiastical architecture and paintings, stylistic ornament might vary with affective intent — delight or marvel, ecstasy or tranquility or pathos.

7.

Even in using the nomenclature of the sixteenth and seventeenth centuries, it is difficult to pin down the meaning of different categories of style. The *genus grande* bears no single sense, nor does the plain or low style. The elements of Senecanism in the style of Thomas Browne may indeed be associated with terseness as in *Christian Morals*, but these elements are frequently, and characteristically, combined with orotundity and deliberate magnificence. The result is a style altogether different from the Senecanism of Joseph Hall or Justus Lipsius. The macaronic style of Robert Burton is a mixture of scholastic and pedantic terminology, racy and breezy epithets, undigested gobbets of erudition, fragments of poetry, uncontrolled *copia* both of matter and language. Its qualities are in some ways reminiscent of the style of Thomas Nashe, the prose of the Marprelate tracts, the manner of Aretino, Folengo, and even Giordano Bruno. The plain style of Ben Jonson's poetry is not that of George Herbert, nor is the plainness of Robert Herrick the plain style of John Denham, Edmund Waller or of John Dryden. Again, though Donne makes use of the low style, indecorously mingling the colloquial with the scholastic, this can hardly be described as plain.

The nomenclature of period styles presents even greater difficulties. The attempt to find a single formula which applies to an alleged historical period and is common to the character of its society, its sensibility, its literature and art is, in some respects, like looking for a mare's nest — a search for the nonexistent. Nor is a single formula valid, in most instances, for either the literature or the art of the period, much less for both. The same author, as we have seen, may employ a variety of styles. Milton's poems on

Hobson the university carrier utilize the academic, scholastic conceits often characteristic of the metaphysicals, though he does so with less ingenuity and more restraint. In "The Passion" and the Nativity Ode, he employs the exaggerated conceits associated both with *marinismo* and with the neo-Spenserian tradition. Jonson's influence is apparent in the epitaph on the Marchioness of Winchester, in *Arcades* and *Comus*, and to a certain extent in both *L'Allegro* and *Il Penseroso*. In many of the sonnets, critics have recognized a debt to Della Casa and Tasso; the influence of Tasso and other Italian poets and theorists has been observed in *Lycidas*, in the blank verse of *Paradise Lost*, and in the partial use of rhyme in the choruses of *Samson Agonistes*. In addition, there are the variations in level of style within the same poem in accordance with the decorum of the speaker and the subject matter or the fictional audience, and the influence of different classical authors.

THREE

The Classical Image and
Renaissance Pedagogy

In comparing "the Renaissance" with other, earlier renascences, Erwin Panofsky noted one distinctive feature of the former: "the reintegration of classical themes with classical motifs." According to Panofsky, although the Middle Ages were "deeply interested in the intellectual and poetic values of classical literature" and "by no means blind to the visual values of classical art," they were "unable and unwilling to realize that classical motifs and classical themes structurally belonged together. . . ." In high-medieval visual art there was a "dichotomy of classical motifs and classical themes"; "classical motifs were not used for the representation of classical themes while, conversely, classical themes were not expressed by classical motifs." It was the privilege of the Renaissance to reunite them, and this reintegration appeared to be specifically "characteristic of the Italian Renaissance as opposed to the numerous sporadic revivals of classical tendencies during the Middle Ages. . . ." Yet, as Panofsky further comments, "this reintegration could not be a simple reversion to the classical past." Artists had to "strive for a new form of expression, stylistically and iconographically different from the classical, as well as from the mediaeval, yet related and indebted to both."[1]

In medieval and Renaissance literature, one may encounter a similar disjunction and reintegration of classical materials and classical forms — though it would probably distort literary history to seek detailed analogies between the arts of discourse and design on this point. Medieval authors could borrow images and phrases from antiquity or adapt *topoi* and narratives from the classical writers, but (with significant exceptions) they did not systematically imitate the ancients as paradigms for both structure and style.

52

Consequently, however great a medieval author's learning might be or however extensive his allusions to classical materials, this work often seemed in Renaissance eyes irregular and barbaric, and in modern eyes "unclassical." In varying degrees, Renaissance authors endeavored to revive the classical genres and classical principles of structure and style: to reform and reorganize narrative and dramatic and lyric modes according to the theory and practice of the ancients.

This was, to be sure, only one facet of Renaissance literature — and it has been, on the whole, altogether too easy to exaggerate the "classical" qualities of Renaissance poetry and prose. Yet this was an important facet. Many authors had little desire to imitate the ancients directly or to follow the canons that their contemporaries were abstracting from classical poetics and poetry; nevertheless, they felt the influence of classical principles of style and form through vernacular tradition. Though the "modelling" of such poems might seem highly irregular to a Jonson or a Milton — and much more so to a Minturno, a Scaliger, or critics of still later generations — they could scarcely avoid absorbing some of the principles of structure and design, characterization and dialogue, that their contemporaries were learning or adapting from the ancients.[2]

Like the dichotomy of classicism and anticlassicism, the formulae of integration and disjunction and reintegration have been applied frequently not only to medieval and Renaissance art and literature, but also to such late-Renaissance (or post-Renaissance) styles as mannerism and baroque. Contemporary critics speak of mannerism in terms of the disintegration and fragmentation of Renaissance style, of baroque in terms of the strenuous labor of reintegration — the dissolution of Renaissance harmony and the endeavor to restore it. In all three of these instances, the qualities of style are regarded not only as the contrived results of conscious art, but as socially conditioned responses to the intellectual and political crises of the period, expressions of the anxiety or assurance, the despair or optimism of the age. Yet it is not, perhaps, either fortuitous or irrelevant that essentially the same formulae — a process of disintegration and reintegration, analysis and synthesis — were operative in the educational programs of the Renaissance: in the methods whereby students were taught to analyze the literature of antiquity and to adapt its form, its matter, and the elements of its style to their own compositions.

To a significant degree, our own conceptions of "Renaissance classicism" have been molded by the views that individuals of the period held of antiquity and their relationship to it. This, in turn, had been strongly influenced by the nature and orientation of their formal and informal education. Many of the external (and sometimes superficial) aspects of the literature and painting of the age — the copiousness of mythological allusions, the imitation of classical figures and motifs and decorative ornament, the frequent glorification of the sages and heroes of antiquity, and indeed the concern for the service of the state and the pursuit or bestowal of secular glory — were in part attributable to the kind of schooling that poets and their patrons were receiving and the character and aims of humanist pedagogy. If one had been specifically trained to mine classical history and myth for images and allusions and for examples of virtue and vice, which could be profitably used in one's academic compositions, it was natural to apply similar techniques in literary composition long after leaving the schoolroom. In learning eloquence from the ancients, one also learned to assimilate them to ethical and political norms, to treat them as models (good or evil) for private and public conduct.

1.

The principal elements in our own stereotypes of Renaissance classicism seem to be: unity of theme and design; proportion or harmony in the relationship between parts and in the subordination of parts to the whole; a balance between naturalistic and idealistic norms in representation; and decorum in the interrelationships between subject and style, action and character and genre.[3] To these we might add (though it is rather an accident than an essential of composition) various techniques that self-consciously emphasized a particular writer's imitation or evocation of antiquity. The writer's treatment of the classical conventions of a genre, for instance: prologue and stichomythia in *Comus*; the role of the Chorus in *Samson Agonistes*; proposition and invocation, epic similes and epic machines, prospective and retrospective narratives, the formulae of epic address in *Paradise Lost*. Allusions to persons, places, or events in classical history and fiction. Imitations and parodies of the style of some particular poet or orator of Greece or Rome. Explicit avowals of inferiority or superiority to the ancients — of an intent to follow them humbly from afar or to surpass them.

The remoteness from antiquity in time enhanced aesthetic distance; Renaissance writers could imitate or evoke antiquity because they had been separated from it by so many centuries of "barbarism." The forms of classical civilization, detached from their original historical context, now possessed (it seemed) an "ideal" reality of their own, a metaphysical validity independent of the historical process. These forms could be abstracted from ancient history and pagan myth and reimposed on the matter of Scripture or on the histories and legends of England, France and other modern states. The preservation of the form, though transferred to a very different subject matter, would evoke the image of antiquity in the very act of displacing it. To substitute the Christian Muse for Calliope and Mount Sion for Parnassus, to introduce the subject matter of Genesis into the epic proposition instead of references to heroes of Troy, and to adapt the epic simile to Biblical material and Renaissance science — these techniques of displacement called attention to the recovery of classical form and style while emphasizing the chronological distance between ancient world and modern, and the spiritual gulf between the classical and the Judaeo-Christian traditions.

In such instances, the basic presuppositions of humanist education tended to bring into clearer focus the underlying opposition between classical form and style and Biblical subject matter. Just as rhetorical tradition emphasized the distinction between content and style (*res* and *verba*) in discourse, Renaissance poetics stressed the dichotomy of matter and form in the choice of an epic or dramatic argument and the construction of the plot.

Nearly all the elements of "classical" style and structure would, in a Renaissance context at least, be subjected to a process of analysis and synthesis. To achieve structural unity, one would consider the formal divisions of a work, the sections of an oration, the several parts of a narrative or dramatic plot. In seeking thematic unity, one would also look for variety of material and for techniques to bring it into focus. With regard to decorum, one would endeavor to accommodate words to matter (*verba* to *res*), but to do so one had to consider them both separately and in combination. The same isolation and correlation of the elements in a work of art or literature would apply to the relationship between action and character, thought and style in an epic; to the sequence of protasis, epitasis and catastrophe in a Terentian comedy; to the relation between reversal, recognition and *pathos* in a tragic plot. One would be trained systematically in the complementary skills of dissolution and reconstruction. In the context of humanist education at least, the rebirth of antiquity was like the rejuvenation of Aeson: systematically dismembered, skillfully reassembled, magically revived.

2.

Like classical authorities on the education of an orator, Renaissance humanists distinguished three essentials for skill in eloquence: native ability (*natura* or *ingenium*), theory or knowledge of the principles of rhetoric (*ars*), and exercise or practice. As an aid to practice and as a complement to theory, both ancients and moderns had advised the close study and imitation of the "best" writers of the "best" period of Latinity, selected for content as well as style.[4] True eloquence must be solidly based on knowledge of the truth: on the speaker's intellectual and moral excellence, wisdom and sincerity of purpose. Perfection of character and range and depth of learning were no less essential for the orator than distinguished utterance. A variety of matter to communicate was necessary, as well as appropriate eloquence to communicate it; the speaker had to possess *copia rerum et verborum*, "infinite riches in a little room."

In the humanist schools of the Renaissance, centered almost entirely on the study of classical authors and directed toward competence in the Latin tongue, emphasis was placed on both content and style (*res et verba*) and on the moral inferences that might be drawn from the works studied. Greek authors were chosen largely for content and as aids to understanding Latin writers.[5] Though the latter were studied for matter as well as for excellence in style, the determining factor in selecting them was (for the most part) the purity and elegance of their Latinity;[6] from them the student must learn not only what to write but also how to write it well.

The complete texts of Quintilian's *Institutio Oratoria* and Cicero's *De Oratore* were rediscovered early in the fifteenth century and were eagerly appropriated by teachers of rhetoric. The former was the only substantial Latin treatise on education surviving, and the fact that it was devoted specifically to the training of an orator was partly responsible (it has been suggested) for the notably philological character and rhetorical orientation of the humanist curriculum. Following Quintilian's advice and example, Renaissance schoolmasters placed heavy emphasis both on prose composition and on imitation of the "best" writers as models. Closely read for both style and erudition, selected poets, orators and historians served both as models for imitation and as repositories of arguments and exempla wherewith students might enrich and reinforce their own lines of argument.[7] In certain schools, students entered the harvested fruits of their reading in separate notebooks according to the familiar dichotomy of words and matter. One book would be devoted to niceties of language: words and phrases, elegancies of diction or verbal ornament. The other might contain *sententiae*, examples and other materials that might furnish arguments pro or con on a wide variety of subjects, arranged methodically under topical headings or "commonplaces" (*loci communes*).[8] In their reading and composition, students became proficient at analysis and synthesis: the complementary labors of dissecting a work into its component elements and subsequently reassembling them — perhaps into a reasonable likeness of the original, perhaps into an image of some other classical author, or perhaps into a self portrait executed in classical style and combining the features of the modern with those of the antique exemplar.

3.

The political and social context of Renaissance classicism was not the principal determinant of style, though many cultural historians have believed it to be. There was a significant interrelationship, however, between style and the political and social circumstances. Aside from the traditional correlation of stylistic levels and literary genres with social classes, the various forms of rhetoric — deliberative, forensic, demonstrative — had been conventionally associated with different aspects of political life: courts of law and public assemblies, public worship, the eulogy of the community's leaders, the denunciation of public enemies, the persuasion of the crowd. The ideal of active service to the state underlay much of the humanist program; a classical education (the humanist argued) combining the eloquence and wisdom of antiquity with moral instruction would provide a firm foundation for a variety of duties in the state: as prince or courtier, ambassador or counsellor, captain or knight, poet or orator or priest. These presuppositions underlay the educational schemes of Vittorino da Feltre and Guarino of Verona, and they were still operative in John Milton's outline for a course of predominantly classical authors designed to prepare the students to "perform justly, skillfully, and magnanimously all the offices, both private and public, of peace and war."[9] Late in life Milton would return to the humanistic educational ideal, parodying its classical substance and its political associations. In the temptation in the wilderness in *Paradise Regained*, Satan proposes an essentially classical curriculum, centered on the best poets and orators and philosophers of ancient Greece.

Echoing the commonplaces of humanist pedagogy, the devil argues that such an education would best prepare the hero for his princely duties, enabling him not only to command himself but to teach and govern others by persuasion.

In Italy the revival of the language and literature of classical antiquity, so closely associated with the greatness of the Roman state, might be regarded as a patriotic duty. So it appeared to Petrarch and to many of his fellow Italians.[10] But in its transmission to northern and western Europe, this classical revival adopted the protective coloration of other political loyalties, regional or national or sectarian. The English and French were urged to enrich or refine their own languages and literatures as the Italians had been doing. Milton aspired, at a comparatively early age, to "fix all the industry and art I could unite to the adorning of my native tongue" and to accomplish for his own people "what the greatest and choicest wits of Athens, Rome, or modern Italy, and those Hebrews of old did for their country. . . ."[11]

Predominantly elitist, the humanistic program gradually reached a much broader spectrum of society. Designed for the education of princes and noblemen, or the children of affluent burgesses, it frequently included students of lesser means and humbler birth; the humanist educators themselves often came from widely diverse backgrounds.

Of the social factors that differentiated Renaissance from medieval culture, one of the more significant for humanist education (it has been argued) was the decline of "the military role of the lay aristocracy" and a shift in emphasis to the ideal of an educated gentry, "active in the service of the state, familiar with the major texts of classical literature, and expert in the rhetorical arts of persuasion."[12] Scholars have also stressed the rise of an urban middle class interested in literature and art and the patronage of the verbal and visual arts by the "despots" and merchant-princes of Renaissance city-states, social diffusion of literacy and learning through charitable schools, printed books and vernacular translations. And they have emphasized the centralization and consolidation of power in the national monarchies of northern and western Europe.[13] The character of the Renaissance humanist schools left its impact on one's tastes in vernacular literature as well as on one's aesthetic and intellectual appreciation of the literature of antiquity. The tastes of the courts — at Ferrara and Mantua and Rome, at London or Paris and Madrid — and the tastes of the urban middle class often played an important part in the formation and diffusion of a style. It was not unusual for

authors to defend themselves against the seeming irregularity of
their work on the grounds of the nature and predilections of their
audience, on the need to satisfy popular or aristocratic taste.

4.

The essentially rhetorical orientation of humanistic education
simultaneously encouraged and distorted the understanding of
antiquity. The primary emphasis fell on Latin authors selected
partly for content but primarily for their pedagogical value at the
various levels of a grammar school as models of Latin style. Writers
of less impeccable Latinity or of exceptional difficulty or idiosyn-
cratic style would scarcely serve the schoolmasters' purpose; students' familiarity with Latin literature in the original tongue would
accordingly be severely limited. Their knowledge of Greek authors
in the original language would be even more restricted. Their
contacts with the natural sciences and philosophy would be largely
literary, directed toward understanding scientific or pseudo-
scientific allusions in classical poets and historians, and enriching
their own store of commonplaces and images. Many of the humanist educators were indifferent or contemptuous toward the
sciences, and in their reaction against scholasticism some of them
restricted the study of logic to the bare essentials that might assist
the student in organizing and developing material. Aside from the
philological orientation of the humanist schools, the fact that Latin
authors themselves had, for the most part, shown greater interest
in the poetry and oratory and history of Greece than in its science
and philosophy — and that medieval European scholars had been
compelled to seek the latter largely through Arabic channels —
also tended to narrow and distort the image of classical civilization.

The humanist educators frequently approached history from the
viewpoint of rhetoric as well. They turned to the classical historians as sources for commonplaces and exempla that might be
utilized in composition, for speeches and orations (often the invention of the historian himself) that might provide models for imitation, and for instances of virtue and vice that might serve as moral
and political *topoi*.

A similar emphasis on rhetoric often conditioned their attitudes
toward poetry. This too could provide exempla and *sententiae*,
phrases and images, model chronographias and topographias,
formal or informal speeches that could be exploited by the student
in predominantly rhetorical contexts. Lucan was often extolled by

educators as a "rhetorical" poet — though sometimes denied the
title of poet by literary theorists on the grounds that he was
essentially an historian.

"Classicism" (even in the variety of senses it possesses for our
own contemporaries) was only one of several strains in Renaissance literary tradition; and, like Erwin Panofsky, Morris Croll
stressed the divergences as well as the affinities between the
moderns and the ancients whom they distantly admired and in
varying degrees imitated. The Renaissance "taste for ornate
prose," Croll suggested, was "caused by the concurrence of the
same elements in the taste of the Renaissance that give the character of ornateness to nearly all of its art, the same mixture of the
classical, the medieval, and the courtly in the culture of the age
that makes the *Orlando Furioso*, for instance, and the *Faerie Queene*
so fantastic and so unclassical." In the evolution of Euphuistic
prose, the major cause was not the imitation of the classics, but
"the novelty of literary prose in the vernacular, and the need of
adapting this familiar speech to unaccustomed uses of art and
beauty." To "attribute the love of a fanciful ornateness to this
cause is to fall into the common error of identifying the Renaissance with the revival of antiquity." In fact (Croll maintained),
"the humanistic imitation of the classics . . . would appear the one
strong influence working for purity and simplicity."[14]

Intellectually, the Renaissance acquired a different "image"
from that of the Middle Ages, for a variety of reasons: reintegration
of classical form and content, its attempt to derive learning and
eloquence from their original sources (Latin, Greek or Hebrew)
rather than indirectly through "barbarian" channels,[15] its dislike of
scholastic methodology and style, its concern for formal beauty
and proportion, its renewed emphasis on the persuasive force and
didactic value of eloquence as the vehicle and instrument of truth.

Yet one should not mistake the image for the reality. The
scholastic tradition remained firmly entrenched at many of the
universities. Though the philological techniques of the humanists
helped to restore the texts of Greek philosophers and scientists —
and though the humanists praised the value of eloquence as the
instrument and vehicle of philosophical truth — the classical vocabulary they extolled and the methods they employed were
generally much less precise and less suitable for the demonstration
of scientific and philosophical doctrines than the neologisms and
hair-splitting distinctions of the schoolmen. The values of humanistic learning were inextricably interwoven with those of antiquity
— with the authority of the ancients and with the intellectual and

social value of rhetoric — and were in part compromised when the latter came under attack: when the veneration of antiquity seemed an obstacle rather than an aid to the advancement of learning, the authority of the ancients an idol of the mind, and the art of eloquence a craft of deception.

5.

A clearly defined image of the Renaissance in terms of the revival of antiquity and the restoration of the classical tradition is possible only if we, as scholars, systematically exclude the greater part of the art and literature of both periods. If one narrows one's definition of classicism to close imitation of the vocabulary and syntax, the imagery and structure, the arguments and commonplaces, and the subject matter of a classical work, then one would be left with comparatively few works in either prose or poetry, in neo-Latin or in the vernacular. In the strictest sense, one would be compelled to write in Latin and to avoid or disguise anachronisms; references to contemporary persons and events, the politics and religions of modern Europe must somehow be made to appear contemporaneous with those of Augustan Rome. The names and offices of living rulers must be accommodated to those of imperial or republican antiquity; and the objects of Christian belief invested with the epithets and attributes of pagan divinities.

Writing in the vernacular, one might adapt the images and *topoi*, the schemes and tropes, the structure and the content of classical models, but one could, only in a very limited degree, hope to imitate their vocabulary or syntax.

One might, finally, endeavor to imitate the structure of a classical model, while drawing one's subject matter and much of one's imagery from nonclassical sources — from the Bible or from British or French or German or medieval Italian history — and utilizing the Christian marvellous (or discarding supernatural machinery altogether) instead of the conventions of antique paganism.

In varying degrees, the image — or in some respects the illusion — of Renaissance classicism has resulted from its exploitation of one or several elements in the classical tradition (syntax, vocabulary, structure, content, etc.), but rarely from a combination of *all* of these.

The most important of these factors was probably structure or design — and in this sense *Samson Agonistes* and *Paradise Lost* are preeminently "classical." Nevertheless, a poet could in fact manage to *appear* classical by piling up phrase after phrase borrowed from ancient authors, allusion after allusion to classical myth or history: the early Latin poems of the young Milton may serve as instances. Most of the classical allusions in the First and Seventh Elegies and in academic exercises like *Naturam Non Pati Senium* and *De Idea Platonica* are ornamental; they belong to the rhetoric of display, and they deliberately illustrate the student's erudition in ancient literature. But he deploys them rather with a respect for *copia* (copiousness of both thought and words) than with a regard for classical form and classical restraint. Subsequently he would acquire a stronger sense of control, a firmer command over the formal organization of language and material.

The "illusion" of classicism is a plausible response to Renaissance affectations of the antique. Though it is partly our own *eidolon*, it was also to a very considerable extent the "idol" of the Renaissance — though not always recognized as such. There was an element of theatrical illusion in the assumption of Latin or Greek names ("Melanchthon" for Schwarzerd; "Oecolampadius" for Hüszgen), in the exchange of epistles modelled on those of Cicero or subsequently those of Seneca or Pliny, in the formal apparel Machiavelli assumed for his nocturnal communion with the ancients. There was also conscious illusion in following the conventions of art; in many instances the author or painter would deliberately sacrifice historical accuracy and verisimilitude for the sake of imitating the ancients.

In many instances, the "illusion" involved a conscious emphasis on the historical gulf separating the writer or artist from antiquity. In imitating a classical author, Renaissance poets might deliberately look for parallels in their own time, for equivalences or "correspondences" between the milieu of — let us say — a Roman satirist or elegiac poet and their own. In this sense, the imitation or adaptation of an ancient author could be in itself a work of wit, a discovery or invention of analogies between individuals or periods widely separated in time and place. This type of imitation — in which the literature of antiquity serves as a comment on modern times — is most clearly exemplified in Pope's treatment of Horace, and Samuel Johnson's adaptation of Juvenal. The method is, in a sense, a legacy not only of the tradition of literary imitation but also of the rhetorical convention of drawing moral or political inferences from the examples of antiquity, whether sacred or profane. Here the classical text functions much like a Biblical text, as a point of departure for indicting the follies and vices of modern times.

For Renaissance poets writing in classical genres, the resemblance to antique models that they sought to achieve through the formal structure and organization of their material could be significantly compromised by the demands of the vernacular. It would be virtually impossible to reproduce either the vocabulary or the syntax of the classical tongues, and most efforts at quantitative verse in the vernacular had failed. At best, these poets could aspire to comparable stylistic effects through a judicious regard for the advantages and limitations of their own language. From the perspective of the twentieth century — though not from that of Milton's own contemporaries — his preference for unrhymed verses in his epics enabled him to achieve an effect more consonant with that of a classical heroic poetry than the use of heroic couplets or *ottava rima* or rhyming quatrains would have permitted. In particular, his concern with the techniques for achieving "true musical delight" in poetry — "apt Numbers, fit quantity of Syllables, and the sense variously drawn out from one Verse into another" — enabled him to produce an impression comparable to that of the heroic verse of antiquity. In point of fact, it was firmly grounded in the English tradition of blank verse, though probably influenced by the *versi sciolti* of Tasso and other poets of the Italian Renaissance.[16] It is significant that in his note on the verse of *Paradise Lost* Milton represented his rejection of rhyme — in true Renaissance fashion — as a revival of classical usage after the barbarism of the Middle Ages: "an example set, the first in *English*, of ancient liberty recover'd to Heroic Poem from the troublesome and modern bondage of Riming."[17]

The veneer of classical allusions, mythological themes and classical phrases and ornaments was, in the long run, less important than the influence of classical models and theory on the structure or modeling of a poem. Aristotle had assigned primary importance to the plot or disposition of an epic or tragedy — it was the "soul" of the poem — yet the influence of his *Poetics*, along with the example of some of the major poets of antiquity, was one of the determining factors in the critical emphasis on formal unity and proportion. No matter how lavishly writers might strew their work with flowers of rhetoric and epithets culled from the ancients, their work would seem unclassical in the eyes of many of their own contemporaries — and certainly in eighteenth century eyes — unless they also followed the structural principles inherent in the poetry of Greece and Rome. Significantly, in composing *Samson Agonistes* Milton regarded the example of the Greek dramatists as a better guide than the theories and arts of poetry: "Of the style and uniformity, and that commonly call'd the Plot . . . they only will best judge who are not unacquainted with *Aeschylus*, *Sophocles* and *Euripides*, the three Tragic Poets unequall'd yet by any, and the best rule to all who endeavor to write Tragedy."[18] What Milton and some of his near-contemporaries learned from such models were the principles of structure: formal and thematic unity, proportion and harmony, the logical relationship between parts and the subordination of the parts to the whole.

A Renaissance poem heavily indebted to classical erudition, adorned with the figures of classical rhetoric and rich with classical references may nevertheless *look* unclassical — as Spenser's *Faerie Queene* appeared to Morris Croll — if the syntax is not classical also, and especially if the structure does not recall that of the classics. Spenser's epic was essentially Italianate — directly through Ariosto and Tasso and others, and indirectly through the Chaucerian tradition. Yet it had also borrowed much from classical myth; and in its treatment of epic conventions like the proposition and invocation, the poem was influenced by Virgilian and Homeric practice, though not closely modelled upon it. In comparison with Tasso's *Gerusalemme Liberata*, it was much closer to the freer and looser structural pattern of Ariosto's *Orlando Furioso*. Consequently, both Spenser and Ariosto have seemed unclassical in the eyes of several critics. Because these critics have preferred to identify the characteristic style of the Renaissance as "classical," they have been compelled to regard both of these poems as "manneristic" rather than truly Renaissance in style. The essential basis for this judgment is the fact that both poets elected to write in the tradition of the romance — a nonclassical genre, as neoclassical critics were quick to point out — and retained many characteristic romance conventions: notably the multiple plots with multiple heroes, interlinked through the techniques of *entrelacement*. Though both poems were actually "romance-epics" (a neologism of our own age), though both combined features of the two genres, and though Spenser had in mind a more unified design than Ariosto's, neither poet endeavored to imitate closely the structure, the syntax, or the verse of classical epic.

On the other hand, Tasso, who endeavored to combine the variety of the romance with the unified structure of classical epic (a concept of the epic derived partly from Aristotle's *Poetics* and partly from the example of Homer and Virgil), has appeared "baroque" to several critics, precisely because of his partial but incomplete endeavor to impose classical form and structure on his chivalric subject matter.

In both of these instances, the basic criterion underlying the use of the term "mannerist" or "baroque" has been the issue of comparative unity and multiplicity in theme and design.

6.

The "classical" elements in the Renaissance are so closely associated with the humanist tradition that the growth and decline of this tradition seem, to many of our own contemporaries, to mark the beginning and end of an era. At one extreme, the polemics of the *humanistas* against the schoolmen introduced themes and arguments that remained commonplaces for centuries. (One reencounters many of these motifs in the polemics of John Milton.) There is the distaste for scholastic logic and especially for the scholastic method of teaching grammar. There are the condemnations of the "living" Latin of the Middle Ages as barbarous, and medieval learning as monkish, ignorant and corrupt. There are the conscious effort to revive the language and the arts and learning of antiquity, the endeavor to imitate the authors of antiquity, and the tendency to regard these authors not only as authoritative in erudition and in style, but also as teachers of moral wisdom. At the other extreme, a changing intellectual climate proved inhospitable to some of the principal humanist ideals — and again one has the sense of the end of an era: the waning of the Renaissance complementing the waning of the Middle Ages.

Most significant, perhaps, were the intellectual crises of the late Renaissance — in epistemology, in metaphysics and cosmology, in religion — and their impact on the arts of discourse. Not only were the systematic philosophies of the ancients frequently at variance with one another and with the Christian faith; the geography of antiquity had been proven demonstrably wrong, and its cosmology was being questioned by the moderns. It was no longer plausible to believe with Erasmus and many other humanists that the encyclopedia of wisdom — the knowledge of all the arts and sciences necessary for humankind — was comprised in the writings of Greece and Rome. It was no longer probable to maintain that the progress and advancement of learning depended on mastering the languages and wisdom of antiquity, to insist that the key to the future lay in the remote past. The new discoveries in the natural sciences and in mathematics — subjects often slighted by the humanists themselves, or subordinated to literary and historical studies — were also undercutting the authority of the ancients and the importance of classical studies as an essential prerequisite for the study of nature. The *eruditio* of the ancient world was beginning to appear increasingly dubious, restricted and unreliable. Moreover, through the labors of the humanists themselves, who had made the knowledge of antiquity more widely available through translations and compendia, individuals had access to much of the learning of antiquity, even knowing little Latin and less Greek.

The humanist program was also compromised, in a sense, through renewed attacks on rhetoric by philosophers, scientists and clergymen, and by poets themselves. Such attacks were no new phenomenon, of course — but in an age of skepticism and uncertainty, when traditional systems and dogmas were being challenged, the uneasy alliance between philosophy and rhetoric was subjected to new and additional strain. How could the orator, however sincere the intent, effectively teach or persuade if truth itself remained in doubt? Moreover, at a time when the nations of Europe were divided by political and religious wars, the power of rhetoric in arousing and exploiting the passions seemed, in the eyes of many observers, dangerous to the peace of both church and state.

In the later phases of the Renaissance, one observes a shift in emphasis from "verbal" to "real" learning. This is apparent not only in the arts of discourse, where it recapitulates issues debated long before in antiquity, but also in the intellectual life of the time, largely through the strength of the Baconian tradition. In the context of rhetorical theory, *res* ("things") normally referred to the content of discourse: its subject matter, its arguments and examples, its inventory of ideas. In this sense it was the contrary of *verba* ("words" or style). But it could also mean matter or "things" in a literal sense, as the contrary of "form." Bacon and many of his followers often exploited this second meaning of the term, applying it to "matter" in the metaphysical sense, to the understanding and use of "sensible things," and to "real" knowledge. In this way, they could turn the *res-verba topos* not only against the humanists and their emphasis on verbal skills, but also against scholasticism (the common target of humanism and "new philosophy"), arguing that many of its concepts had a purely verbal existence and bore no demonstrable relation to reality.

FOUR

Classical and Anticlassical Modes: Analogies Between the Verbal and Visual Arts

Both Ben Jonson and John Donne were born in the early 1570s and lived until the 1630s, and Abraham Cowley was born in 1618, just ten years after the birth of John Milton. Yet, in both instances, the differences between the two contemporaries are more impressive than their similarities; critics have tended on occasion to contrast them as examples of classical or mannerist, humanist or metaphysical techniques: in short, as representatives of modes frequently regarded as period styles. The fact that these contrasts occur among contemporaries should perhaps make us skeptical about associating them too closely with a particular period. On the other hand, the occasional similarities between authors who are otherwise quite different in technique should also discourage us from exaggerating the differences between them. Jonson expressed admiration for Donne's poetry as well as negative criticism, and indeed scholars have sometimes ascribed the same poem to both. Cowley was one of Milton's favorites among modern poets, and critics have observed analogies between Cowley's conceptions of the Pindaric ode and Milton's practice.[1]

The tension between "classical" and "nonclassical" (or "anticlassical") underlies both the art and the literature of the sixteenth and seventeenth centuries; it provides one of the frameworks for the comparison between verbal and visual modes of expression. But it also raises problems of definition: the question of the evolution or decadence of styles, the differentiation between Renaissance or mannerist or baroque, the continuity or discontinuity of

aesthetic modes, the applicability of art historical terms to literature and vice versa.

In discussing the nomenclature of styles, E.H. Gombrich
argued, some years ago, that the familiar "procession of styles and
periods" — "Classic, Romanesque, Gothic, Renaissance, Mannerist, Baroque, Rococo, Neo-Classical and Romantic" — was "only a
series of masks for two categories, the classical and the nonclassical." All of these "various terms for nonclassical styles" were
actually "terms of exclusion."

Deploring the tendency to elevate these styles into "systems in
their own right embodying alternative values, if not philosophies,"
Gombrich observed that the same passage in Vitruvius, attacking
the "license and illogicality of the decorative style fashionable in
his age" and contrasting this style with the "rational method of
representing real or plausible architectural constructions," served
as a pattern for Vasari in his condemnation of the "corrupt architecture of his time" (i.e. baroque) and for Winckelmann in his
attack on the rococo. Gombrich also noted that, even though the
eighteenth century "sometimes used the terms Gothic and Baroque interchangeably" as derogatory terms for the nonclassical
and for "bad or bizarre taste," these epithets gradually acquired
different senses: "Gothic being increasingly used as a label for the
no-longer classical, the degenerate."[2]

Vasari himself regarded early attempts by Renaissance artists to
imitate or emulate the ancients as a reaction against "Gothic" or
Byzantine styles. Subsequently, as both Walter Friedlaender and
Anthony Blunt suggested, mannerist painters reacted against the
styles of the High Renaissance,[3] and baroque theorists in turn reacted
against mannerist principles in favor of Renaissance precedents.
Neoclassical critics would react similarly against baroque art.

The pattern of reaction or interaction between "classical" and
"anticlassical" styles in Renaissance art is paralleled in literature.
George Williamson regarded "the purely classical or Ciceronian
style" of the Renaissance as "a recovery, and a revolt against the
medieval tradition."[4] Morris Croll called attention to attacks by
Father Vavasseur and Father Caussin on the conceited style fashionable in the Seicento and the imitation of Silver Age authors.
Father Vavasseur's oration *Pro Vetere Generi Dicendi Contra Novum*
attacked the "Anti-Ciceronian, the post-Augustan (style), which
had become almost universal in his time." Croll saw the task of
Caussin and Vavasseur as one of rallying "the taste of their time to
pure Augustanism" against the tendencies that had been "set
going by Lipsius and his school."[5]

1.

The notion of the rhythm of history — the alternation of periods of growth and decay, cycles of achievement and decadence and revival — occurs frequently in the Renaissance, often in association with the personification of Fortune or the schema of the four ages of the world. Individuals of the period applied it to politics and religion, to language and Hermetic magic, to the several arts and sciences. It was in these terms that writers of the Renaissance conceived their own relationship to classical antiquity and the Middle Ages, that antimannerist critics frequently judged Cinquecento painting, and that neoclassical theorists evaluated baroque art and *concettismo*. In protesting against alleged barbarism or decadence of styles, many of these critics took the classical tradition (and sometimes the art of the High Renaissance as well) as a standard, regarding departures from this tradition (however they might define it) as stylistic aberrations, deviations from correct norms and the "right way." As Gombrich observed, sixteenth and seventeenth century criticism of medieval and baroque styles echoed Vitruvius's strictures against the painting of his own day in comparison with older traditional styles.[6]

In the schools and ateliers of the Greco-Roman imperium, a loosely defined classical tradition had already begun to emerge, and even in antiquity it was invoked as a standard of taste for judging vices of style and censuring new or barbarian modes. In the Middle Ages, the Renaissance, and well into the nineteenth century, one encounters attempts to revive the classical tradition (however loosely it might be defined), along with repeated departures from it. These departures might be largely due to alien influences, to the requirements of imported religions, to the quest for novelty, or to conscious reaction against pagan antiquity or classical authority. In the art and literature of antiquity as well as in Renaissance and post-Renaissance culture, there is a continuing dialogue between what may be loosely termed classical and anticlassical modes.

Yet in applying the "classical/anticlassical" antithesis to literature we are apt to encounter major difficulties.[7] In the first place, the classical tradition is so comprehensive and so widely diffused that it would be difficult to divide authors into "classical" and "anticlassical" categories. Many who appear (or appeared to sixteenth and seventeenth century critics) to fall into the anticlassical category had borrowed themes and motifs or adapted phrases, images or narratives from classical sources. Others, who appeared to be reacting against one classical author, might be following the example of some other writer of antiquity. A writer critical of the stricter Ciceronianism of Pietro Bembo or Étienne Dolet might counsel the student to emulate the "spirit" of Cicero instead of imitating him to the letter; another might advise an eclectic approach, forming one's style through eclectic study of a variety of authors and culling from each what seemed best and most appropriate to one's own personality; another might substitute Seneca — or Tacitus or Pliny or Vellius Paterculus — as a model for close study and imitation.

In many instances, moreover, allegedly anticlassical writers were themselves writing in classical genres — satires, verse epistles, Pindaric odes and the like. They were often reacting against the influence of a particular classical model or authority, not against the classical styles and genres *per se*; and even in these instances, their real target might well be the meticulous imitation of an ancient writer by the moderns. An "anti-Ciceronian" was rarely hostile to Cicero; this criticism was generally directed against the exaggerated veneration of Cicero as an exclusive model for stylistic elegance — against the "Ciceronianism" of Bembo and Longolius and Dolet.

2.

The tension between "classical" tradition and "anticlassical" variations has been, in many respects, a recurrent feature in the longstanding quarrel between ancients and moderns; but it has been, for the most part, a quarrel of contemporaries or near-contemporaries. Though this tension could be (and often was) formulated in purely stylistic terms, it was frequently assimilated to a historical framework and interpreted in terms of successive periods of perfection and decadence, renovation and decay. The pattern of civilization bore a striking resemblance to the theological schema of the fall of humankind: antique excellence, decline, regeneration. Alternatively, it could follow the schema of nature's progressive decay — a *topos* adapted by Donne to the demands of funebrial encomium and elaborated by Godfrey Goodman through a detailed demonstration of the superiority of the ancients to the moderns.[8]

Like the quarrel between "ancients" and "moderns," reactions against Ciceronian eloquence — and reactions against these reactions — were prominent in antiquity. Yet neither the antithesis between ancients and moderns nor the dichotomy of classical and anticlassical modes is altogether satisfactory. The terms are too general, the antinomies too rigid; and in many respects the framework commonly associated with these schemas — a framework of convention and innovation, tradition and revolt — is both simplistic and confusing.

The stereotype of an "orthodox" classical tradition — interrupted by periods of seeming decadence or reaction, but also marked by classical or pseudoclassical attempts (or pretended attempts) to return to the "antique manner" — produces the appearance (or illusion) of a series of renascences.[9] (An analogous phenomenon occurs in the tension between individualists and traditionalists in Chinese art.) Even the reactions, however, are often justified by appealing to the example and precedent of the ancients: their originality and their superiority to rules. In many cases, the apparent reaction is really a protest against the contemporary "establishment," and reflects a tension between academic tradition and the individual talent.

Mannerist artists did not, in fact, repudiate the Renaissance tradition. They extended or developed certain of its aspects and minimized others, borrowing at will from Italian primitives, artists of the Northern Renaissance like Albrecht Dürer, and from painters of the High Renaissance. Neoclassical writers and artists of the seventeenth and eighteenth centuries often regarded themselves as perfecting rather than rejecting the Renaissance tradition, refining and polishing it and bringing it into closer conformity with classical principles. For example, Dryden's attitude toward Shakespeare was one of distinctly qualified admiration. He believed that, of all modern (and perhaps ancient) poets, Shakespeare possessed "the largest and most comprehensive soul" and that in most of Shakespeare's "irregular" plays, there was "greater spirit in the writing" than in any French drama. Nevertheless, even though Shakespeare frequently wrote better than any other English poet, he often wrote "below the dullest writer of ours, or any precedent age," according to Dryden. Furthermore, the English language had become so much refined since Shakespeare's time that "many of his words, and more of his phrases" were scarcely intelligible.[10]

In English neoclassical prose, there was a partial return to the balanced and periodic structure of the Ciceronian tradition — but purged of excessive verbal ornament — and in neoclassical painting and architecture, one encounters a partial return to Renaissance models. If there was indeed an element of reaction, it was against the excesses of mannerist, baroque or metaphysical style;

yet even here there was substantial continuity, and it may be more
accurate to speak of compromise rather than reaction. For, in fact,
the English neoclassical stylists assimilated — but chastened and
refined — the pointed wit of the "anti-Ciceronians" and their
concern for the plain style, just as they moderated the Ciceronian
tradition. In achieving a more graceful, more natural and less
mannered style, the neoclassicists were indebted partly to French
neoclassical models like Boileau and Racine and Molière, and
partly to classical ideas of the Attic mode, but their success consisted primarily in finding a mean between the Ciceronian and
anti-Ciceronian traditions. In the same way, baroque painting
incorporated many of the achievements of mannerist as well as
High Renaissance art, achieving a temporary compromise between
tradition and revolt.

One cannot define a period by its moods: the manic or depres-
sive phases of a society, its optimism or pessimism, faith or
skepticism, its hope or despair. Still less can one define it by such
fits of cosmic sensibility as "world-longing" or "world-affirmation," as "world-negation" or *Weltschmerz*. An awareness of the
limitations of human reason does not necessarily mark the end of
the Renaissance, any more than a recognition of the value of
rational moral decision marks its beginning. Both are constants in
Western thought. The overseas expansion of several Western
European powers during the seventeenth century and the development of an ambitious program for the renovation of science and
technology occurred during a period formerly regarded by cultural
historians as an age of artistic decadence, morbid introspection and
disillusion.

Nor is one altogether justified in defining a period or a culture
by its styles. The "classical" styles of the Renaissance continued to
exist alongside mannerist and baroque modes. If nothing else had
changed — the structure of society, the methods of natural science,
the attitude toward epistemology, the conception of the cosmos,
the attitude toward rhetoric and the conventional topics of invention, the reverence for classical authority — one might well regard
eighteenth century art and literature as basically an extension of
the Renaissance tradition. *Concettismo* and *culteranismo*, which
were in large part exaggerations of certain facets of that tradition,
as well as reactions against other aspects — could be regarded as
temporary lapses in taste, fashionable aberrations from the low but
steady revival of the *maniera antica* and the reconquest of classical
style. Yet, for all the neoclassical strictures against the excesses of
the metaphysical style, the wit of the Augustans was in part

derivative from the metaphysical conceit: the urbane child of a fantastic eccentric.

Neither the Reformation nor the Counter-Reformation — both heavily influenced by Renaissance philology and historiography — marks the end of the Renaissance, though they undoubtedly exaggerated the gulf, always present in the Renaissance mind but judiciously concealed by many of the humanists, between Biblical and pagan antiquity, sacred and profane tradition.

3.

The Renaissance understanding of other periods — classical antiquity, the Middle Ages, even the earlier stages of the Renaissance — was in many respects limited and distorted. Thus Francis Bacon associated humanist rhetorical ideals with the influence of the Reformation rather than with the influence of Petrarch and Quattrocento educators.[11]

In their understanding of antiquity, Renaissance humanists were strongly influenced by the primary orientation of their school curricula: acquiring an accurate and fluent command of the Latin tongue. Relying in part on Quintilian's program for the education of an orator, they reflected his views concerning the close study and imitation of authors of the "best" period of Latinity as an aid to stylistic elegance. Even though the schoolmasters themselves were advised (by Erasmus and others) to read widely among classical authors in order to select the best of them as school texts, and to choose these texts on the basis of content as well as style, they tended (like Quintilian long before them)[12] to concentrate their attention upon "Golden Age" authors largely on the basis of stylistic superiority. Their attitude toward antiquity was thus significantly conditioned by the nature of their profession: as teachers of the Latin language and the arts of discourse.

Similarly, their views of the Middle Ages were frequently prejudiced by their vocation as Latinists. If the interval between classical antiquity and their own age seemed "barbarous" in their eyes, it was not only because the arts and sciences appeared corrupt and decadent, but also because the language itself had been corrupted by "barbarisms." The Latin of the schoolmen — so unlike the Latin of Cicero and Quintilian — had incorporated new coinages and various uncouth idioms borrowed from non-Latin tongues. These were literally barbarisms. The Celtic and Germanic languages were, of course, "barbarian" tongues; and the Romance tongues represented a corrupt, decadent, "barbarized" form of the Latin language. In these respects the word retained its original sense of "foreign" or "alien," and in the context of Italian literary and artistic controversy, it frequently continued to do so. Thus Antonio Minturno condemned the romance, so popular among his fellow citizens in his own day, as "barbaric" and "ultramontane" in origin, an import into Italy from France. In much the same way, the "Gothic" style could be denounced as an alien invader and obliquely associated with early Germanic incursions into the Roman Empire — though in fact, of course, it had no connection either with the Goths or with the period of the barbarian migrations. The northern humanists, not surprisingly, adopted the term and extended it to the entire period — or to literary fashions of their own time that they disliked. Erasmus could speak of the barbaric character of the Middle Ages, and Milton, in defending his use of blank verse in the urbane era of the heroic couplet, could denounce rhyme as the "invention" of a barbarous age.

Renaissance references to preceding ages and to their own were often distorted by the diatribes of humanists against schoolmen or by the polemics of advocates of the "rules" of genre against the conventions of the popular theatre and such fashionable but new-fangled genres as the romance and the tragicomedy. In pressing their arguments, the humanists tended to emphasize the superiority of the ancients over the moderns and the authority of ancient precept and example. In defending themselves and rebutting the arguments of their opponents, however, the partisans of the moderns appealed to the principle of historical relativity. The tastes of the moderns were as valid, they argued, as those of the ancients, and a modern author need not be bound by the literary conventions of antiquity. Strict adherence to these could suppress individuality, imagination and invention, and result in formally correct but lifeless imitations. They maintained that if Aristotle had lived in modern times, he would surely have expressed other opinions concerning unity of action in epic and drama; he would have recognized the merits of variety as a source of beauty and pleasure, and he would have done justice to Ariosto and other writers of romance.

The framework of literary and artistic controversy during the Renaissance was itself an important factor in fostering stereotypes of periods and of period styles, and in relating the development of the visual and verbal arts to the larger patterns of intellectual and political history — or to the pattern of world history itself. Pitting ancients against moderns, the rules of antiquity against fresh invention and modern taste, and the imitation of classical models against the liberty and imagination of the individual talent, the essentially polemical context of Renaissance criticism tended to foreshadow the goal of later periods: to correlate the study of styles with the dialectics of history.

4.

Though there is a limited validity in such a dialectical approach to the history of literature and art, it can be a misleading approach — even if one is fairly scrupulous about defining one's terms. Petrarchism and anti-Petrarchism, or Ciceronianism and anti-Ciceronianism are not only hard to pin down; they have shifted their meaning with different critics. If the somewhat rigid Petrarchism and Ciceronianism of Cardinal Bembo is accepted as a norm, a large proportion of Renaissance lyric poetry and oratorical prose would have to be regarded as "anti-Ciceronian" or "anti-Petrarchist" even though it was strongly influenced, directly or indirectly, by both of these authors. If these definitions are broadened to include an eclectic approach to problems of style, and variants and offshoots of the Petrarchan and Ciceronian traditions, a number of writers often regarded as anti-Petrarchist or anti-Ciceronian would have to be included among the Ciceronians and Petrarchists. The themes of the Petrarchan sonnet, its inventory of conceits and the *topoi* and imagery associated with them, persist among writers who elaborated or parodied them or endeavored to introduce innovations. There were varieties of Petrarchism, just as there were diverse strains of Ciceronianism, in the Renaissance. Donald Guss has even argued plausibly that John Donne belongs to this tradition.[13]

The strict Ciceronianism of Bembo and Dolet did have its disciples and apostles, but many Renaissance writers preferred an eclectic approach, choosing what appeared to them best and most appropriate from a wide range of authors, and sometimes appealing to the legendary example of Zeuxis and his image of Helen of Troy. W.H. Woodward compared the Ciceronian in letters to the Vitruvian in architecture. Serlio had insisted that every architect ought to follow "Vitruvius's rule and most certain and infallible directions"; in every art there was one primary authority, who was recognizably superior to the others and whose words were "fully accepted and without doubt believed."[14] On virtually the same grounds, Bembo had asserted Cicero's supremacy as an exclusive model for Latin style. Since the ancients had exhausted all conceivable styles and since an eclectic style would lack unity, an original style was no longer possible. Hence a modern writer should "seek out the one supreme stylist and imitate him, and him alone. . . ." Dolet similarly believed that Cicero had provided all that was necessary to meet the full demands of the present. "Human character and social life are not variable quantities," he asserted, and the models established by the ancients remained universally valid.[15]

Pico della Mirandola, on the other hand, maintained that, as every person was an individual, each writer ought to evolve an individual and personal style, following the example of the painter, appropriating and combining from all schools what would best serve the writer's purpose. "You try to rebuild," he wrote to Bembo, "*as it stood* a wall which has been torn down. The material . . . is the same, but . . . the ordering of the bricks, and . . . the cementing will be new, and will be yours." Poliziano likewise regarded a good style as intimate, personal and inalienable. According to Poliziano, the writer whose "method is that of direct imitation is hardly different from a parrot"; such writing lacks reality and individuality. The style of a truly learned writer "emerges from a continued process of erudite study, of comparison of styles, and of actual effort at composition." Erasmus himself, in deploring the excesses of Ciceronianism, pointed out stylistic defects in Cicero and observed that Quintilian had "found it necessary to deprecate an ignorant worship of his oratorical method."[16]

5.

The schema of tradition and revolt may be partially valid in the context of *auctoritas*: the selection of a particular writer as the principal authority in a particular art or science or as a "model" for close study and imitation. Aristotle and Galen in philosophy and medicine, Cicero and Quintilian in rhetoric, Horace and Aristotle in poetics, Vitruvius in architecture — all of these were, in their own fields, considered the "masters of those who know." Their works were standard guides in the various arts and sciences; they provided impressive testimony in controversies; and, for the most part, they enjoyed the prestige of school-authors either at the universities or in grammar schools. Yet their very prestige could make them an obstacle to the further advancement of learning or to the study of other authors, ancient or modern. Francis Bacon included them among his "idols of the theater," and indicted the principle of authority and the excessive veneration of antiquity as major barriers to further progress in the arts and sciences.

In the sciences, the authority of the ancients seemed to hinder the advancement of "real" learning; in the arts, it tended to fetter imagination and clip the wings of poetic or artistic invention. It increased the gulf between popular and learned taste, and undercut many of the principal authors and favorite literary genres among the moderns: the major poetry of Ariosto and Dante, the popular tragicomedies and romances.

That there should be protests and remonstrances directed against the authority of the ancients in the name of the arts and sciences alike, then, is hardly surprising. But in reexamining the formulas of reaction in the Renaissance and the paradigm of classicism and anticlassicism, one should not mistake these complaints against the despots of the schoolroom for implacable hostility: a kind of intellectual tyrannicide. The opponents of Aristotle or Cicero rarely succeeded in freeing themselves altogether from their influence; nor were they, for the most part, seriously endeavoring to do so. In attempting to dethrone a school-author, they were not, in most instances, trying to silence him forever. In some instances, these opponents wished to substitute another authority — Plato or Seneca or Epicurus — or to substitute a variety of authors for a single model. In other instances, they were chiefly concerned with defending modern poets from hostile criticism by their own contemporaries, to demonstrate that the moderns were independent from the "rules" and the examples of the ancients. In setting these poets free from bondage to classical authors, then, they left modern writers at liberty to write as they chose, borrowing from antiquity or modernity or relying altogether on their own imaginations. The modern poet was (in their view) the equal of the ancients in liberty if not always in merit, a fellow citizen rather than a subject of the classical poets.

There is a significant difference between deliberately choosing a particular classical author as a model for imitation and being influenced by his work in more general and less systematic ways. Various authors of the Renaissance who explicitly rejected the former were actually influenced by the style and content of classical poetry — and in view of the classical orientation of the grammar schools, they could hardly have avoided it. Conversely, writers who professed their admiration for the classics and a resolve to emulate them sometimes imitated them very loosely, influenced less by the example of the ancients than by that of their own contemporaries and immediate precursors.

6.

Attempts by Renaissance poets and artists to revive the *maniera antica* by imitating or adapting the style (or styles) of the ancients[17] were, in large part, a response to contemporary fashion. These poets and artists were molded by contemporary taste, and though they helped to reshape and redefine it, they were also subject to its vagaries. Poets and artists usually learned the basic principles of style from their own contemporaries. Italian painters and sculptors imitated their masters, and after forming their own styles, they might consciously alter it under the influence of other artists, as Raphael assimilated the example of Michelangelo. Elizabethan playwrights usually learned their techniques largely from their fellow dramatists. However scrupulously neo-Latin and vernacular writers might attempt to imitate classical authors, the standards by which they chose and interpreted their models and decided what features should and should not be imitated were inevitably conditioned by contemporary pedagogical techniques, the discretion of their schoolmasters and their own personal tastes. The imitation of the ancients was frequently a practical, as well as a theoretical, ideal — but the choice of authors and the manner of imitation were, in large part, a reflection of contemporary fashion, and they sometimes varied widely with different poets and place and time. In professing to imitate the ancients, poets or orators could be merely imitating their contemporaries. In other cases, their fidelity to the classics might be more scrupulous, but even then their interpretations and manners of imitation may reveal more of Renaissance taste and fashion than of the spirit and rhetoric of antiquity.

The imitation of the classics was in part a pedagogical technique, a means of mastering the principles of composition and stylistic decorum — principles that could be applied to vernacular as well as neo-Latin eloquence. It was also, in part, an aesthetic ideal and a response to contemporary taste. For some, at least, of the generations of schoolboys reared on close study of classical authors, "the love of sacred song" and the companionship of the Muses was not an empty cliché; and in writing for such men, poets might indulge their own classical tastes more freely than in addressing a more popular audience. On occasion, moreover, the emulation of the classics became a national and an ecclesiastical ideal. The English and the Italian, the Protestant and the Catholic, might hope to accomplish for their own societies what Horace and Virgil, through close study of Greek masterpieces, had done for Rome and the Latin language. In aspiring to equal or surpass the ancients, they were enhancing the glory of their own nations or of the Christian church.

In most instances, the imitation of antiquity essentially involved adaptation or accommodation of the classical tradition, rather than meticulous fidelity to classical models. In this respect, the Renaissance differs from other approximations of the *maniera antica* — medieval "renascences" and eighteenth and nineteenth century classical revivals — only in degree. The continuity of classical learning in European civilization precludes a sharp distinction between "classicizing" and "barbarian" periods (whatever the people of the Renaissance themselves may have thought or said about the matter). Since the principal authorities for the major arts and sciences (with the notable exception of theology and certain branches of mathematics) were, for the most part, classical authors, it is not surprising that medieval scholars should have attempted, from time to time, to go back, as far as possible, to the original and primary authorities themselves. This was the case with scholastic logic and ethics, physics and metaphysics, as with humanistic rhetoric and grammar and history. If the continuity of the classical tradition had been greater, such "revivals" might not have seemed necessary; if it had been less, they might have occurred much later, or never at all.

The respect for the *auctoritas* of the ancients in most branches of learning made such apparent "renascences" probable, if not inevitable. The Renaissance sought and achieved in the sphere of rhetoric and other "humane studies" what the scholastic "renascence" (if we may call it that) accomplished in the domain of logic and the intellectual and physical sciences. Both attempted to return to primary authorities, but (for the most part) in different branches of learning and through different techniques. The strength of the humanist approach resided in its philological and historical techniques, which made possible the restoration and interpretation of both Latin and Greek texts. The neglect of philology, conversely, had been one of the principal defects of scholastic erudition. Few of the schoolmen possessed sufficient Greek or Arabic to read their authorities in the original, and in explicating the essential texts, they were compelled to rely largely on translations and commentaries — frequently of dubious reliability.

In part at least, the attacks of Renaissance humanists on scholastic methodology were an extension of the medieval quarrel of the arts — the rivalry between rhetoric and logic, the graces of eloquence and the subtleties of philosophy, issues that had pitted the medieval humanists of Chartres and Orleans against the dialecticians of Paris. In seeking to "restore" the classical styles as exemplified by the major orators, poets and historians of antiquity, Renaissance humanists were, in a sense, attempting to accomplish in the field of rhetoric what late medieval schoolmen were accomplishing in the field of logic — both were appealing to the text and example of the classical writers traditionally regarded as the major authorities in their respective branches of learning. The return to antiquity is, in many respects, essentially, a return to primary authorities — often long-acknowledged as such, but sometimes neglected, corrupted by inadequate translations and scribal errors, or obscured by later commentaries. This reversion to classical authorities is analogous to patristic revivals and the renewed emphasis on the primary authority of the Biblical text in late medieval and Renaissance theology. It parallels the claims of artists in other fields — painting and sculpture, architecture and occasionally music — that their own theory and practice represented a return to the principles of the ancients as their primary authorities.

In the case of painting or music, such claims might seem very tenuous indeed, insofar as there was altogether too little evidence of classical practice. Actual models for painting were few, and there were no surviving examples of classical music. Accordingly, artists and theorists were compelled to depend largely on the statements of ancient historians or on analogies with rhetoric and poetics. The scarcity of data did not prevent them from appealing to such classical authority to justify their own stylistic innovations or adaptations.[18] Renaissance prose-writers reacting against the overemphasis on Cicero's authority and example also appealed to classical authority, frequently endeavoring to legitimize their revolt by imitating or professing to imitate the styles of other classical writers, Caesar or Seneca, Tacitus or Velleius Paterculus.

Such appeals to classical authority might reflect a conscious reliance on antique example as a rule and guide in literary and artistic composition, but in many instances their function was primarily logical or rhetorical. The citation of written authority functioned as a form of inartificial proof; orator, poet, painter, sculptor and architect alike could justify their own practices most effectively by appealing to the authority of ancient precept and example, as well as to reason and nature. In actual practice, these arguments tended to converge, with God and nature and reason bidding the same, with art and nature alike imitating the ideas in the divine intellect, and with the example of the ancients providing the best evidence for the rule of nature and hence the most reliable rule for art — an idealized image more perfect than the actual creations of nature and closer to the divine archetype or universal idea of the species.

7.

Sharing many of the same theoretical assumptions and critical terms, Renaissance painting and poetics exploited the same topics of invention, recognized the same dual end of utility and delight, and faced the same problem of portraying intelligible essences through sensuous forms. They imitated action, character, passion, nature and the ideas underlying or transcending nature. They acknowledged the same unities of time, place and action; the principles of verisimilitude and probability; and decorum in style, genre and subject matter.[19] Further, these Renaissance theorists professed the same respect for the authority and example of the ancients and for the ideal of the learned poet or painter, the *poeta* or *pictor doctus*. They cited the same mythographers, the same rhetoricians and the same classical treatises on poetics. They emphasized the distinction between formal disposition or structure and verbal or visual ornament; for many artistic theorists, design corresponded to the plot or fable of narrative or dramatic poetry, as the essential form or idea — the "soul" — of the work.[20]

Theorists of both painting and poetics oscillated between emphasis on the rules of art and imitation of the ancients, on the one hand, and (on the other hand) assertions of the liberties of the individual artist, the divine *furor* of the inspired poet or painter, and this artist's independence from the rules of art, and freedom from the obligation to imitate predecessors. Both possessed, so to speak, a bill of rights as well as a legal code and a corpus of precedents. Both possessed a theory of "ideal imitation," which bore more than a superficial resemblance to the methods of Platonic dialectic and Aristotelian induction; by selecting or abstracting the elements of beauty (or other ideas) from various works of nature or of art and combining them in a new or ideal form, the artist not only improved on nature by eliminating the inevitable imperfections inherent in particular objects (thanks to the drag of matter), but also succeeded in fashioning a clearer and more refined image of the universal idea, an image more fully emancipated from nature and matter and therefore capable of realizing more effectively the perfection of the archetype.[21] Finally, both may also have shared on occasion (as recent literary critics have argued) a respect for mathematical structure as a key to ideal form. In addition to this common theoretical background, poets and painters borrowed themes and inventions, iconographical motifs and mythological details, images and concepts and allegories from one another.

In view of these interrelationships between the visual and verbal arts, as well as their common indebtedness to rhetorical theory and the aesthetic cliché *ut pictura poesis*, it is by no means improbable that changing tastes in plastic styles may have conditioned literary tastes and techniques, and vice versa. Moreover, since the sister arts shared the principle of ideal imitation, catered to the private tastes of the same patrons or to the public ends of the same ecclesiastical or political institutions, and frequently derived their commonplaces and conceits from the same philosophical and theological sources, it is not unreasonable to associate the development of artistic styles with contemporary social and intellectual developments and to emphasize parallels between artistic or literary history and the history of ideas and institutions.

Such analogies can be valid, however, only when they make due allowance for the technical problems peculiar to each individual art or science and for the degree to which specific artists or poets consciously relied on another discipline — anatomy or geometry or optics — in pursuing the ends of their own art. Otherwise the critic is apt to perpetuate the Spenglerian fallacy of seeking a single formula for a period or style and finding in a single discipline (geometry or differential calculus or music) the key to the entire intellectual and aesthetic culture of an age. The safest way to avoid such fabulous reconstructions of cultural history as ritual epiphanies of a *Zeitgeist* is to reexamine the technical problems peculiar to each art or science and the degree to which the nature of these problems and their solutions has conditioned changes in philosophical or artistic methodology and alterations in style.

FIVE

The "Sensibility of Mannerism"

In this chapter, I shall attempt to survey some of the conflicting definitions of mannerism[1] proposed by literary critics and art historians and discuss the difficulties of classifying specific poets — as opposed to painters — under this label. Though the terms "mannerism" and "baroque" come from art history and are alien to literary criticism, they have become thoroughly naturalized. Dryden's "sister arts" — painting and poetry — did not exercise joint sovereignty. They ruled divided and distinguished domains, each subject to its own code of laws. In both fields, artists attempted to reinforce their own authority by appealing to the same ancient texts, or by citing analogous rules and decisions. They were not primarily concerned, however, with establishing a system of international law — a universal aesthetics. The problems they faced were, in part at least, peculiar to their own self-conscious discipline; and much of their judicature was, in fact, casuistry — a reinterpretation or redefinition of the rules in order to justify or condemn the practice of particular artists or poets.

1.

In attempting to differentiate "mannerism" from "baroque"[2] or in stressing the affinities between "mannerist" or "baroque" painters and poets, critics have sometimes reduced both arts to a sort of cultural ectoplasm — manifestations of the spirit of the age, the spirit of a generation, or "a spirit of the forms."[3] In mannerist art, Max Dvořák perceived the "manifestations of a general 'spiritual crisis' in the sixteenth century,"[4] and in "mannerist distortion and torment" other critics have perceived the symptoms of contemporary "malaise and distrust."[5] Its restless energy reflected a "Schizothym" world "no longer organized in stable relationships," a universe "not wholly determinate," but "open and shifting," in which the equivocations of casuistry paralleled the "elastic logic" of mannerist art and the double meanings and ambiguities of mannerist verse. Mannerist art "already shows the disturbing disrelationship of mind and body which became a major problem in Descartes"; "mannerist drama utilizes sensational acting even if the actor is not placed within any 'logical framework of events,'" and the ambiguity in mannerist tragicomedies results partly from "decisiveness of gesture within a fluid or dissonant context. . . ."[6]

Critics of mannerist and baroque trends, both in literature and in art, have often been fully aware of the ambiguity and imprecision of these terms, and the need for a more exact terminology. "It would be best," in Walter Friedlaender's opinion,

> if all these terms such as Gothic, Renaissance, Mannerism, Baroque, Classicism, and so forth, which were apparently willfully promulgated and defined, were only used when they meant something very definite and circumscribed. In any case a period should always be restricted to one or two generations, and not used to include completely different trends under a common denominator like "The Art of the Baroque."

According to Friedlaender, the term mannerist was

> immediately applicable only to the second part of the period [c. 1550 to c. 1580], the phase of the *maniera*, and was extended to include the first period by virtue of its being the foundation. Similarly *barocco* was applied as a term of contempt to all that was hated by the rational, classicistic trend toward the end of the *seicento*, and later down to Milizia. It applied to what from the classicistic point of view were the explosive, inflated, extravagant works of a Bernini, a Borromini, or a Pietro Cortona, to these "pestilential diseases of good taste," but not on any account to the works of the Carraci. . . .
>
> Here again the art historians of the nineteenth century must be held responsible for causing confusion, placing the beginning of the Baroque in painting around 1580 . . . and contrasting it to the Renaissance. Actually and historically the painting in the period under discussion arose in opposition to the *maniera* of the late *cinquecento*, but not at all to the same degree, nor in antithesis to the High Renaissance. On the contrary, the temper of the generation growing up around 1580 had its spiritual foundation in the painting of the early, or earlier, *cinquecento*, which served as their model, and can therefore be called "classic" for them.

In Friedlaender's opinion, "it would be more correct to call this time of reform . . . a neoclassical or neo-Renaissance period. . . ."[7]

For Friedlaender, then, the style that other critics would designate as baroque or early baroque represented a conscious reaction against late Cinquecento mannerism and a deliberate return to the classicism of the so-called "High Renaissance." The second phase of mannerism, in turn, had been rooted in the "anticlassical style" of the early Cinquecento. This was "not a mere transition, not merely a conjunction between Renaissance and Baroque," but an autonomous style, a "new style that cast off the classic, and against the Renaissance pattern of canonical balance, set up a subjective rhythmic figuration and an unreal space formation. . . ." Developing "out of the Andrea del Sarto circle as an outspoken reaction against the beauty and repose of the Florentine High Renaissance," it was already "fully formed" between 1520 and 1523; and as a result of the sack of Rome in 1527, the "seeds of the new tendency" were subsequently scattered "far and wide" through northern Italy and France.[8]

In differentiating the idealistic element in mannerism from the "ideal art" of the High Renaissance, Friedlaender suggested that, unlike the latter, mannerist art

> does not rest on an idea of a canon, [but] rather upon a "fantastica idea non appogiata [*sic*] all imitazione," an imaginative idea unsupported by imitation of nature. Thus the canon apparently given by nature and hence generally recognized as law is definitively given up. It is no longer a question of creating a seen object in an artistically new way, "just as one sees it," or, if idealistically heightened and ethically stressed, "just as one ought to see it." Neither is it a matter of recreating the object "as I see it," as the individual person observes it as a form of appearance. Rather, . . . it is to be recreated "as one does not see it," but as, from purely autonomous artistic motives, one would have it seen.[9]

In attempting a "restaurazione della pittura," seventeenth century critics like Carlo Cesare Malvasia and Giovanni Pietro Bellori had objected to the fantastic and unnatural distortions of the later mannerists: "They relied totally upon their imagination and applied themselves to a sort of hasty and wholly mannered way of doing" (Malvasia); "Abandoning the study of nature, artists vitiated art with their manner, or (shall we say?) with their fantastic idea" (Bellori). In Friedlaender's opinion, the reform movement, which commenced around 1580, was directed against the "mannered Mannerism of the second phase," and its purpose was "to cut loose from the degeneration of form just as much as from the degeneration of the spiritual into the playful and allegorical." The reformers shared a "desire for simplicity and objectivity instead of complexity, for truth to nature (or that part of nature that could be objectively tested) instead of to the 'imaginative,' and for solid and dedicated work instead of painting by rote with only a glib and facile 'effect' in mind."[10] These reformers, he argues, formed the vanguard of the baroque movement.

2.

Ernst Curtius likewise associated mannerism with anticlassical trends; but, in applying this concept to literature, he not only dissociated it from art history, but regarded it as "a constant in European literature," the "complementary phenomenon of the Classicism of all periods." As the "common denominator for all literary tendencies which are opposed to Classicism, whether they be preclassical, postclassical, or contemporary with any Classicism," he preferred this term to "Baroque" — a term that in his opinion had "caused such confusion that it is better to eliminate it." Curtius's definition centered on the "mannerist" use of rhetorical ornament. Whereas "the standard classicist says what he has to say in a form naturally suited to the subject," decorating the discourse with judgment and restraint, "in mannerist epochs, the *ornatus* is piled on indiscriminately and meaninglessly. In rhetoric itself, then, lies concealed one of the seeds of Mannerism," and it "produces a luxuriant growth in Late Antiquity and the Middle Ages."

Tracing "seven leading varieties of formal Mannerism" from antiquity into the Renaissance, Curtius argued that "medieval Latin Mannerism . . . finds its way into vernacular literature, and there, unaffected by the Renaissance and Classicism, it can be traced through the centuries," taking "deepest root in Spanish soil" and flaring up "for the last time in the seventeenth century." In his opinion, "to separate seventeenth century Mannerism from its 2,000 years of prehistory and, contrary to all historical testimony, to call it a spontaneous product of [Spanish or German] Baroque is possible only as a result of ignorance and of the demands of pseudo-art-historical systems."

Emphasizing the close association between formal mannerism and "mannerism in thought," and between the formal epigram and the "pointed style," Curtius stressed the "relations between Spanish Mannerism and the Latin tradition" and the indebtedness of Gracián's *Arte de Ingenio* and *Arte de Prudencia* to the conventional rhetorical distinction between invention and disposition or *ingenium* and *iudicium*. Gracián's originality "consists precisely in the fact that he, first and alone, declares the system of antique rhetoric to be insufficient and supplements it by a new discipline, for which he claims systematic validity," by subjecting "the conceit (*concepto*) to rules."[11]

3.

In the Florentine Mannerism of Vasari and Bronzino, Anthony Blunt perceived a "lowering of the intellectual and emotional tone of art." Painting had become "a game of skill, appealing to the love of ingenuity and leaving the rational faculties undisturbed." In Vasari's emphasis on grace and facility, Blunt found an echo of Castiglione's stress on *sprezzatura* ("recklessness" or spontaneity) as a source of grace.[12] In imitating nature, the artist must study "the choicest ancient and modern works" in order to "improve the grace and perfection in which art goes beyond the scope of nature"; through much study and exercise, "attitudes in any position can be drawn by help of the imagination without one's having the living forms in view." The "judgement of the eye" was a better standard for proportion than mathematical calculation; by correct judgment artists could achieve, "in due relation to their dimensions, a grace exceeding measurement." In Vasari's *Lives*, "all the elements surviving" from High Renaissance theory "have been altered and given a new meaning."[13]

The principal characteristics of Cinquecento mannerism, in Blunt's opinion, were intelligible only against the background of the Counter-Reformation — the alliance of the Papacy with Spain after the sack of Rome, and the decrees of the Council of Trent. In many ways, "the Mannerists are nearer to the artists of the Middle Ages than to their immediate predecessors," abandoning "the Renaissance ideals of convincing space and normal proportions" and making "almost as free use as a medieval artist of arbitrary construction and deliberate elongation," substituting "tones which appeal directly to the emotions" for the "restrained and realistic coloring of the Renaissance." The mannerists show a preoccupation with "developing new methods of drawing and composition" rather than with "the reconstruction of the visible universe. . . ." In the later mannerists, Blunt detected "almost mystical doctrines . . . about the nature of beauty" along with "other anti-rational features" such as the superiority of the judgment of the eye to mathematical methods, the close association of grace with

taste (*gusto*), the emphasis on unfettered invention, the tendency
to base the rules of art on authority rather than experience and
"individual rationalism," and a "non-naturalistic conception of
maniera or style.[14]

Both Erwin Panofsky and Rensselaer Lee associated mannerism
specifically with Renaissance neo-Platonic doctrines. Divine inspiration (*il furor di Apolline*) exempted the artist from the rules, while
the idea of beauty — a divine emanation within the painter's soul
— served as a release from the obligation to imitate natural forms
as they actually existed in nature or as they appeared to be. In
Lee's opinion, "the Mannerist doctrine that the Idea of beauty
which the artist should follow is not gathered from nature but
exists a priori in his mind . . . has its counterpart in the well-
known deviations from nature in Mannerist art." This "mystical
and Platonic point of view" was characteristic of mannerism, while
"an empirico-idealistic, or generally Aristotelian, point of view"
was just as "thoroughly characteristic of the Baroque seventeenth
century. . . ." The fundamental distinction lies between the idea
"as an archetype of beauty existing a priori in metaphysical independence," and the idea "as derived a posteriori by a selective
process from the artist's actual experience of nature."[15]

In some instances, moreover, mannerism was closely associated
with "fantastic" imitation in contrast to the restrictions of naturalistic or "icastic" mimesis. In defending Dante's *Commedia* against
charges of violating probability and verisimilitude, Jacopo Mazzoni
argued that "phantastic" imitation is the proper mode of the poet,
whose office is to feign "idols." Though Torquato Tasso challenged Mazzoni's views, it is significant that Gregorio Comanini
based his discussion of the mannerist painter Arcimbaldo partially
on the Platonic category of phantastic mimesis. For Comanini, this
is the principal delight of poetry, whereas "icastic" imitation is that
of the painter.[16]

4.

Arnold Hauser approached the problem of mannerism in terms
of the history of ideas, using art historical connections primarily as
a means rather than as an end. In giving "preferential treatment"
to painting, however, he pointed out that "it was the concept of
style established by art history that made it possible to isolate
trends of spiritual development from their personal representatives, and to take a collective view of individual endeavours and

purposes." Even though "the origin of mannerism is connected with factors far more complex and involved than any phenomena restricted to the visual field," mannerist works were "being produced in painting while no trace of the style was yet apparent in the other arts, and . . . for a long time it was possible to conceive of a 'mannerist' outlook in other fields only by analogy,. . . only on the basis of ideas drawn from the visual arts."[17]

In mannerist literature and art, Hauser recognized a symptom of the crisis of the Renaissance and the disintegration of the Renaissance sense of harmony. Stressing the "anticlassical," "antihumanist" and "antinaturalistic" aspects of mannerism, he noted its inability to "state its problems except in paradoxical form." The key to mannerism, he suggested, was alienation; nevertheless, it was "not so much a symptom and product of alienation . . . as an expression of the unrest, anxiety and bewilderment generated by the process of alienation of the individual from society and the reification of the whole cultural process." This sense of alienation, however, constituted the raw material for art rather than "a formal element." The mannerist artist expressed "concern, dismay and despair at a world in which the spirit of alienation, depersonalization and soullessness prevail, but his work, as an expression of protest against this world or a way of escape from it, in the artistic respect need bear no marks of alienation."

Hauser objected to the tendency to confuse the "manneristic" with the "mannered" and to reduce mannerism to "a mere epilogue to classical periods and thus a regularly recurrent phenomenon in the history of styles." Friedlaender's emphasis on the "anticlassical" and unnaturalistic aspects of mannerism seemed to him useful as a starting point for analysis but inadequate if "applied without qualification." According to Hauser,

> A proper understanding of mannerism can be obtained only if it is regarded as the product of tension between classicism and anticlassicism, naturalism and formalism, rationalism and irrationalism, sensualism and spiritualism, traditionalism and innovation, conventionalism and revolt against conformism; for its essence lies in this tension, this union of apparently irreconcilable opposites.

A completely satisfactory definition would "emphasize the tension between conflicting stylistic elements which finds its purest and most striking expression in paradox." The "artists and writers of the mannerist period were not only aware of the insoluble contradictions of life; they actually emphasized and intensified them." They "singled out the contradictory quality of things, cultivated it as artists, and tried to perpetuate it and make it the basic formula of their art."[18]

Mannerism in literature, Hauser believed, "began and ended later than in the visual arts." Criticizing the "continual confusion of mannerism with the baroque" by literary historians, he attributed their errors not only to "insufficient art historical experience" but also (and primarily) to an inadequate conception of the baroque. In emphasizing its "subjectivism, immoderation and exuberance," literary scholars had ignored "the fundamental factor": that the baroque was essentially "an emotionally determined artistic trend appealing to broader sections of society, while mannerism is essentially an intellectually and socially exclusive spiritual movement." In Hauser's view, efforts to transfer "the formal principles of the visual arts to literature" had generally resulted "not in establishing any real identity, but in equivocation, as, for instance, when a sonnet of Spenser is called 'linear' in contrast to Milton's 'painterly' *Il Penseroso*. . . ."

In every art, Hauser continued, "the problem of form is tied up with its own medium, . . . and the solution of a problem in one is not automatically transferable to another. . . ." The "formal peculiarities of mannerist painting, sculpture and architecture have no precise equivalent in literature, and the stylistic unity in this instance appears in a common spiritual disposition rather than in similar formulations." Hauser insisted that Heinrich Wölfflin's contrasts between plane and recession and between the painterly and the linear were "inapplicable to the other arts," and his concepts of closed and open form could be transferred to them "only by stretching their meaning. . . ."[19]

Hauser followed Max Dvořák and Wilhelm Pinder in stressing the "mannerist character" of the works of Cervantes and Shakespeare. In his opinion, mannerism offered the "best approach to an explanation of Shakespearian form. . . ." The

> continuous mixture of tragic and comic motifs, the mixed nature of the tropes, the gross contrast between the concrete and abstract, the sensual and intellectual elements of the language, the often forced ornamental pattern of the composition . . ., the emphasis on the a-logical, the unfathomable and contradictory in life, the idea of the theatrical and the dream-like quality, the compulsion and restraints of human life — all these are arguments for taking mannerism as the starting point of the analysis.

Similarly, the "artificiality, affectation and mania for originality in Shakespeare's language are also manneristic and to be explained only by the manneristic taste of the age."[20]

In Hauser's view, the essential novelty in Cervantes's *Don Quixote* was

> not the ironic treatment of the chivalrous attitude to life, but the relativizing of the two worlds of romantic idealism and realistic rationalism. What was new was the indissoluble dualism of his worldview, the idea of the impossibility of realizing the idea in the world of reality and of reducing reality to the idea.

Cervantes's approach to the problem of chivalry was "entirely determined by the ambivalence of the manneristic approach to life," wavering between "the justification of unworldly idealism and of worldly-wise common sense." Thence arises his own "conflicting attitude to his hero," who is both "saint and fool in one and the same poem." The "wavering sense of reality" in *Don Quixote*, the "effacement of the frontiers between the real and the unreal," is essentially manneristic. Other mannerist features include the element of the comic in the tragic — and vice versa — and the hero's "dual nature," which made him appear alternately sublime and ridiculous. If "a sense of humor is the ability to see two opposite sides of a thing at the same time, then the discovery of this double-sidedness of a character signifies the discovery of humor in the world of literature — of the kind of humor that was unknown before the age of mannerism."[21]

5.

John Shearman's analysis of mannerism is especially useful for its discussion of tensions between unity and variety in literature and art. He regarded mannerist styles as sophistications of Renaissance style (and baroque styles as developments of mannerist style) rather than as reactions *against* the Renaissance. He also noted the influence of ancient examples of "manneristic" decorative motifs on Renaissance artists. He stressed the continuity of tradition, but analyzed the transformation of mannerism by El Greco, Bellange and other artists. He discussed the affinities of mannerism with Gothic (though utilizing classical and Renaissance motifs instead of medieval Gothic motifs) and with *chinoiserie*, and the relationship between mannerism and rococo. Emphasizing the relationship between rhetoric and art, he criticized twentieth century psychological interpretations of mannerism, with their exaggerated stress on tension, malaise, divided sensibility and disturbed social conditions as determinants of style. He contrasted the unified viewpoint of baroque and High Renaissance art with the multiple, uncoordinated viewpoints of mannerist achitecture and garden design. Noting the elements of lightness and pleasure as well as marvel in mannerist art, he stressed the stylistic virtuosity of mannerist artists, their delight in variety and strangeness and jeu d'esprit, and their preoccupation with surmounting technical difficulties.[22]

In mannerist art, Shearman also detected an exaggerated emphasis on the decorative element at the expense of content, meaning and function. He endeavored to link the style of mannerism with "Bemboism" in literature and with the Renaissance concern for *copia*, devices of amplification, and grace and variety of style. Shearman's argument is not altogether convincing, however, in actually differentiating or explaining the basic features of mannerism. In several respects, these emphases would seem to be fairly typical of the humanist movement as a whole. If pushed to its logical conclusion, using these criteria as denoting mannerism would tend to subsume virtually the entire Renaissance (including both Neo-Latin and vernacular literature) under the mannerist label.

Wylie Sypher's study, in turn, tended to overemphasize the expressive quality and the psychological motivation of style. Attempting to "outline the changing configurations of the worlds revealed and created by the changing styles of art from the fourteenth through the seventeenth centuries," he argued that, since "styles have a life of their own," there are "analogies between types of formal organization in different arts," even though the arts themselves differ in "medium and content." Every art technique has a "social context," and style itself becomes a form of syntax, expressing the way a society "feels, responds, thinks, communicates, dreams, escapes. . . ."

By tracing "changes in literary syntax," Sypher suggested, the critic could "interpret the varying modes of consciousness in different eras of European culture." Moreover, since "a style serves as a syntax of consciousness, many of the definitions of style in the visual and plastic arts should have certain uses in analyzing the structure of literary experience erected by the world." Syntax is "conditioned by the structure of the world in which we believe we live; and the whole organization of the artist's sensibility is a screen through which appears the world he represents." A "prevailing style in the arts" constitutes a "configuration" or *Gestalt* of "our experience of reality. . . ." Thus the "abrupt phrasing in *The Song of Roland*" indicated that the poet "thinks and sees in sharply divided categories," while his paratactic constructions reflected a "rigidly feudal view of the world" and a "limited, static, simplified, hierarchal, unarticulated" concept of reality. Rabelais's syntax in turn was adapted to the "disorderly, disoriented, expanding world opening before the renaissance consciousness."[23]

6.

Despite obvious differences in methodology and critical assumptions, most of these scholars have agreed that mannerism — either in literature or in art — should be associated with "anticlassical" and "antinaturalistic" trends, a desire for novelty and surprise, and an emphasis on technical virtuosity and facility at the expense of truth to nature and the rules of art. These scholars have disagreed, however, as to the chronological limits of mannerism and its distinction from baroque. Some of them have emphasized its "mystical" and nonrational qualities, its conscious reversion to medieval or northern styles in the early Cinquecento, its neo-Platonic sympathies toward the end of the same century, and its pronounced allegorical and mythological element, especially among the later mannerists. Most of them have recognized the range and diversity of the style in the hands of various artists or in different milieus, and the difficulty of making valid generalizations about the style as a whole.

Like the mannerist painters themselves, however, these scholars have approached the problem from different angles and with different perspectives. Friedlaender was primarily concerned with the "anticlassical" style of the early Cinquecento, Blunt with the antithesis between an art based on human reason and an aesthetics subservient to an otherworldly faith and an authoritarian church, Curtius with the recurrent opposition between classical (i.e. natural) eloquence and mannered rhetoric in European literature. Sypher was chiefly preoccupied with analogies between verbal and visual styles as a reflection of cultural sensibility and an expression of a changing worldview, Panofsky with the changing fortunes of the term "idea" from Plato through the seventeenth century, and Lee with parallels between literary and artistic theory. These diverse approaches, complementing rather than contradicting one another, indicate the difficulty of defining a style or a movement already notorious for its complexity, and the inevitably tentative and hypothetical status of any attempt at a comprehensive definition.

Blunt's frame of reference tended to exaggerate the rational and

secular element in High Renaissance art as well as the mystical and
otherworldly character of the styles and periods that preceded and
followed it. In the generation of Masaccio, Donatello and Brunel-
leschi, he perceived "a new ideal of art," an emergent style which
expressed people's "new approach to the world, their Humanist
confidence and their reliance on the methods of reason." The
naturalism apparent in painting and sculpture was "based on
scientific study of the outside world by means of the new weapons
of perspective and anatomy," while in architecture "the revival of
Roman forms" fostered a style that answered "the demands of
human reason rather than the more mystical needs of medieval
Catholicism." Whereas medieval theories of painting, subordinat-
ing art to the Church and an otherworldly scale of values that
"emphasized the spiritual and had no interest in the material,"
had "made no demand that artists should imitate the outside
world," the generation of 1420 believed that "painting consisted
first and foremost in the rendering of the outside world according
to the principles of human reason."[24]

This frame of reference scarcely does justice to the naturalistic
and realistic tradition in late medieval poetry and art, to the
emphasis on verisimilitude and decorum in medieval poetics, to
the element of lower or middle class realism in the fabliaux and in
classical and medieval definitions of comedy in terms of a realistic
representation of common life. In certain respects the development
of Renaissance style, in art and literature alike, involved a movement away from late Gothic realism in the interests of greater
dignity and elevation of style and a heightened emphasis on
idealized representation.

In large part, the differences between realistic and idealistic, or
natural and mystical, emphasis resulted from distinctions in genre
or in subject matter rather than from chronological differences. In
classical and medieval, Renaissance, baroque and neoclassical art
or literature alike, realism was more likely to be associated with the
low or middle style than with the high style, with the lower and
middle classes of society rather than with princes and demigods
and heroes, and with comedy and satire rather than with tragedy
and heroic poetry. This is hardly surprising. The persons and
events of epic and tragedy are themselves extraordinary and often
mythical or legendary; in practice and theory alike, tragic and
heroic poets based their arguments on distant places or the remote
past. Comedy and satire, on the other hand, conventionally dealt
with the contemporary scene, with lower or middle-class persons,
and with familiar everyday incidents. Their styles varied likewise

— the grand style involving the greatest departure from the vocabulary and syntax of ordinary speech, the low and middle styles preserving greater conformity to familiar and colloquial usage. In literature, the pitch of style and the degree of idealism or realism were partly contingent on genre and the relative altitude of characters and subjects. In view of the close relationship between poetry, painting and rhetorical theory, variations between the extremes of idealism and realism in the visual arts would seem, in part at least, to have been similarly conditioned by notions of decorum.

The emphasis on the dichotomy between sacred and secular, or spiritual and natural values, as the basis of the contrast between medieval and "mannerist" art, on the one hand, and the art of the High Renaissance, on the other, tends to distort the character of all three ages or styles. This dichotomy was, in fact, inherent in the European literary and artistic tradition from late classical antiquity well into the eighteenth century. It does not really differentiate the Middle Ages from the Renaissance, though it may on occasion clarify trends within the art or literature of a particular period, or tensions within the same peom or painting. On occasion, poets or artists might deliberately emphasize the tensions or oppositions between these extremes; in other instances, they might minimize the antithesis or ignore it altogether, mixing sacred and secular or mystical and rational elements for a common end or consciously employing the natural as the symbolic vehicle of the spiritual.

7.

The essential points at issue in late Cinquecento controversies over "mannerism" and subsequently over "baroque" art were, on the whole, questions concerning regularity in design and verisimilitude in representation: in short, truth to nature and the principles of artistic imitation. The same issues were raised with regard to the rhetorical excesses of *culteranismo* and *conceptismo* in Spain and the irregularities of metaphysical and dramatic poetry in England. Moreover, in sixteenth century Italy, criticism of Dante's *Commedia* and the romance-epics of Boiardo and Ariosto had centered on similar principles. Tasso sought a formula for reconciling the unity of the epic plot with the variety of the romance and for representing the marvellous without sacrificing verisimilitude, probability and decorum — and, like many of his near-contemporaries, artists as well as poets, he found his solution in the Judaeo-Christian marvellous.

   Others sought *maraviglia* through paradoxes, conceits, inge-
nuities of invention and style. These were not always dissociated
from probability or credibility. The paradoxes and mysteries of the
Christian religion were articles of faith and commanded assent;
neo-Platonic mysteries and Stoic paradoxes possessed the authority of Greco-Roman philosophy. In these and in the representation
of miracles, the poet and painter could deliberately emphasize the
element of wonder, while relying on theological doctrine, Biblical
history, or ecclesiastical tradition for authority and conviction. In
mock-encomiums and burlesque paradoxes, they could "demonstrate" an absurd thesis with apparent probability by relying on
sophistic proofs; among these was the argument from analogy.
Often a notoriously specious form of proof, this was the foundation of the majority of conceits; rhetorically and dialectically, these
conceits functioned not merely as ornaments of discourse but (as
Rosemond Tuve has argued) as probable, or apparently probable,
arguments.
   Poets could also combine probability and surprise by basing
their conceits (in Gracián's definition, recognitions of analogy or
correspondence)[25] on one or more of the numerous "correspondences" that the tradition of "universal analogies" conveniently
afforded.[26] Or a poet could adapt and alter the familiar images and
motifs of the classical and Renaissance poetic tradition; hackneyed
though they often were, these images and motifs derived apparent
probability from the fact that they had become commonplace, and
the poet might invest them with "marvel" by presenting them in a
new and different way.
   Ingenuity and novelty of style could arouse wonder. Heroic
poets sought *maraviglia* through the rugged and lofty grandeurs of
the magnificent style, portraying extraordinary virtues and actions
in an extraordinary vocabulary and syntax, and employing a level
of discourse removed as far as possible from the familiar patterns
of common speech. The followers of Góngora and Marino sought
novelty and wonder through a highly ornamented style, involved
elaborate figures of sound, disrupted syntax, or abstruse and
complex metaphors. The novelty of Góngora's conceits resided
primarily in his incongruous juxtaposition of qualities that properly belonged either to the metaphorical image or to its actual
referent; his well-known trope "plumed citharas," for instance,
transfers an epithet literally applicable to birds to his metaphorical
substitute for birds. The Greek rhetorician who described vultures
as "living sepulchers" and the fliers who piloted the "Flying
Coffins," employed the same device. This conceit serves merely as

rhetorical ornament and does not serve as logical proof. Both the metaphor and the epithet are conventional; moreover, the novelty resides in their juxtaposition. The followers of Quevedo and Donne endeavored to achieve surprise through comparisons no less farfetched but frequently drawn from scholastic sources or common life and often presented in a colloquial style, or with dramatic verisimilitude.

With Góngora's type of conceit, effective in its own way and in its own context, we may contrast Donne's comparison of the lovers to twin compasses. Introducing his image as a simile rather than as a metaphor, he develops it consistently as an argument from analogy, using it as a basis for emphasizing various aspects of the lovers' relationship. Unlike Góngora, he does not blur the identity of either the image or its referent by fusing their respective qualities into a figure that belongs fully neither to the literal nor to the metaphorical object — a sort of hermeutical or ontological oxymoron belonging partly to two different levels of meaning and reality. Donne's novelty lies primarily in the invention itself — in the terms of his comparison and in his quasi-logical elaboration of the analogy; Góngora's in the concious conversion of a familiar metaphor into a form of oxymoron or paradox. Góngora's image, credible when analyzed and interpreted by the intellect, is incredible (and marvellous) when read according to the terms in which it is presented to the imagination.[27]

Painters similarly sought the effect of novelty or wonder through a variety of means, including stylistic ingenuity as well as miraculous subject matter or metaphorical and allegorical elements. The miracles of the Old and New Testaments, the *mirabilia* of saints and the paradoxes of the Christian faith were simultaneously marvellous and credible. The metamorphoses and similar marvels of classical myth could be credible as allegory. The fantastic or monstrous shapes with which iconographical tradition had invested the divinities of the Gentiles and the personifications of abstract concepts like Fortune and Time were simultaneously marvellous and impossible on the literal level, but nonetheless credible as symbol. A masque, a pageant, a triumphal arch, the programme for the painted ceilings of a palace or the walls of a church, or the mythological poetry celebrating the victories or nuptials of a patron could exploit the incredible simultaneously as a source of marvel and delight and as the vehicle of a credible or commonplace idea. In cases where the nature of the occasion and the identity of the persons honored were already common knowledge, or in instances where the ideas symbolized were doctrinal commonplaces, the meaning of the allegory conferred credibility on the symbol.[28] Images of Fame and Victory or representations of Mars, Jove, Venus, Diana or Minerva might lack verisimilitude in the strictest sense, but in the context of a national victory or royal marriage their meaning was as credible as any other mode of demonstrative oratory. In such instances, allegory and emblem functioned as encomium, suggesting the universal — fortitude or justice, beauty or chastity or wisdom — and applying it to specific persons or events, "subsuming" (so to speak) the specific qualities of Henry IV or Marie de Medici or Queen Elizabeth under universal ideas.

Biblical types might similarly combine the marvellous and the credible, as in Vasari's representation of the Biblical prophecy of the woman's seed (Gen. 3:15) who would bruise the serpent's head. Whereas Protestant commentators interpreted this passage as a prophecy of Christ, Catholic exegesis applied it to the Virgin. Accordingly, in his "Immaculate Conception" at Lucca,[29] Vasari places beneath the Virgin's feet the human-headed serpent (conventional in representations of the temptation of Eve) coiled about the tree of knowledge.

Conscious distortions in the proportions and disposition of figures and in the treatment of space · could also enhance the element of the marvellous (as in the paintings of Pontormo, Bronzino, Parmigianino and other artists analyzed by Friedlaender), though critics have apparently exaggerated the importance of "unreal space" in mannerist art.

Nevertheless, it is impossible to reduce "mannerist" art or poetry to a single formula or to ascribe it to the influence of a specific factor — the emphasis on *ingenium* and free invention, the conception of *disegno interno* and its superiority to nature, the desire for novelty and *maraviglia*, the fashionable taste for conceits and "points," the doctrine of universal analogies and cosmic correspondences, or the restlessness and spiritual malaise of the age. Medieval poets had recounted "ferlies" and wonders, and — long before Tasso and Marino — Pontano had defined the end of poetry as marvel. The "conceited" style in poetry and prose had been a "constant" in European literature, as Curtius and Gracián himself recognized. The doctrine of correspondences was likewise a "constant" from antiquity through the Middle Ages and Renaissance and into the eighteenth century. Though all of these factors may have conditioned "mannerist" literature and art, they were not primarily responsible for the style (or styles) itself.

The term "anticlassical" as applied to mannerist prose, poetry and the visual arts has limited validity, since it frequently involves arbitrary or specialized definitions of classicism. Curtius redefined classicism in terms of natural expression and an existing canon of authors based essentially on the standard of correct Latinity that remained in favor, with few radical changes, from late antiquity throughout the Renaissance.[30] Art historians usually employ this term in a specialized sense, applying it to the art of the High Renaissance and to academic styles based on this tradition. Though "mannerist" artists and writers might have asserted their freedom from servile imitation of the ancients, they nevertheless continued to borrow from them and to justify their practice by antique example and precedent. Seventeenth century theorists sometimes designated the fashionable "conceited" style of their period as a *novum genus dicendi*, but its roots (as most of them recognized) were to be found in the Latinity of the Silver Age. "Anti-Ciceronians" appealed to classical authorities for support, just as mannerist painters appealed to Plato's theory of ideas to justify their own divergences from classical and High Renaissance conceptions of proportion.

In their variety, their irregularity, their emphasis on spontaneity and ingenuity, and their appeal to a higher principle than the literal imitation of nature, "mannerist" artists exhibit certain affinities with the "individualists" and "eccentrics" of Far Eastern painting. These very qualities make it all the more difficult to reduce their styles to a common denominator, without underemphasizing their individuality. The common link between these artists is less the possession of a common body of theory or a common style than their emphasis on personal style and their variation from canonical norms. In attempting to define mannerism and to evolve a comprehensive stylistic formula, critics are paradoxically endeavoring to reduce individuality of style and subjective taste to a single and universal idea. Unless critics are willing to distort the very qualities they are attempting to define, they should focus their study primarily on the styles of individual artists and only secondarily on the characteristics these artists seem to have in common.

Like the anticlassical label, the emphasis on the "unnatural" element in mannerist painting is not altogether applicable to literature. Though critics of metaphysical poetry regarded its scholastic terminology and metaphysical arguments as inappropriate for the *suasoria* (suasion) of a lover courting a mistress, recent criticism has attempted to associate "baroque" or "libertine" prose style with the natural expression of the act of thinking, the attempt to mirror in syntax the processes of thought.

Finally, the technical problems that a poet or artist must inevitably face in structuring and designing a composition are not identical. Though both might consciously strive for unity of design in the imitation of thought or character, action or passion, the methods whereby they must achieve such unity must inevitably be peculiar to their diverse media.

Despite the tendency of certain cultural historians to seek in the "feeling for space"[31] a more or less unconscious response to the spirit of the age, and the tendency of several art historians to emphasize the irrationality of mannerist art, some of the principal characteristics of mannerist and baroque painting result apparently from thoroughly conscious attempts to resolve problems of spatial composition that are peculiar to the arts of design and have no exact parallel in poetic and rhetorical composition. To approach these art historical problems as though they were problems in literary or intellectual history can only result in distorting them. Conversely, metaphysical poetry and anti-Ciceronian prose involve specifically literary problems that can be solved only on literary grounds and cannot be understood in terms of art history or social psychology.

Though there are in fact a substantial number of principles and aesthetic problems common to the visual and verbal arts, there are nevertheless technical problems peculiar to each art, and the critic must distinguish carefully between them. Appeals to vague criteria like "feeling for space," "sensibility" and "taste," or the "mind and spirit of the age" usually beg the question; these are valid only when supported by concrete examples. Through ignoring the specific problems peculiar to each art, historians have sometimes confused aesthetic effects and the principles of composition with social attitudes, interpreting symmetrical or asymmetrical compositions as evidence of social balance or imbalance, scenes of repose or violent movement as signs of cultural stasis or restlessness, the artistic juxtaposition of contrary masses and energies as indications of spiritual tensions, and distorted contours as symptoms of a twisted psyche.

The implicit assumption underlying this approach differs little from the nineteenth century approach to Shakespeare, which confused genre and style with emotional biography: reading "joyous comedies" as an expression of personal joy, "bitter comedies" as a record of disillusionment, tragedies as the confession of a psychological crisis or even a nervous breakdown, tragicomedies and pastorals as the mellow serenity of middle age. In much the same way, the youthful optimism of the Renaissance psyche, the confident worldliness of its maturity, the disillusion and doubt of its middle years, and the fideistic dogmatism or morbid introspection of its old age are (it has been assumed) mirrored in the changes of Renaissance art — the spirit of the age trapped in an enchanted glass.

SIX

The "Age of the Baroque"

In this chapter, I shall consider some of the definitions of the
baroque[1] proposed by various art historians and literary critics,
and discuss the difficulties of arriving at a stable denotation for this
term. The question of the precise meaning of art historical terms
and their relevance to literary history is more complicated in
criticism of the "baroque" than in studies of "mannerism." Art
historians were slow to emphasize the mannerist phase in late
Renaissance art, and its relationship to baroque styles, High Renaissance art and "Gothic" modes still remains controversial.
Heinrich Wölfflin's influential book on the development from the
"classic" styles of High Renaissance painting, sculpture and architecture to the flowering of seventeenth century baroque largely
ignored the problem of mannerism. Friedlaender's lecture on the
early mannerist painters, though delivered in 1914, remained
unpublished until 1925, ten years after the publication of Wölfflin's
study.[2] Morris Croll's essay "The Baroque Style in Prose" appeared in 1927. Before literary critics were fully cognizant of the
implications of mannerism, the term "baroque" had already become well-established in the theory of literature. As a result,
critical terminology, already ambiguous enough, has been further
complicated by conflicting classifications. The same writers —
metaphysicals, *concettisti*, *marinisti*, Gongorists — have been labelled baroque or mannerist by different critics. Many of the poets
and prose writers whom Ernst Curtius classified as mannerist are
"baroque" in the opinion of other scholars. A few recent critics, on
the other hand, have endeavored to preserve the art historical
distinctions between these terms, dividing the metaphysicals (for
instance) into mannerist and baroque poets and sometimes differentiating between mannerist and baroque styles in works by the
same writer. Such distinctions can be useful, however, only insofar

as the terms themselves are clearly definable; and in many cases, the problem of nomenclature appears to be an accident of literary history, the result of a cultural lag between art theory and the theory of literature.

Insofar as literary scholarship endeavors to exploit the terminology and techniques of other arts or sciences, its conceptual framework is likely to be anachronistic. In making use of the methods and concepts of art history, we frequently experience the same "delayed reaction" that we encounter in other fields: depth psychology and *Gestalt* theory, phenomenology and *Geistesgeschichte*, anthropology and iconography. The latest modes in literary methodology are, in many instances, the discarded fashions of other disciplines.

1.

Heinrich Wölfflin's *Renaissance und Barock* first appeared in 1888. In this work, he attempted to clarify the origins of the baroque style — "the style into which the Renaissance resolved itself or, as it is more commonly expressed, into which the Renaissance degenerated" — and to define its geographical and chronological limits. In his opinion, the baroque was essentially an Italian (and, more specifically, a Roman) achievement. This "stylistic change" possessed a radically different significance for Italian and for northern art, inasmuch as the north did not experience the same "progression from a strict to a 'free and painterly' style" that occurred in Italian art. Moreover, Wölfflin asserted, "Roman baroque alone has a right to be regarded as . . . the typical manifestation."

Though he found a comparable phase in ancient art (which "dies" from "symptoms analogous to those with which the Renaissance ended"), Wölfflin regarded the year 1580 as "a convenient starting point for the fully formed baroque style." In contrast to the Renaissance, the baroque style "developed without models" and theoretical rules; and since there was apparently "no sense of breaking fundamentally new ground," the new style was nameless. The term *stilo moderno* "embraced equally all that was neither antique nor of the 'stilo tedesco' or gothic style," though new terms such as "capricious, bizarre and extravagant" were applied to it, and "anything unusual and uncanonical was greeted with approval."

Noting that the modern meaning of *baroque* is of French origin,

Wölfflin cited Diderot's *Encyclopaedia* for its early application to architecture in the sense of *bizarre*. Regarding the change from the classical Renaissance style to the baroque as inevitable, Wölfflin suggested two alternative explanations of its causes: the theory of "blunted sensibility" (which he wisely rejected) and the hypothesis that "style is an *expression* of its age, and changes with the changes in human sensibility." According to the latter theory, the "Renaissance had to die because it no longer responded to the pulse of the age. . . ." The "change in mood," he maintained, was apparent not only in art but also in literature. In the "difference of language" between the epics of Ariosto and Tasso, and also between Boiardo's *Orlando Innamorato* and Berni's more polished revision of this romance, Wölfflin detected a significant contrast in sensibility: a contrast between the "gay variety" of the early Renaissance and the "grandeur" sought by a later period.[3]

Though Wölfflin's study was centered primarily on art historical problems (and still remains valuable where it does not exceed these self-imposed limits),[4] it nevertheless involved historical assumptions that derived in large part from Hegelian theories of cultural history. Through his formal analysis of "period styles" and the response of various sixteenth and seventeenth century artists to the technical problems of composition, Wölfflin managed to achieve a systematic explanation of certain stylistic developments in Renaissance and post-Renaissance Europe primarily in terms of purely artistic principles. There was no imperative (as is to frequently the case in criticism of seventeenth century poetry and prose) to explain artistic developments on social and cultural grounds. As a product of his own historical milieu, however, he took such cultural conditioning for granted, adapting the historiography of art to the assumptions of contemporary *Geistesgeschichte*. In a sense, then, his book is itself the representative of a "period style."

For Wölfflin, nothing was "more natural to art history than to draw parallels between periods of culture and periods of styles," and in "the transition from renaissance to baroque" he recognized a "classic example of how a new *zeitgeist* enforces a new form." In the art of Rubens, he perceived the powerful influence of "a particular cultural current, the mode of feeling of Roman baroque," and in the "columns and arches of the High Renaissance" a visible expression of "the spirit of the time. . . ." A "new ideal of life . . .," he said, "speaks to us from the Italian baroque. . . ." In the contrast between classical and baroque types, he detected a "change of the form of beholding," a "transformation of the imagination. . . ." The "idea of reality has changed as much as the idea of beauty," and the new modes of artistic representation reflected a new mode of vision.[5]

Just as Curtius perceived a tension between mannerism and classicism throughout Western literature, Wölfflin found "classic and baroque not only in more modern times and not only in antique building, but on so different ground as Gothic." The linear style of classical art and the painterly style of baroque artists expressed two different "conceptions of the world. . . ." The one was an art of being, the other of semblance. The latter "does not body forth things in themselves, but represents the world as seen, . . . as it actually appears to the eye. . . ." The contrast between these styles

> corresponds to radically different interests in the world. In the former case, it is the solid figure, in the latter, the changing appearance: in the former, the enduring form, measurable, finite; in the latter, the movement, the form in function; in the former, the thing in itself; in the latter, the thing in its relations.

Similarly, the "style of close composition" in classical art and the "a-tectonic style" of baroque reflected different conceptions of the world. The former "builds, as nature builds, and seeks in nature what is akin to it. . . . At all points the style strives to grasp the firm and enduring elements of form. Nature is a cosmos and beauty is revealed law." In the latter,

> the interest in the constructed and self-contained declines. . . . The significant element of form is not the scaffolding, but the breath of life which brings flux and movement into the rigid form. In the one case, beauty resides in the determinate, in the other, in the indeterminate.

An analogous antithesis appeared for Wölfflin in the contrast between classical and baroque attitudes toward absolute and relative clarity in form. Whereas "all renaissance design everywhere aimed at a presentment which might be regarded as an exhaustive revelation of form," the "baroque avoids this acme of clarity," finding beauty in forms which "cannot quite be apprehended and always seem to elude the spectator. Interest in moulded form yields to the interest in indeterminate, mobile appearance." Whereas "classic clearness means representation in ultimate enduring form[,] baroque unclearness means making the forms look like something changing, becoming."[6]

Like other European historians of his generation, Wölfflin was reluctant to exorcise the specter of historicism. A historical era was still a haunted house, and a period style was the ectoplasm in which the invisible spirit of the age became manifest. He could still regard "temperament, *zeitgeist*, or racial character" as determining the "style of individuals, periods and peoples." He conceived styles "primarily as expression, expression of the temper of an age and a nation as well as expression of the individual temperament," and his analysis endeavored to "show in what ways styles express their epoch." Nevertheless, he was aware of the limitations of this approach, acknowledging that an "analysis with quality and expression as its objects by no means exhausts the facts." His own inquiry was focussed on the "mode of representation as such," the "visual possibilities" confronting the artist in a particular period. Qualities of style could not be explained altogether in terms of expressional content. In the history of style, there was "a substratum of concepts referring to representation as such," and their discovery and analysis was the proper task of the art historian. The "tectonics" of Raphael, for instance, could not be entirely

> attributed to an intention born of a state of mind: it is rather a question of a representational form of his epoch which he only perfected in a certain way and used for his own ends. . . . By attributing everything to expression alone, we make the false assumption that for every state of mind the same expressional methods were always available.[7]

Wölfflin was content, on the whole, to concentrate on the formal analysis of style and to leave the problem of its expressional content to others. Unlike later students of Renaissance or baroque style, he did not analyze the sixteenth or seventeenth century worldview in detail, nor did he attempt to examine in detail its expression in literature. His underlying assumptions — that style is an expression of personal or national temperament or of the spirit of the age and that different period styles reflect different conceptions of the world — were shared by many of his contemporaries in other disciplines. This common frame of reference made it comparatively easy for literary historians and specialists in intellectual and social history to adapt his findings to their own fields of study. The influence of Croce's aesthetic theory, his emphasis on art as expression, and his conception of *concettismo* as a manifestation of the baroque made the literary application of Wölfflin's principles seem appropriate. For students of *Geistesgeschichte* and disciples of Hegel and Spengler, it seemed logical to assume that the formal manifestations of the *Zeitgeist* in Cinquecento and

Seicento art would be paralleled in the literature and sciences of the period. From a darker quarter, the hypothesis of depth psychology, in turn, gave unsuspected support to the literary and social exploitation of Wölfflin's art historical analysis. As expressions or projections of the unconscious, the characteristics of literary and artistic styles could mirror the inner tensions and emotional conflicts within an individual or the larger society.

2.

René Wellek credited Wölfflin with first transferring the term *baroque* from art history to literary history, and its subsequent development as a literary historical term has been strongly conditioned by Wölfflin's categories. To a certain extent, literary historians have turned to the history of art for explanations of literary phenomena that might (in part at least) be more satisfactorily explained in terms of the literary theory of the age. This is also true, to some degree, of other — and non-Wölfflinian — conceptions of baroque and mannerist traits in late Renaissance literature. Like the Wölfflinian antitheses of multiplicity and unity or clarity and obscurity, other points of emphasis in art criticism — the logical and ornamental value of antitheses and *contrapposti*, the exploitation of the sensual or sensuous to illustrate the spiritual and the noumenal, the conscious pursuit of novelty and variety and marvel, and the yoking together of different levels of reality — are common in Renaissance treatises on the verbal arts. (Even the juxtaposition of "real" and "unreal" or of varying degrees of detail and verisimilitude finds a partial parallel in the rhetorical concepts of amplification and diminution.) The theory of "ideal" imitation and the delineation of universals through sensuous examples or analogues persists, though in altered form, in the theory and practice of *concettismo*. Finally, the scholastic elements that Renaissance critics sometimes recognized and deplored in "metaphysical" poetry offer a suggestive parallel to the scholastic connotations of the term *baroco* on the Continent.

The origin of the term *baroque* is still controversial. Benedetto Croce regarded it as a derivative from the fourth mode (*Baroco*) of the second figure of the syllogism: every P is T; some S are not T; ergo, some S are not P. In sixteenth and seventeenth century Italian literature (he observed), the term "argomento in baroco" had been applied pejoratively to pedantic, captious or sophistic reasoning.[8] Other critics traced this word to the Portuguese *barroco*, an irregularly shaped pearl. During the eighteenth century, the baroque label was applied to both art and music. Wellek has suggested that the Czech music historian August W. Ambros was "first to use it as a period term, in 1878," observing that the "enormous vogue of baroque as a literary term arose in Germany only about 1921–1922."[9]

Twentieth century critics have varied widely in their interpretations of baroque style and its relationship to the intellectual and spiritual crises of the sixteenth and seventeenth centuries. Croce associated it pejoratively with the Counter-Reformation and the "decadence" of Italy. In his opinion, it was an "esthetic sin," an "artistic ugliness" rebellious to the law of artistic coherence and responsive to another law: "the law of license, convenience, caprice, and hence utilitarian and hedonistic." Transferred from scholastic logic, the term was applied to the "bad artistic taste of Seicento architecture, sculpture and painting."[10]

Austin Warren likewise emphasized the links between baroque style and sensibility and the spirit of the Counter-Reformation. Arguing that the Church "found in the baroque appeal to the senses a mode compatible with her tradition," he regarded the baroque as a "Catholic counterstatement to the reformer's attacks on the wealth of the Church and her use of painting and sculpture." From the Ignatian method in meditation (which sought to "localize both the historic and the psychological, to realize, in pictorial or symbolic form, the whole of religion") the "transition to emblems, *tableaux vivants,* and paintings designed to stir the pious emotions is but slight." The emblem and the *impresa* were "admirably suited to Jesuit use"; and, exploiting "the happy blend of *dulce et utile,*" the Society of Jesus devised *imprese* for princes, and books of sacred emblems for popular consumption. Characterizing the baroque style as "exuberant, rhetorical, sensual, grandiose," Warren commented that the "repose and symmetry of Renaissance art have yielded to agitation, aspiration, ambition, an intense striving to transcend the limits of each genre."[11]

In an essay on "The Baroque Style in Prose," Morris W. Croll stressed the baroque preference for "expressiveness rather than formal beauty," "effects of contortion or obscurity," its predilection for forms expressing "the energy and movement, its dramatic qualities, and its asymmetry." The "motions of souls, not their states of rest, had become the themes of art." In Croll's opinion, these were likewise characteristic features of anti-Ciceronian prose, and later critics have emphasized the same qualities in the poetry of *culteranismo* and *conceptismo*. Croll regarded them as an expression of the "baroque impulse." The change "from Ciceronian to anti-Ciceronian forms and ideas" in the prose style of the period was "exactly parallel with those that were occurring in the other arts. . . ."

The "baroque" prose style, as Croll conceived it, was a loose periodic style distinct from the closely knit Ciceronian period and from the "curt" style (*stile coupé*) derived from Seneca and other writers of the Silver Age and revived by Muret and Lipsius. Though its "members are usually connected by syntactic ligatures," unlike those of the curt style, it resembled this curt style in its attempts to "portray the natural, or thinking, order; and it expresses . . . the anti-Ciceronian prejudice against formality of procedure and the rhetoric of the schools." The baroque style's "progression adapts itself to the movements of a mind discovering truth as it goes, thinking while it writes," erecting and breaking symmetries, rapidly adjusting "form to the emergencies that arise in an energetic and unpremeditated forward movement," exhibiting "spontaneity and improvisation" in passages heavily loaded with conceptual content. This style combined the "effect of great mass with the effect of rapid motion, and there is no better formula than this to describe the ideal of the baroque design in all the arts."

The baroque style in prose was thus "the informal, meditative, 'natural' loose style." Croll found characteristic examples in French and English writers of the period. Montaigne, in his opinion, had "exactly described" this style when he wrote, "I write voluntarily without a fixed design; the first dash (of the pen) produces the second." Pascal similarly had observed the order of nature, writing in "the exact order in which the matter presents itself." The writings of Sir Thomas Browne gave the "effect of being, not the result of meditation, but an actual meditation in process."[12]

Croll praised Browne's mastery of "what Montaigne called 'the art of being natural'"; it is significant that both Browne and Montaigne had emphasized their own mutability of temperament and idea, their alternations in opinion and in mood. In his variability and susceptibility to change, Montaigne's human microcosm exhibited the same flux and transience that he perceived in the external world. "Others form man," he had written, "I describe him, and portray a particular, very ill-made one. . . . Now the features of my painting do not err, although they change and vary. The world is but a perpetual see-saw," and "I cannot fix my object. . . . I seize it at this point, as it is at the moment. . . . I do not portray the thing in itself [*l'estre*]. I portray the passage. . . . I must adapt my history to the moment." The fantasies of music, he said, are "guided by art, mine by chance."[13]

3.

In baroque art, Arnold Hauser found a reflection of the "new scientific worldview" based on the Copernican hypothesis, the "conception of the universe as an unbroken systematic whole," a universe without a fixed center. With this new cosmology, he associated pantheistic sentiment and belief, a "worldview of divine immanence. . . ." As a result of the "intellectual revolution" in European society, the ancient "fear of the judge of the universe is superseded by the '*frisson métaphysique*,'" by Pascal's anguish in face of the '*silence éternel des espaces infinis*,' by the wonder at the long unbroken breath which pervades the cosmos." In Hauser's opinion, the "whole of the art of the baroque" was

> full of this shudder, full of the echo of the infinite spaces and the interrelatedness of all being. The work of art in its totality becomes the symbol of the universe as a uniform organism alive in all its parts. [Everything] is the expression of an overwhelming, unquenchable yearning for infinity.[14]

In Hauser's view, Wölfflin's categories of the baroque represented "the application of the concepts of impressionism to the art of the seventeenth century," or rather to "a part of this art. . . . ." Hauser believed that the clarity of Wölfflin's concept of the baroque had been obtained "at the price of mostly neglecting to consider the classicism of the seventeenth century." Accordingly, in Wölfflin's analysis the art of the period appeared "almost exclusively as the dialectical opposite of the art of the sixteenth century and not as its continuation." Wölfflin had underestimated the importance of subjectivism in the Renaissance and overestimated it in the baroque. He had failed to recognize that "the subjectivization of the artistic worldview, the transformation of the 'tactile' into the 'visual,' of substance into mere appearance, conceiving the world as impression and experience," had been "prepared for to a far-reaching extent by the Renaissance and mannerism." Wölfflin had also, according to Hauser, overlooked "the real origin of the change of style by ignoring its sociological presuppositions." Finally, most of his categories could not be applied to the "classical art of the baroque period." Claude Lorrain and Poussin were neither "painterly" nor "unclear," and the structure of their art was not "a-tectonic."[15]

With the "cool, complicated intellectualistic" style of mannerism, Hauser contrasted the "sensual, emotional, universally comprehensible style" of the baroque.[16] Franco Croce similarly stressed the "theme of sensual delight" as a symbol of "what is new in the Baroque sentiment," won at the "cost of minimizing and exteriorizing the patrimony of the Renaissance, from Petrarch through Tasso." In his judgment, Torquato Tasso's poetry was "both proto-Baroque and Late Renaissance at the same time." Croce believed Giambattista Marino to be the first of the baroque poets because "he was the first of them to be completely free of doubts concerning the originality of his work and concerning the [element in it that we call] Baroque."[17]

To Roy Daniells, the baroque seemed "the logical continuation and extension of High Renaissance art, with conscious accentuation and 'deformation' of the regular stock of techniques"; in the hands of baroque artists, these techniques had become "more dynamic" and more theatrical. The marks of the baroque were "a sense of triumph and splendour, a strenuous effort to unify the opposite terms of paradoxes" and "a high regard for technical virtuosity." In the "development of a cult of significant darkness" in the English literature of the early seventeenth century, Daniells observed a significant parallel to "the deliberate obscurity in graphic and plastic design" that Wölfflin had analyzed in his fifth category: the shift from absolute to relative clarity. Daniells also noted a deliberate rejection of the baroque on the part of the "Royal Society" and an "absence of Baroque features from the styles of . . . Addison and Swift. . . ."[18]

In Daniells's opinion, the "overlapping of cultural influences" posed special problems for the study of the baroque in England. In both dramatic and nondramatic poetry and prose of the English seventeenth century, he observed analogies with Wölfflin's categories, but he also noted correctly that it was "impossible to tip Wölfflin's concepts over into another kind of art and use them immediately as criteria." He found a "clear analogy between the ingenious use of metaphor and the baroque employment of perspective to condense a great deal into a single line of vision," and he regarded Donne, Crashaw and Milton as "probably the three most interesting exponents of baroque form in poetry: Donne on account of his early and deliberate dislocation of conventional shapes, Crashaw because of his direct connections with continental Catholic art, and Milton for the large structure and very delib-

erate artistry of his major works. . . ." Examining the poetry of
Spenser and Milton to discover "whether there are points of
correspondence between the differences which separate them and
those which lie between high renaissance art and baroque," Daniells perceived in *Paradise Lost* numerous resemblances between
"Milton's structural methods and those of the baroque architect"
— but he warned against pushing such analogies too far. In his
view, there existed some fundamental principle in the baroque
aesthetic which produced "bold clashes of color, difficult equilibrium in design, effects of tension and straining movement, and the
unification of what individually is unbalanced into the wholeness
of a designed composition"; Milton utilized "similar devices in his
thinking and in the formal handling of his poetry."[19]

For William Fleming, the baroque period was essentially "an age
of movement, activity, exploration," in which time was of the
utmost importance. Baroque society first adopted the "symbol of
the flow of time and made it a part of everyday living," while the
scientific thought of the age was preoccupied with "movement in
calculation, in measurement, in exploration, in transportation."[20]

Wylie Sypher regarded the baroque as an art of "reintegration"
and invested its differences from mannerism with epistemological
and theological significance.

> After the crisis in mannerist conscience, with its repressions, defini-
> tions, complexities, and double evasive answers, its dissonant,
> involved contours, baroque performs a . . . catharsis by spectacle,
> by an expressive power. The baroque canon of style does not
> depend upon mannerist contingencies, but upon assurances and
> certainties — certainties lacking the mannerist subtlety and discrimi-
> nation.

The baroque then, reflects the attitude prevailing after the Council
of Trent, which had convened in "a climate of mannerist doubt"
but had eventually "laid the foundations for a settlement in theology and a reintegration of style in the arts. . . ."

Richard Crashaw was, in Sypher's opinion, possibly "the most
characteristic poet of baroque piety," as he brought "to the conceit,
and to wit, a sensuousness more ornate and voluptuous than
appears in the other English devotional poets. . . ." Tasso lacked
"the full baroque energy," and the supreme achievement in baroque literature belonged to Milton's *Samson Agonistes* and *Paradise
Lost*. Exhibiting the full "plenitude of baroque," *Paradise Lost* represented "a formal expression of the baroque will-to-space because it
sets up huge 'classical' boundaries and then exceeds them." Mil-

ton's "baroque vision amplified the renaissance art of Spenser."
Throughout *Paradise Lost*, Milton exploited the baroque principle of
emphasizing the foreground. The image of Satan in Hell and the
description of the infernal conclave were "composed in baroque
space," and the "spatial relations in Milton's cosmos are illusory in
the technical baroque sense. . . ."[21]

For Frank J. Warnke, the term *baroque* could most profitably be
employed as a "generic designation for the style of the whole
period which falls between the Renaissance and the neoclassical
era." As "the designation of a period," the word referred "not to a
precisely definable style but to a cluster of related styles." The
"unity of a period style," Warnke believed, "appears not in the
dominance of a set of identical techniques but in the way in which
differing, even contrasting techniques articulate a common group
of preoccupations and emphases. . . ." Classifying metaphysical
poetry as a subdivision of the baroque, he stressed the "stylistic
variations" apparent in the treatments of hyperbole, conceit and
dramatic contrast by various writers of the period: notably Marino
and Donne, Gryphius and George Herbert. Denying the existence
of a mannerist period, he preferred to classify marinism, *concettismo*, *culteranismo*, and metaphysical and *précieux* poetry as types
of the baroque. Distinguishing two principal movements within
baroque literature, a mannerist trend and the High Baroque, he
criticized attempts to associate the style of the baroque with any
particular worldview.[22]

On the issue of a specifically mannerist period and on the
relationship between baroque style and *Weltanschauung*, Harold
Segel disagreed, but he concurred in applying the term baroque to
the period between the Renaissance and neoclassicism. In *The
Baroque Poem*, Segel described the baroque "reaction against mannerism" as essentially a "movement to restore the unity and relative
significance of subject that had been diminished by the excessive
Mannerist concern with form." In the baroque, he observed

> a new respect for unity and the use of style to elucidate a particular
> subject. Variety, ornament, the search for ways of exciting wonder-
> ment still had a place in Baroque art, but because of the resurrected
> passion for unity they were not used indiscriminately, as was often
> the case among the Mannerists.

In an endeavor to recover unity and symmetry, the antimannerists
in the visual arts "turned away from the asymmetrical lines and
disproportionate shapes of mannerism and attempted to restore
the balance and harmony of the Renaissance."[23]

In his interpretation of baroque sensibility, Segel emphasized its inherent paradoxes and contradictions: the struggle between Catholic and Protestant and between Europe and the Islamic Orient, "intense spirituality in a time of sensuousness," and an

> inclination to reject the world paralleled by a passionate attachment to it. . . . The perception of these apparent irreconcilables gave rise to the antithesis, paradox and incongruity so frequently encountered in Baroque art. . . . But the 'tension' generated by the coupling of seemingly irreconcilable or remotely related concepts differs in a very essential way from the tensions in Mannerist art. In the latter, the tension results not from the perception of and attempt to reconcile the extremes, but from a sense of dissolution, of fragmentation. The Baroque artist worked instead toward unity, toward reintegration; aware of antitheses and paradoxes and incongruities in the world about him, he sought their reconciliation in the same manner that flesh and spirit were reconciled

in Catholic thought and in "much Protestant teaching. . . . Far from detracting from unity, as in mannerism, space and line, variety and novelty in Baroque art are all managed in such a way as to convey a unified vision."[24]

Contrasting the "sensuousness of Baroque imagery" with the Renaissance, Segel suggested that the "nature of the Baroque age, with its profound calamities, on the one hand, and its pervasive sensuousness, on the other, lent new immediacy to the familiar conflict of flesh and spirit."[25] Among English and American "baroque" poets, Segel included such diverse figures as John Donne, George Herbert, Robert Herrick, Henry King, William Habington, Richard Crashaw, Lord Edward Herbert of Cherbury, John Milton, Andrew Marvell, Michael Wigglesworth and Anne Bradstreet. In Spain and Italy, he associated the baroque primarily with the traditions of Góngora and Marino, but he also included the work of Calderón, Lope de Vega and Campanella.

4.

Within recent years, the concept of the baroque as a period style has been subjected to extensive criticism, revaluation and redefinition. Among the more valuable of these reassessments are essays by Wolfgang Stechow, R.A. Sayce and René Wellek.

In a study of the baroque in the visual arts, Wolfgang Stechow distinguished three different meanings of the term as it had traditionally been used. In the first sense, *baroque* designates "a style quality diametrically opposed to . . . classical composure and restraint," indicating "exuberance, dynamic stress, emotional grandeur" and similar qualities. Secondly, it merely designates "a certain period in Western European art, mostly the period between 1580 or 1600 . . . and 1725 or 1750." Thirdly, it denotes a "recurrent" or "typically *late* phase of every Occidental style. . . ." Stechow challenged the validity of the first sense: "a universal acceptance of the term is impossible if we continue to use it as synonymous with grandeur, heroic sweep, or the like. . . ." The third sense might be valid for a particular phase of ancient art, he asserted, but not for Gothic art. The second definition hinged on the "stylistic unity of the entire epoch"; although this had yet to be demonstrated, it nevertheless remained a useful *"working hypothesis."* In the baroque epoch, he detected "a basically new and optimistic equilibrium of religious and secular forces," largely attributable to the "progressive revolution" of the Reformation and the "conservative revolution" of the Counter-Reformation.[26]

R.A. Sayce attempted to counter some of the objections that had been raised against the term baroque, including: "the variety of senses," the inutility of "all such general designations of styles," the transference of concepts of the baroque from "the foreign world of the visual arts," and its association with the generalizations of *Geistesgeschichte*. In his opinion, the current usage of this word implied two alternative hypotheses: first, "that there are at any given moment (or specifically at some time between 1550 and 1750) affinities between literature and the other arts, between the arts and other human activities" and secondly, "that there is at any given moment . . . a perfect unity of all the arts and of all human activities and that this unity is the expression of the *Zeitgeist*." To Sayce, the first seemed incontrovertible and the second unlikely. In its most useful sense, then, the baroque was essentially "a stage in the development of . . . Renaissance classicism, from which it is inseparable; it involves the distortion . . . of classical forms in order that something different may be expressed." The alleged confusions in the use of this term could be largely dispelled if the critic would hold fast to three principles: "the hierarchy of terminology, *décalage* or time lag, and the fact of the French resistance to and transformation of the baroque." Sayce also emphasized "the difficulty of finding a theory of the baroque in contemporary writers; on the whole, classical principles are expounded even by those who violate them in practice."[27]

René Wellek's essay, "The Concept of Baroque in Literary Scholarship," summarized the history of this term in literary criticism and provided both an analysis of its definitions and validity and a chronological bibliography of writings which "definitely use the term Baroque applied to literature." In recent descriptions of the baroque, he distinguished two distinct trends: "one which describes it in terms of style and one which prefers ideological categories or emotional attitudes." The term entered literary criticism, he suggested, when Oskar Waltzel applied Wölfflin's antithesis between closed and open form to Shakespeare. In Wellek's view, "even the more sober transfer of Wölfflin's categories" apparently "achieved very little for a definition of the baroque." Although four of these ("painterly," "open form," "unity" and "relative clarity") could be applied fairly easily to baroque poetry and prose, they actually achieved "little more than ranging baroque literature against harmonious, clearly outlined, well-proportioned classical literature." Transferring Wölfflin's categories to literatures, Wellek believed, tended to blur the sense of *baroque* and to compromise its value as a "clear period-concept." Efforts to define it "in terms of its most obvious stylistic devices run into the same difficulty"; therefore, it was "probably necessary to abandon attempts to define baroque in purely stylistic terms." In Wellek's opinion, the most promising method for "arriving at a more closely fitting description of the baroque is to aim at analyses which would correlate stylistic and ideological criteria."

Wellek also distinguished sharply between those critics who regarded the baroque as "a recurrent phenomenon in all history" and those who treated it as "a specific phenomenon in the historical process, fixed in time and place." As a period-concept, baroque could not be defined in the way that "a class-concept in logic can be defined," inasmuch as all individual works of a given period could not be "subsumed under it." A period, according to Wellek, is "only a regulative concept, not a metaphysical essence" nor a "purely arbitrary linguistic label." Even as a period-term, moreover, the "chronological extension" of the term *baroque* becomes "bafflingly various." In England it could "include Lyly, Milton, and even Gray and Collins." In France it could refer not only to Rabelais, Ronsard, Du Bartas, and the *précieux*, but also to Racine and Fénelon. The "figures and metaphors, hyperboles and catachreses" so often interpreted as evidence of the inner tensions of the tortured baroque poet "frequently do not reveal any inner tension or turbulence and may not be the expression of any vital experience at all, but may be the decorative overelaboration of a highly conscious, skeptical craftsman, the pilings-up of calculated surprises and effects."[28]

Neither the application of this term to English literary studies nor the attempt to make "the baroque a recurrent type throughout history" had been successful, Wellek noted. More promising, in his opinion, were "attempts to approach the problem of the baroque through a study of the history of poetic theories. . . ."[29]

5.

For Wölfflin and numerous other critics, "classical" and "baroque" art reflected radically different sensibilities or "interests in the world." In these different period styles, they perceived contrasting orientations toward fixed reality and changing appearance, toward static "being" and shifting semblance, toward absolute and essential existence ("the thing in itself") and relativity.[30]

Like the contrast between Cinquecento and Seicento worldviews, these stylistic differences have probably been exaggerated, and the attempt to ascribe them to antithetical *Weltanschauungen* (a hypothesis that is by no means essential to Wölfflin's major thesis) also appears to have been overstrained. An emphasis on change and movement and momentary appearance is inherent and potentially operative in the very conception of poetry or art as the imitation of an action, or as a mimesis of passion, character and thought. In part, the dramatic emphasis on the tensions and surprises generated in the course of a changing external situation, or in the mind of a character who is responding emotionally and ethically to such changes, is responsible for this attention given to mutation and movement and momentary appearance. Passion and admiration are to be sought, as Milton observed, not only in the "changes of that which is called fortune from without," but also in the "wily subtleties and refluxes of man's thoughts from within."[31]

In the drama, an emphasis on change is not inevitable, though both comedy and tragedy were traditionally defined partly in terms of the kind of "mutation" — from woe to weal, or vice versa — they depicted. Aristotle had preferred the "complex" plot in tragedy, where the change occurs suddenly and paradoxically, "contrary to expectation," as this produces greater marvel and surprise, or where the shift is accompanied by a sudden recognition on the part of one or more of the central characters of their real identity or the true nature of their relationship. In a comic plot —

especially in comedies constructed according to the model of
Menander, Plautus and Terence — the dramatic situation is constantly shifting and altering, creating and dissipating fresh tensions, new hopes and doubts and fears, until the "perturbations"
are finally resolved. With the evolution of an analogous "intrigue-
plot" in tragedy, it was possible for the dramatist to exploit ambiguities of character and situation, presenting abrupt and paradoxical changes and counterchanges in terms of the tragic emotions.
Moreover, popular taste often demanded variety, novelty and
change — a succession of "thrills" like that which once delighted
spectators of American silent films. As a result, the dramatist was
often required to alternate rapidly between tragic and comic materials, widely diverse geographical settings and social contexts,
and to introduce more frequent and sudden alterations in the
development and "unraveling" of the plot than were customary in
classical tragedy.

In many Renaissance era plays, accordingly, the dramatic situation is fluid, shifting, and (except in the eyes of the gods) ambiguous and indeterminate. The critical moments, apparently, are
many; at each of them the action may conceivably veer for or
against the protagonist. Plot and counterplot produce sudden and
surprising reversals, expectations and counterexpectations, true
and false surmises, multiple illusions and manifold ironies. In
many instances, the plot, when analyzed, can be divided into a
series of dramatic moments, each containing a mixture of truth and
illusion, each affording only a partial glimpse of the full significance of the dramatic action, each relative to each and to the
whole.

In attempting to portray an action, the painter might strive for
these and similar effects. The painter, however, inevitably had to
face the problem of rendering dramatic movement in a static
medium, freezing gesture and passion and event in a single moment. That so many visual artists succeeded so well in an enterprise that might superficially seem impossible is testimony to the
skill of the baroque painter and sculptor, and (even more) of the
baroque architect, who managed to convert building itself to
drama, the imitation of an action.

In addition to the "turns" and surprises in the dramatic presentation of the action, and their effects on the mind and will and
passions of the *personae*, the late Renaissance drama demonstrated
(in many cases) a developing mastery of the techniques for delin-
eating inner conflict; unexpected and sudden turns of thought or
changes of purpose, and alternations of emotion. Hitherto dra-

matic *ethos* or character had been considered, all too frequently, in terms of comparatively fixed norms, typed according to the traditional *attributa personarum* and the principle of decorum, with little allowance for seeming inconsistencies. As long as the *persona* continued to act in character — and as long as this character conformed more or less to a standard pattern — there would be comparatively little scope for the element of novelty and surprise. Moral conflict could be objectified by pitting two antagonists against one another, or partly internalized through inner debate, but it remained on the whole schematized and predictable, like the struggle between love and honor or the contention between flesh and spirit, body and soul.

The mastery of the seemingly incongruous in characterization — the unexpected and apparently contradictory refluxes in thought, purpose and emotion — had yet to be achieved. In the late Renaissance, however, vernacular dramatists displayed greater facility and naturalness in portraying the process of moral decision in dialogue or in monologue. The process of debate appears, in many instances, less formal and schematic than in earlier drama. Apparent inconsistencies break the more rigid decorum of conventional character types. As a result, the "turns" in the meditations and resolves of the principal characters not only seem more natural, but also more unexpected, more various and more "marvellous."

One encounters a similar flexibility and variety in the representation of the passions. Instead of portraying a single emotional state or even a conflict between two simple emotions, the dramatist may attempt a less predictable and more variable imitation of passion.

Such essentially dramatic emphases, stressing movement and paradox and surprise in the representation of *ethos* and *dianoia* and *pathos* are to be found not only in the drama proper, but in epic, lyric and other genres as well.

The representation of shifting appearances in baroque art, moreover, essentially holds to the time-worn principle of verisimilitude in a new and fresh guise. Both medieval and Renaissance authors and artists had acknowledged this principle. It had been discussed at length in manuals of rhetoric and poetics; they could find it in Horace and later in Aristotle. Though Wölfflin perceived in Holbein's portraits "an unsurpassable embodiment of the art of being, from which *all terms of semblance* have been eliminated,"[32] it is doubtful that either Holbein or his contemporaries would have concurred in this judgment. They would probably have praised instead the painter's verisimilitude, his ability to make his portraits "like the reality."

Likeness to reality — verisimilitude — is a relative and variable standard. It varies not only with custom but with the available terms of comparison. In comparison with Byzantine and "Gothic" art, the sculptures of the ancients seemed as impressive for their naturalness and verisimilitude as for their grace of proportion. Against the background of medieval art, Giotto's paintings impressed his contemporaries by their resemblance to nature and their dramatic quality; in comparison with the art of the High Renaissance, however, they would seem lacking in verisimilitude. To Seicento artists (many of whom extolled the painters of the High Renaissance and advised a return to their principles as an antidote to the excesses of mannerist style), even the art of the High Renaissance might seem deficient in *vraisemblance*. For even though the proportions and modeling of the figures might seem natural, and the composition of place mathematically correct, their arrangement, their disposition in space, and the handling of space itself were frequently and all too obviously the results of conscious art. They seemed deliberately and artificially posed. As Wölfflin observed, in connection with closed and open form, "The final question is . . . whether the figure, the total picture as a visible form looks *intentional* or not."[33] In Renaissance "classical" art, it often does.

6.

Though Wölfflin exaggerated the effect of *Weltanschauung* on baroque composition ("the general tendency is to produce the picture no longer as a self-existing piece of the world, but as a passing show, which the spectator may enjoy only for a moment"),[34] he was right in emphasizing the artist's pursuit of the changing appearance. This emphasis was primarily based, however, not on a radically different sensibility or worldview, but on further development of the principles of verisimilitude and the dramatic rendition of external and internal actions and movements: the imitation of thought and feeling, meditation and passion.

The emphasis on style as a more or less intuitive projection of personal or collective sensibility may (to be sure) provide a timely corrective to the comparatively narrow and overrationalized conception of style as a reflection of theory or as a solution to technical problems of invention, imitation and disposition. The experiments of Gestalt psychologists and analyses of the painting and poetry of schizophrenics have undoubtedly produced fresh insights into the psychological foundations of aesthetic modes and styles. Nevertheless, the expository value of these viewpoints is severely limited. For the most part, the styles of both the verbal and the visual arts involve a mixture of rational and irrational, theoretical and technical, personal and impersonal factors. These styles cannot be fully and satisfactorily explained either as conscious artifices or as projections of the unconscious. An exclusively psychological approach can be as misleading as a purely philosophical or a systematically sociological interpretation. Neither mannerist nor baroque nor neoclassical style is a true "configuration" in the Gestaltist sense, and attempts to account for the evolution and decline of literary and plastic styles on purely psychological grounds are no less biased than efforts to reduce stylistic modes to new developments in aesthetic theory and the theory of knowledge. Historians cannot, of course, afford to ignore twentieth century psychology any more than they can neglect sixteenth and seventeenth century epistemology or questions of literary or artistic technique. To correlate such diverse approaches, however, is difficult; it requires a syncretistic and eclectic methodology, and in the final analysis, a historical synthesis will probably be a fabrication of the individual historian's own imagination. As scholars, we cannot escape our own subjectivity, nor is it desirable that we should.

Attempts to correlate syntax with cosmology may easily be carried to irrational extremes. To associate hypotactic structure and closed form with one kind of worldview or ideal of society, and paratactic structure and open form with a radically different conception (as many students of the Seicento have done) is to elevate a grammatical distinction into a metaphysical principle, perceiving contradictory worldviews in coordinate and complex sentences and projecting upon the medieval or Renaissance cosmos the comparative unity or disunity, coherence or incoherence, of a hypotactic or paratactic sentence structure. The critic who searches long enough may easily detect the signature of the macrocosm itself in a circular sentence — a miniature world revealed in a Ciceronian period — but it is questionable whether such evidence is more reliable than a poet's vision of a world in a grain of sand, and a mappamundi in his mistress's tears. Like the medieval and Renaissance exegetes who invested grammatical categories with allegorical senses, critics have not hesitated to convert syntax to emblem and grammar to hieroglyph, interpreting complex sentences as symbols of historical periods and cycles and the grammatical *circuitus* as an image of the *ouroboros*, the serpent of eternity. In the same way, the "ring-structure" conventional in the epic simile has been transmogrified into a cosmic emblem.

This type of analysis has been common in both literary and art historical criticism. Geometrical analysis of the structure of Homeric or Virgilian or Miltonic epic stems from Sir John Myres's endeavor to associate the structure of Homer's poems with that of protogeometric pottery. Recent attempts to interpret the syntax of sixteenth and seventeeth century prose and poetry as a reflection of a contemporary *crise de conscience* have been strongly influenced by similar tendencies on the part of art historians, who have analyzed the "syntax" or figural and spatial organization of mannerist and baroque painting.

Finally, it seems probable that art and literary historians alike have exaggerated the importance of philosophical differences in the theoretical works of the period. The majority of poets and painters are not infallible logicians. Moreover, their statements concerning the nature and origin of the artist's "idea" are often polemically conditioned, relative to the defense or condemnation of a particular artisan or a specific style. One should not attach undue significance to doctrinal discrepancies on such points in different treatises or even in the same treatise. The essential issue, in many of the Cinquecento or Seicento discussions cited by Anthony Blunt and Rensselaer Lee, is not the writer's preference for an Aristotelian or neo-Platonic theory concerning the ontological status of ideas, but rather the writer's attitude toward the relative importance of formal rules (whether of nature or of art) and free invention, studied composition and spontaneity, and the relationship between external nature and the painter's design. The point at issue is not, as a rule, a choice between contradictory and incompatible alternatives, but is the question of degree, the selection of a mean between extremes. Both the defenders and opponents of the "mannerists" frequently accepted the same principles, but differed in the relative emphasis that they accorded to them.

In some instances there is substantial agreement among mannerist, baroque and neoclassical critics as to the importance of studying nature and works of antiquity, learning the rules and developing one's natural bent and genius. Most of these ideas were, in fact, commonplaces of neo-Horatian poetic theory; and for this very reason, disputants on either side might expediently appeal to them for support in controversy. The particular *topos* one chose to emphasize, and the degree of emphasis accorded it, varied with the style or practice a particular writer was committed to attacking or defending. Although theory cannot be altogether divorced from practice — or vice versa — and though theory could and often did influence practice in a significant degree, it was sometimes, certainly, little more than a thinly disguised mode of demonstrative or judicial rhetoric: an instrument of defense or offense, praise or blame.

SEVEN

The Metaphysicals

In one respect, the term *metaphysical poetry* possesses an apparent advantage over rival designations. It originated in literary criticism rather than in art historical theory. Nevertheless, like *mannerism* and *baroque*, it was first used pejoratively. To take it literally, as a defining term, or to look for specifically "metaphysical" elements in Donne or Crashaw is almost as meaningless as listening for the echoes of Bow-bells in the cadences of Keats or Leigh Hunt. It is, as Helen Gardner observed, a "kind of nickname" — like "the Cockney poets," "the School of Night," or "les Fauves."[1] Moreover, it is scarcely less ambiguous than *baroque* and *mannerist*. Indeed, all three terms have been distracting; they divert the attention of critics from the pursuit of the author's meaning to the meaning of their own technical vocabulary — to the denotation and application of critical terms that were originally terms of abuse.

Much ink and ingenuity have been expended, for instance, in endeavors to rationalize the label "metaphysical," to distinguish its several senses, and to demonstrate its relevance or irrelevance to various Seicento poets both in Britain and on the Continent. Some critics would extend this term to Dante and Saint Thomas Aquinas, to Góngora and Marino and Théophile de Viau; others would exclude Crashaw. Some would admit a broader range of sixteenth and seventeenth century poets, both British and continental; others would restrict the term in its purest sense virtually to Donne and Marvell and perhaps to Cowley. Some would classify metaphysical poetry as a subspecies of the baroque; some as a branch of mannerism; others, as practically synonymous with either or both of these terms. Some have taken the word literally and attempted to justify it in terms of theme and content, emphasizing the speculative and ontological subjects of metaphysical poetry, its affinities with Platonism and Hermeticism, and its

124

alleged concern with the invisible realm of spiritual essences and transcendental ideas. Others (more sensibly) have rationalized the *metaphysical* label primarily on the grounds of method rather than content, stressing the poet's exploitation of images and arguments derived from scholastic philosophy, the poet's dialectical method and its affinities with the methodology of formal disputation in the schools, and the conscious manipulation of logical or sophistic proofs. Still others have pointed out similarities and differences between metaphysical poetry and late Renaissance arts of meditation.[2]

1.

Contemporary critics are well aware of the difficulties involved in defining a "metaphysical" school or tradition, and are fully conscious of the impressive differences among the so-called metaphysicals. To attempt to reduce them to a common denominator of style or sensibility is comparable to seeking a single formula for the "individualists" and "eccentrics" in Chinese painting.

Yet despite its ambiguity, the term is too well-established to be conveniently displaced. Alternative classifications would be, in some respects, even less satisfactory. To refer to these English poets as *concettisti* would be accurate, but this category is much too broad. *Fantastic* — appropriate for the play of wit in Cleveland or the allusion of the flight of the imagination in Crashaw — might suggest analogies with Italian burlesque verse, the prose of Burton, and the paintings of artists like Arcimbaldo; but it would scarcely fit the closely reasoned and tightly constructed poems of George Herbert. Emphasis on the poet's aesthetic exploitation of *dialectical* and *scholastic* methods and terms, or on the conscious *sophistry* underlying the play of wit would be too narrow; it could be applicable to certain poems by Donne and Cleveland, but not to Vaughan or Traherne or most of the other metaphysicals. *Anticlassical* would hardly do justice to the influence of the classical elegiac poets, epigrammatists and satirists, to the prominence of Aristotelian rhetorical concepts in the theory of *concettismo*, or to the Latinate stylistic features in the poetry of both Góngora and Marino.

For the earliest critics to use the term with reference to seventeenth century English poetry, "metaphysical" referred to style and manner rather than to theme and content. Drummond and Dryden — and, much later, Samuel Johnson — applied this term to

Donne, Cowley and others not because they had elected to write about separated substances (although many poets, both metaphysicals and nonmetaphysicals had indeed chosen such themes), but because they frequently drew their images and arguments from metaphysics (and from many other branches of philosophy and science) or because they argued and disputed like metaphysicians, scholastic philosophers, and school-divines. Such poets as Cleveland and Donne (it was implied) wrote *more philosophico* rather than *more poetico*, eschewing the customary ornaments of poetry and deliberately substituting the methods and imagery of pedantic and esoteric erudition.[3] Abandoning the pursuit of grace, formal beauty and "harmonious numbers," these poets turned to the subtle distinctions, hair-splitting definitions and jejune terminology of scholastic demonstrations or to the intricacies of Hermeticism and Neoplatonism. For the sweet (*dulce*) they substituted the sour; for the smooth and harmonious, the rough, the harsh and the discordant; for easiness, difficulty. In brief, they preferred thistles to figs, and brambles before roses.[4]

There would be little need to belabor this point, were it not for the fact that several "metaphysical" poets (some of them "rediscovered" in our own century) did indeed write on metaphysical themes — time and eternity, being and nonbeing, the signatures of God in nature, the ascent of the soul through contemplation, mystical ecstasies — and for the occasional tendency to explain the metaphysical label in terms of content rather than method. Herbert Grierson sensibly dissociated Donne and his followers from "Metaphysical Poetry, in the full sense of the term": the poetry of Dante and Lucretius and Goethe, which was "inspired by a philosophical conception of the universe." In his opinion, the "metaphysical strain" in these seventeenth century poets appeared primarily in the philosophical nature of their conceits, in "the *concetti metafisici ed ideali* as Testi calls them in contrast to the simpler imagery of classical poetry" and of "mediaeval Italian poetry. . . ."[5]

Yet, even if one confines this term largely to manner and style, it would be difficult to find a single formula applicable simultaneously to Donne and Crashaw, Herbert and Cleveland, or Cowley and Vaughan. The English metaphysicals exhibit wide stylistic diversity, as do the *concettisti* on the Continent. Although Frank J. Warnke regarded the metaphysical style as a variation of the baroque, and emphasized the international character of both, he also stressed the differences between Donne and Marino: "Donne cannot properly be called 'Marinistic' any more than Leopardi can be called 'Wordsworthian'; yet, as Wordsworth and Leopardi are both Romantic, so Marino and Donne are both baroque."[6]

2.

Despite their differences, Marino and Donne, Góngora and Quevedo, Cowley and Crashaw and Cleveland are *concettisti*. They are all, in a sense, priests of the contemporary cult of *ingenio*, even though they belong to different literary sects. These terms are not, however, either synonymous or convertible. Although the majority of metaphysical poets were *concettisti*, the majority of *concettisti* were by no means "metaphysicals." Most of these poets (metaphysicals and nonmetaphysicals alike) possessed in common a search for novel, surprising and ingenious metaphors. Sometimes, though not invariably, they made use of "strong lines,"[7] of terse and obscure aphorisms and riddles, of emblems and proverbs and epigrams. But not all *concettisti* were terse or epigrammatic; Marino and his imitators were often highly diffuse. In diction, these poets ranged from plain to ornate, from low to elevated, from colloquial to the extremes of the "cultivated" style. Some achieved ingenuity without obscurity. Others deliberately darkened their work by a variety of techniques: through abstruse allusions and terms of art, unusual diction and syntax, learned and far-fetched metaphors; or through their dialectical feints, shifts and dodges as they wound their way through the mazes of a complex and paradoxical argument.

What primarily distinguished the metaphysical poets from other *concettisti* was not the farfetched conceit or the frequent use of the epigram, but the choice of philosophical material as the basis for their conceits, and/or philosophical techniques of demonstration in developing them. In defiance of the views of Renaissance humanists, who counseled the poet and orator to eschew technical terminology or "terms of art" and excessive subtlety in their reasoning, the metaphysicals borrowed from the vocabularies of philosophy and science, based their metaphors and analogies and exempla on philosophical and scientific doctrines, and exploited scholastic methods of proof and disproof in elaborating them. In both of these respects, one encounters great variety not only among different poets, but even in works by the same author. Donne did not consistently dispute and argue like a schoolman, nor did the majority of English metaphysicals debate, wrangle and split hairs with the scholastic subtlety and ingenuity of Donne. The majority

of his conceits (as we need hardly remind ourselves) were not
derived specifically from metaphysics but from other branches of
learning or from common experience; this is also the case with
Herbert, Crashaw and the other metaphysicals. In this respect, as
in others, the term *metaphysical* can be used only as trope. It is
rarely valid in the literal sense.

3.

To seek a single formula or a single origin for *concettismo* or for
its "metaphysical" variants seems unprofitable. Scholars have
already examined a wide variety of contributing factors: the classical epigram and elegy, Ramist logic and neo-Aristotelian theories
of metaphor, and the conception of *admiratio* or *meraviglia* as a
principal effect of poetry and rhetoric. They have associated it
alternately with Petrarchist and anti-Petrarchist traditions, with
medieval and Renaissance Platonism and Aristotelianism. They
have stressed the influence of the Counter-Reformation and of
Jesuit spirituality in particular, but they have also recognized a
Protestant strain in the baroque and a Jansenist element in the
baroque literature of Catholic France. Scholars have also emphasized the analogies with mannerist and baroque painting, with the
vogue of emblem literature and the fashionable taste for enigmas
and paradoxes. They have noted the influence of the burlesque
tradition, Biblical typology and cosmic correspondences, the new
cosmology, formal techniques of meditation, and contemporary
attitudes toward *culteranismo* and toward the plain style. As forma-
tive influences, they have included the epistemological crisis of the
late Renaissance; the political and intellectual tensions of the age;
the revival of Stoicism and Pyrrhonism; the traditional affinities of
poetry with rhetoric, logic and sophistic; the rhetorical ideal of
copiousness in matter or in words; the rhetorical exploitation of
proverbs, *sententiae* and epigrams; and the conventions of
academic disputations and civic theatrical performances.
   To varying degrees, most of these factors were indeed operative
in both British and Continental poetry of the seventeenth century.
Yet the principal factor would seem to have been the conscious
preoccupation with *ingenio*, even though the more exhaustive
Continental treatises on this subject did not appear until long after
the major work of Marino, Góngora and Donne. The ideal of wit[8]
(in the sense of native ingenuity, acumen and facility in invention)
provided a link between several of the major features of the

"conceited" style: the farfetched metaphor, the penchant for epigram and aphorism and emblem, the straining for novelty and surprise, the subtle dialectical reasoning. In Aristotle's opinion, the choice of a middle term[9] in dialectical or logical argument, and the perception of similarities and analogies between different things in the invention of metaphors, depended largely on native intelligence or ingenuity. Thus a poet like Donne might exhibit his natural wit (as well as his acquired learning and his art) both through his dialectical skill (discovering a convenient middle term for demonstrating and proving his proposition) and by inventing a new and unusual metaphor or conceit: either discovering an unsuspected analogy between two very different things or finding new analogies and grounds of argument in a conventional comparison. Donne's conceits not only functioned as arguments from analogy; they also, in many instances, provided points of departure for other kinds of argument. His metaphors constantly beget arguments, and his arguments in turn engender new and fresh metaphors.

The antitheses (*contrapposti*) and points (*acumina* or *acutezze*) and the sudden turns of thought characteristic of many *concettisti* were likewise closely associated with the cult of *ingenium*. Aristotle had regarded antitheses, like metaphor, as a grace of style; he had also stressed the delight resulting from surprising the reader through an unexpected turn of thought: consciously fostering a false expectation only to dissipate it. The pointed style, moreover, had been closely associated with the epigram, which in practice often hinged on a conceit.

Insofar as the conceit involved an enthymeme or syllogism, it constituted a form of logical or quasi-logical proof, and thus crossed the frontier of dialectic. Many a seventeenth century epigram, consequently, is in effect a compressed syllogism.

Moreover, a sudden turn in thought in a lyric or satire or epigram, like the unexpected reversal in a dramatic plot, could arouse surprise and marvel. It is significant that Milton himself emphasized the analogy between the reversals or "turns" in *Dianoia* and *Mythos*, finding passion and admiration not only in the external changes of fortune from without but also in the wily subtleties and refluxes of the person's thoughts from within. Already conventional on the stage and in Renaissance lyric — and often associated with the decorum of the moody and volatile lover — such turns and reversals in the representation of thought and emotion could enhance the effect of novelty and *meraviglia*.

Even in developing the most serious themes, *concettismo* was usually a sportive art. Angling for souls like a true fisher of human beings, the parson of Bemerton does not hesitate to mask his hook with the "bait of pleasure":

> A verse many finde him, who a sermon flies,
> And turn delight into a sacrifice.

The sacred poetry of Richard Crashaw hails the "wit of love"[10] in the weeping saint, much as Vaughan's secular verse extols sack as the source of wit. Ingenuity is a game played for its own sake, practiced by gifted amateurs (or professionals claiming amateur status) on public and private occasions — feasts and fasts of the church, weddings and funerals, the publication of a book, the parting of friends, the birth of a prince. Even on the death of a friend, the *concetto* often retains its sportive quality; it remains a contest of skill, frequently marked by unseasonable jests — a metrical funeral game.

4.

Many of the *concettisti* were clergymen; and some of them, with the example of the Greek and Latin fathers in mind, argued the merits of enlivening a sermon with ingenious metaphors and sallies of wit. Others were courtiers, lawyers or university wits. Much of their work is coterie poetry — private, informal, intended for circulation among friends or for publication as testimonials to some acquaintance recently dead and buried or alive and publishing. In England, the poetry of conceits and "strong lines" was often associated (sometimes disparagingly) with the wit of the universities. It is referred to as a fashionable and modish style, cultivated by young men of fashion or by aging wits still eager to appear *au courant* — a poetry composed by wits for wits, by gentlemen for gentlemen. It is a sophisticated art not far removed from sophistry, enjoyed by worldly persons, and rusticating hermits, beaux in lace ruffs or clerical vestments. It is an elitist poetry; its erudition, its obscurity — and, in some cases, its dialectical subtlety — tend at times to exaggerate its character as a coterie art.

In such coterie poetry, one encounters not infrequently a deliberate affectation of esotericism, a pretense of excluding the vulgar and the profane. Frequently, in secular and sacred verse alike, the poets are in a sense initiates, writing for other initiates of their sect. George Chapman had professed to veil the truths of philosophy from the vulgar; and in making this claim, he could rely on the authority of the classical and Renaissance allegorical traditions and the myth of the veiled "wisdom of the ancients." Donne and many of his followers sometimes treat love as a religious mystery or as an art or science requiring the instruction of a master.

Among their many variations on the theme of *eros* — cynical and quasi-mystical, carnal and spiritual, posing as the lover of Many or of One, emphasizing the mutability and inconstancy of passion or the stable and unchanging form of a devotion immune to fortune or absence or death — the metaphors of love as philosophy or science recur frequently. Love is described in terms borrowed from scholastic and mystical theology, hagiology and angelology and astronomy, cartography and geometry, physics and metaphysics, natural history and alchemy. All-sufficient in themselves, the lovers in the Donne tradition often exclude not only the vulgar but the entire world, forming a society of one or a single microcosm. Like Chapman,[11] Donne had an extensive tradition behind him — the Platonic philosophy of love as a cosmic principle and dialectical process; the Ovidian stance of teaching the principles of love as an acquired art; the medieval analysis of *hereos* and its causes, symptoms, diagnosis, prognosis and cure; and the theological doctrine of love as a divinely infused virtue, the ground of merit and good works, creator of the world and poet of the Scriptures, the means of uniting (or reuniting) the human soul with the divine, and (*in gradu heroico*) as the principal basis of sanctity and the glorification of the saints.

Though all of these traditions encouraged a scholastic or academic elaboration of erotic themes, Donne and his posterity extended this approach to a veritable encyclopedia of arts and sciences, outstripping earlier poets in converting the *topos* of love as philosophy into fresh inventions and ingenious sources of wit. Though these *invenzioni* may range (in tone at least) from earnestness to game, their effectiveness often depends on an awareness of their innovations on a commonplace — i.e. on the *topos* of the lover as the master of a learned discipline, a philosopher and the master of an art of persuasion. They are, in a sense, a *reductio ad absurdum* of well-established conventions in Renaissance erotic poetry and treatises on the philosophy of love — and their value as a source of wit consists, in part at least, in the conscious breach of expected decorum, which provoked Dryden's censure of Donne. To treat a physical passion as a mystical philosophy, an affection of nature as an acquired art or science is inherently paradoxical; and the poet is usually well aware of the fact. In developing this paradox, the "refined" lover — academic or courtier, rhetorician or philosopher, sophist or quasimystic — exaggerates the gulf between the initiate and the common herd by treating love as a cult-mysterium or as a philosophical discipline. In doing so, the poet-lover may argue in apparent earnest (as in "The Ecstasy") or clearly in jest (as in "The Flea").

In one respect, this esoteric and elitist stance is a bizarre and at times burlesque elaboration of the Platonic distinction between the vulgar Venus and the heavenly Venus of the philosophers: Aphrodite Pandemos and Aphrodite Urania. In other respects, this stance is reminiscent of the contrast between *fin' amor* and the passion of the common people. The veil of learning interposed between the poet and the common reader serves (much like the veil of allegory in an earlier tradition) to separate the sacred mysteries — the true cult of love — and the initiated few from the rude multitude.

In much the same way, the combination of erotic and philosophical conventions is reminiscent of earlier traditions — the poetry of the *dolce stil nuovo* and of Renaissance Platonism — yet with significant differences. The metaphysicals tend, at times, to apply the methods of philosophy to the subject of love. Earlier poets, on the other hand, had frequently applied the conventions of love poetry to philosophical themes. Philosophy or theology or virtue — or a variety of arts and sciences — may be represented as the objects of love, either through personification-allegory or under the names of real or imaginary ladies. Or a real woman may be eulogized by assimilating her to the transcendental archetype or Idea of beauty or wisdom, chastity or virtue itself.

5.

That some of this coterie poetry should seem to border at times on "high camp" is not surprising. The poet is fully aware of being extravagant, fantastic and bizarre. The poet is also conscious of breaking the "rules" of poetry — realizing that lovers do not ordinarily argue like schoolmen, that "terms of art" and the technical vocabulary of the sciences are inappropriate for poetic and rhetoric, that humanistic apologies for eloquence had ridiculed the dialectical subtleties of the metaphysicians, and that both classical and Renaissance theorists had exalted the poet and the orator over the philosopher precisely because verbal ornaments and passionate language could move an audience more effectively than a concatenation of syllogisms. The fact that the poet could triumph in spite of the rules and in the teeth of orthodox literary tradition, then, would be proof of a special skill.

The metaphysical poets were also conscious of the fallacies in their demonstrations. Much of this dialectic was sophistical, based on apparent proofs, fallacies of equivocation and dubious arguments from analogy. Every university graduate or student of the law knew that metaphors and equivoques were out of place in logical demonstrations, and that they had been banned from Athenian courts. Seventeenth century philosophers, contemporary with many of the metaphysical poets, frequently denounced metaphors as deceitful and banished them from philosophical discourse. The metaphysical poets were therefore breaking the rules of logic as well as those of poetics, yoking heterogeneous modes of discourse together by the same violence that characterized their imagery. Theirs was a hybrid art, neither purely philosophical nor purely poetic; it achieved its effects by uniting methods that Renaissance critical theory regarded as disparate and distinct, if not mutually contrary. The metaphysical poets were conscious of creating a new kind of poetry through deliberately defying the rules of reason and art and thumbing their noses at tradition.

It is this conscious extravagance and *bizzarria* which chiefly differentiates the more mannered *concettisti* from their neoclassical contemporaries. Both on occasion employed the plain style, sported with conceits and paradoxes and equivoques, and were sometimes accused by later critics of deliberate harshness or roughness (*asprezza*). Many English poets of the seventeenth century were influenced by both Jonson and Donne — sometimes writing (as did Henry Vaughan) in different styles, sometimes combining features of both poets in the same poem. (Samuel Johnson noted the influence of Jonson as well as Donne and Marino on the metaphysical poets). For this reason, it is unwise to distinguish sharply between a "school of Jonson" and a "school of Donne." Metaphysical and neoclassical poets alike wrote epigrams and elegies, epithalamions and threnodies, encomia and verse epistles. Both showed the influence of classical poets: Ovid and Horace, Catullus and Propertius and Tibullus, Martial and the epigrammatists of the Greek Anthology, Anacreon and Pindar. Both displayed a taste for the "false wit" of pattern-poems, anagrams and acrostics. Both extolled wit, ingenuity and the faculty of invention.

If the metaphysicals, like many of the Continental *concettisti* and "mannerist" painters, sometimes seem "unclassical" or "anticlassical," it is because they prize originality and singularity of manner over fidelity to orthodox and traditional forms, refusing to be bound by formal rules or classical models. Where the cult of *ingenio* stresses novel and imaginative inventions, the neoclassical school frequently places equal emphasis on the faculty of judgment as well, on the painful and laborious exercise of art, the restraint of fancy by reason, on careful and studied imitation of the ancients and fidelity to the principles of verisimilitude, decorum and the rules of the classical genres. The difference between the metaphysicals and the neoclassicals is often one of relative emphasis and of degree. Many seventeenth century poets combine elements of both styles. Metaphysical poets may on occasion be no less concerned with the exercise of art and "judgment" — craftsmanship and formal organization — than the neoclassical writers. Conversely, the latter (like their metaphysical contemporaries and indeed their classical predecessors) may cultivate the vatic stance of the ecstatic bard, rapt by poetic *furor*, inspired by passion or contemplation or the force of wine; a prophetic visionary momentarily translated into a poet's Elysium or a pagan Olympus, a lover's Paradise or the Christian heaven.

Equivoques and logical or sophistic proofs, hyperbole and oxymoron and paradox, allusions to types and emblems and hieroglyphics, surprising metaphors and conceits, points and antitheses occur frequently in both neoclassical and metaphysical writers, though the former usually employ them with greater restraint and economy. The British metaphysicals and many of the more mannered *concettisti* on the Continent sometimes cultivate an abundance of arguments or *copia rerum* as strenuously as an earlier generation of Renaissance poets and orators had sought abundance of words (*copia verborum*). Similarly, in manneristic painting on the Continent, the very multiplicity and complexity of ornament (as later critics objected) often tended to obscure the clarity and simplicity of the principal invention or design.

The metaphysicals themselves sometimes ridiculed the abuses of the conceited style. Cowley's "Ode Of Wit" condemned the excess of ingenious ornament; to "adorn and gild each part," he said, is as bad as hanging jewels at nose and lips, and it is better to display no wit at all than to have "all thing wit." Wit does not consist in rodomontade or puns ("Jests for *Dutch* men, and *English* boys") any more than poetry consists in anagrams and acrostics. True wit is not to be found in extravagant imagery ("a tall *Metaphor* in the *Bombast* way,"[12] in the aphoristic brevity of the *stile coupé* ("the dry chips of short lung'd *Seneca*") nor in a farfetched conceit:

Nor upon all things to obtrude,
And force some odd *Similitude*.

True wit, rather, is to be found in variety, harmony and decorum: "In a true piece of *Wit* all things must be, yet all things there *agree*." A later generation of neoclassical critics would affirm very similar principles — and condemn Cowley for violating them.

Donne himself, for all his affectation of the language and methods of the schools, had satirized the lawyer[13] who wooed his mistress "in language of the Pleas, and Bench" (Satyre II):

> . . . I have beene
> In love, ever since *tricesimo* of the Queene,
> Continuall claimes I have made, injunctions got
> To stay my rivals suit . . .

The vocabulary of the bar — so common in medieval love-complaints, in Elizabethan lyrics, and even in the sugared sonnets of Shakespeare — is scarcely more pedantic than the medical terminology associated with conventionalized descriptions of the lover's malady or than the scholastic idioms and disputations of the metaphysicals themselves. Donne ridicules the unfortunate Coscus in almost the very terms that Dryden would apply to Donne himself:

> . . . words, words, which would teare
> The tender labyrinth of a soft maids eare,
> More, more, then ten Sclavonians scolding. . . .

Lord Herbert of Cherbury, in turn, had pushed the allegorical fashion in erotic verse to a *reductio ad absurdum*, by recounting a vision of a lady combing her hair: a bark of ivory in a curled sea of gold and concluding with a challenge to the "Philosopher of Knowledge" to unriddle his enigmatic vision. In one poem, Cleveland had parodied his own style; in another he had boasted that his lady's beauty defied all "Tinseyl'd Metaphors" and the art of "Phantastick Postillers in Song. . . ." She is the "Metaphysicks of her Sex," the "very Rule of Algebra," and hyperbolic praise is merely sacrilege.

6.

Though the *concettisti* were usually less scrupulous than their neoclassical contemporaries in observing stylistic levels and the decorum of genres, they did not ignore these considerations altogether, and the same writer might (like Góngora) command a variety of styles. Large-scale generalizations are dangerous, especially as many of these authors consciously affected individuality or eccentricity of manner. Both metaphysical and neoclassical poets sometimes (but by no means consistently) endeavored to capture the tone of colloquial, informal speech, appropriate for intimate personal discourse among close friends or lovers, for private meditation, or for colloquies with the Deity. Such a style would be especially appropriate for coterie poetry, for the fashionable Renaissance themes of love and friendship, and for genres like the familiar letter or verse epistle. It could facilitate the dramatic representation of thought and the process of invention or discovery; and it could heighten the suggestion of an impromptu, the impression of overhearing an interior monologue or an intimate dialogue or the "pious ejaculations" of a soul in devout meditation.

The plain style could be adapted to a variety of effects — Senecan brevity and "terse Asiatic," Attic neatness and elegance, the colloquialisms and slang of informal discourse, and the logical demonstrations and technical vocabulary of the sciences. In their exploitation of the plain style, the metaphysicals and the neoclassical writers differ not only from each other but often among themselves. The plain style of "An Execration upon Vulcan" is not the plain style of "A Celebration of Charis," nor is the plain style of "A Valediction Forbidding Mourning" identical with that of "The Good-Morrow" or "The Sun Rising." Within the same poem or essay, a skillful writer might introduce several variations of the plain style; and within the same *genus dicendi*, seventeenth century poets could assimilate and combine, often without apparent inconsistency, the diverse influences of Jonson and Donne. The Attic style had been traditionally associated with subtle *argutiæ*, elegant jests and nice wit. It was an appropriate vehicle for epigrams and conceits.

The neoclassical writers usually kept these epigrams and conceits firmly within bounds; the metaphysicals (like many of the Continental *concettisti*) exaggerated the conceits, and (in addition) sometimes introduced the vocabulary and methods of scholastic disputation. In this way, they frequently achieved a new and startling style which combined several variants of the plain style: informal discourse, the language of philosophy, and a "conceited" distortion of the Attic mode.

7.

If there is indeed a decorum of paradox, it has been observed with some faithfulness by most critics of the "metaphysical" style — or styles — no less than by critics of mannerism and the baroque. Once excoriated by neoclassical critics as an aberration from good taste and sound judgment, subsequently resurrected like Saint George as a patron or pattern for poets of "entre deux guerres," the metaphysical style has been lauded for its unified sensibility and for its clever exploitation of a divided sensibility and a "fragmented" worldview. Paradoxically condemned by the very poets and critics who were indirectly its heirs in the genealogical succession of "wit," the metaphysical style has invited contradictory assessments through its manifest diversity; and attempts to pin down its nature and its origins have sometimes been no less heterogeneous than metaphysical wit was believed to be.

One of the recurrent difficulties has been the tendency to look for a single formula applicable not only to the different styles of very different poets, but also to the prose writers of the seventeenth century. At one stage historical scholarship reflected the procedures of a paternity suit. It was once virtually an article of faith that "libertine" Jack Donne was the father; that later poets, his heirs, formed in effect a "school" of Donne; that the line of wit was a bloodline, impeccably English in genealogy and manners, a coterie of "old boys" sporting its cultivated eccentricities like an old school tie. All of these views have subsequently been challenged, if not altogether discredited.

Louis Martz emphasized the affinities of the metaphysical tradition with Roman Catholic techniques of meditation, and Barbara Lewalski with Protestant meditations. The essential elements of the metaphysical style were already well established (Martz argued) in the meditative poetry of sixteenth century writers like Southwell and Alabaster. Walter J. Ong found still earlier precursors of metaphysical wit in medieval sacred poetry. Frank J. Warnke pointed out continental analogies in the poetry of La Ceppède and Théophile di Viau, Quevedo and Lope da Vega, and other continental authors.[14] Since Samuel Johnson first called attention to the influence of Ben Jonson on some of the later metaphysicals, scholars have usually recognized in the putative descendants of Donne some genes of the "tribe of Ben."

Still other critics have stressed the community of values shared by "metaphysical" poets and writers of "anti-Ciceronian" prose.

Some have emphasized the affinities as well as the differences between the alleged "metaphysicals," the cavalier poets, and the Augustan poets and critics in their manipulation of "wit." Others have endeavored to correlate the style and content of metaphysical poetry with the manifestations of "mannerist" or "baroque" aesthetics in the visual arts and with the cultural history of the age.

Aside from its rhetorical exploitation of paradox, the actual practice of the metaphysicals was riddled with paradoxes. Many of the more important treatises on wit — those of Graciàn and Tesauro, for example — appeared far too late to influence Donne himself. Though the cult of wit supposedly centered on native ingenuity, the poetry it produced frequently seemed studiedly artificial, heavily dependent on the jocose (or sometimes serious) exploitation of dialectics. To its early critics, this poetry appeared forced and unnatural. Though it might affect an appearance of roughness, spontaneity and unfettered fancy, it might, just as often, display the high polish of a finished piece of sculpture. Deliberate art and judgment complemented invention and fancy, and many of the later metaphysicals shared the views of Horace and Jonson on revision: the necessity for striking a second heat upon the muses' anvil. Many sacrificed the effects of naturalness and spontaneity — *sprezzatura* — for the sake of cleverness and erudition, while in others the effect of spontaneity was achieved through skillful technique. Herbert's artistry may seem far more controlled than that of his precursor, John Donne; yet in the eyes of Thomas Carew, Donne was notable not only for his originality and novelty, but also for the strict "rules" which he had imposed upon himself.

Finally, multiple cross-influences have complicated the problem of defining the metaphysical tradition. What appears to be "the Donne tradition" might in some instances be more appropriately labelled "the tradition of George Herbert"; Herbert's poetry is more directly relevant to that of Vaughan and Crashaw than is Donne's. This too would be unsatisfactory, however; in varying degrees, both of the latter poets reflected the influence of *The Temple*, but nevertheless assimilated what they had borrowed, pursuing the natural (or artificial) bent of their own inclinations — just as Herbert himself had assimilated and transformed the influence of Donne. If Crashaw's poetry seems closer to that of continental authors like Marino than to the English tradition, he nevertheless transformed these influences also, much as he had assimilated the influence of the classical and the neo-Latin epigram. In his translations and paraphrases, "baroque" authors like

Marino and Famianus Strada are subjected to much the same kind of heightened embellishment as medieval Latin hymns. (In some respects, moreover, marinism in England could build on a well-established tradition of elaborated "conceits," on the figurative style of the neo-Spenserians, as well as the "metaphysical" mode.)

Within the metaphysical tradition itself, one may detect a process of continuous adaptation, reformation and restructuring, roughly comparable to the stylistic reforms of the cavalier poets and the Augustans. Though there is a significant difference in degree, both of the latter were directly or indirectly indebted to the metaphysical experiments with the resources of wit. Stripped of the adroit pedantries of Cleveland or the scholastic sophistries of Donne, and adapted alternately to the decorum of the light lyric or the formalities of a more polished heroic couplet, the wit of the metaphysicals may seem almost unrecognizable — but (like the first matter) it is substantially there.

To a significant degree, the "metaphysicals" — in poetry and prose alike — were consciously attempting to dramatize the internal action of discovery and invention, the inner processes of imagination and understanding. They were deliberately avoiding the appearances of revision and afterthought, or concern with formal principles of "method" and arrangement. Some of them also attempted to present their views as tentative and open-ended: subjective and temporary opinions, "pious ejaculations" and sudden insights, rather than considered and reconsidered judgments. Moreover, though they might violate decorum in their choice of farfetched images — just as they violated logic in their sophistical arguments — they achieved a different kind of decorum: a difficult and paradoxical decorum, apparent not to the senses but to the mind. This was a decorum frequently based not on apparent propriety but on seeming impropriety and oxymoron: on conceptual and ideal similarities rather than on sensuous analogies between the image and its referent. This was a decorum often achieved in overt defiance of external verisimilitude and probability, of common opinion and common sense, and of the conventional rules and ornaments of poetry.

To discover and to recognize these analogies exercised the ingenuity of author and reader alike. In the author's own eyes, these analogies might be little more than *jeux d'esprit*; but in other instances they might involve typological symbolism and "hieroglyphics" in nature and history, the works of God or humankind, that would, in the author's opinion, have a real existence. As the "wit" of the Creator, these analogies belonged to the rhetoric of "things": the poet's task was to "discover" them in nature and society and to express them in words. "Real" wit (in the sense of *res*) could sometimes be, especially for writers like Henry Vaughan, the foundation and inspiration for verbal wit.

Joseph Anthony Mazzeo and Ruth Wallerstein have emphasized the divine "wit" that seventeenth century writers perceived in nature (the "book" of creatures), and Louis L. Martz the "wit of love" which Richard Crashaw and other metaphysicals recognized in the operations of divine grace in the human soul.[15] Not only did such analogies — drawn from without and within — constitute an important strain in the poetry of the age; they were also, as Martz pointed out, closely associated with techniques of meditation and with the process of invention.[16] Turning to nature or to Scripture or to the operations of their own minds, poets discovered arguments of divinity or morality, much as a contemporary divine (and many of these poets were in holy orders) might derive axioms of theological doctrine or topics for exhortation from a Biblical text.

The structure of a comparatively short poem or prose composition might indeed recapitulate this process: imitating the act of discovery, developing the hidden analogies implicit in the original metaphor (much as Marvell elaborated the metaphorical correspondence between the soul and a drop of dew), and adapting facets of the same central conceit to the presentation of doctrine and to personal applications. A longer work, like Donne's *Devotions Upon Emergent Occasions*, might consist of a series of such metaphorical discoveries, interconnected through the central analogy between his own illness and the morbid condition of fallen humanity. Or, alternatively, as in *The First Anniversary*, the work might take the form of a more tightly structured meditation, developing a series of analogies based on underlying correspondences between microcosm and macrocosm: the sickness and death of Elizabeth Drury and dissolution of the corrupted world, the hyperbolic identification of the dead maiden with incorruptible Virtue itself and metaphorically the soul of the world. Or — as in the collected lyrics of Herbert or Vaughan or Crashaw — the sequence of "inventions" might be more loosely connected, associated more or less by common approaches (the discovery of spiritual truths implicit in nature or Scripture, in the ceremonies of the Church or in the mind of the poet; the figurative or unadorned expression of naked truth; the evocation of ecstatic devotion) and by recurrent themes, motifs and images.

In some of these cases, metaphysical poets may actually have believed that the analogies they elaborated so cunningly or so

daringly possessed "real" metaphysical and epistemological validity: that these analogies were truly operative in nature and in the
divine economy; that they were indeed an invention of the divine
"wit" and not merely a figment of the individual poet's own fancy.
But in the majority of instances, the poet would seem to have been
fully conscious that the wit was, in large part, a personal invention
(though possibly spurred by divine inspiration). As Donne was
well aware, there was no "real" intrinsic relationship between the
death of Elizabeth Drury and nature's decay; moreover, his own
illness was directly relevant to the "miserable" condition of humanity only insofar as his disease was theologically explicable as
an indirect result of Adam's fall. In developing both analogies, he
was (like other poets) using figurative language figuratively: taking
one truth (Elizabeth's death, his own illness) as a point of departure for analyzing and illustrating general and universal truths of
doctrine. In the eyes of the church, humankind and nature were
indeed diseased and moribund, but these analogies depended
both on a metaphor and on an equivoque. Nature and humanity
were not "sick" in the same sense that Donne and Elizabeth were
ill; the impressive correspondences were based less on the nature
of things as the poet believed them to be than on his own cleverness. In other contexts, Donne could draw his analogies from the
"truths" of science or philosophy, but press them sophistically to
conclusions ingenious but logically absurd. In such instances,
there could be little question of either the epistemological or the
metaphysical validity of correspondences. The rhetoric of "things"
could be as illusory, as sportive, or as powerful as the rhetoric of
"words."

Despite the prominence of this approach — a typology of nature
and the spirit as well as of Scripture — in "metaphysical" poetry
and prose, it did not constitute the "sufficient reason" for the
metaphysical style (or styles). This typological approach represents
one of several applications — one of the most significant, in fact —
that poets made of this style, and it was surely a significant factor
in the development and dissemination of the metaphysical mode.
Yet for all the innovations in style, little in this approach was
radically new. The doctrine of cosmic correspondences was not
new; it had long been a commonplace in medical doctrine and
astrological theory, in several of the natural sciences, in "occult"
philosophy, and in the theory of human proportions. Typological
approaches to Scripture were not new; they could be found in the
gospels and in the epistles of Saint Paul, and throughout the
tradition of Christian hermeneutics. The moral and theological

interpretation of nature through metaphysical analogies was not new; medieval exegetes had transferred this kind of interpretation from the figurative reading of Scripture to the objects of nature and art, just as they had moralized and theologized the mythological poetry of Ovid. The emphasis on the "eloquence" of God in nature was not new; it was implicit in the Psalms and explicit in Saint Augustine's praise of the divine poetic (*The City of God*, Book 11): "the beauty of the course of this world . . . achieved by the opposition of contraries, arranged . . . by an eloquence not of words, but of things."[17]

For the principal origins of the "metaphysical" style, one should look, on the whole, less to seventeenth century conceptions of nature and more to specifically literary sources: the study of Aristotle's *Rhetoric* in the schools of the late Renaissance; the structural function of conceits in the Petrarchan tradition (and, on a more extensive scale, in medieval allegory); the epigrams of Martial, the satires of Persius, the poems of other Latin writers in these genres; the influence of Seneca and Tacitus on contemporary prose; the techniques and terminology of scholastic disputations, still well-established at the universities; the stylistic eccentricities affected by legalists in both France and England; the conventions of Catholic and Protestant meditations; the emphasis on adapting the devices of style to the requirements of privy and personal expression as contrasted with public oratory; the closely associated interest in the familiar epistle (in verse or prose) and the essay as vehicles of private opinion, individual character and personal sentiment. And perhaps, as Rosemond Tuve maintained,[18] a principal origin lies in the Ramist emphasis on dialectics as the essential preliminary for rhetoric, and (in particular) on the invention of arguments inherent in the nature of the matter — like the statue in the block of marble — awaiting discovery and artistic elaboration. Primarily, it was the contemporary preoccupation with "wit" or *ingenio* which directed the "metaphysical" poets to nature or Scripture or the hidden resources of their minds in order to discover and bring into light the implicit "wit" of the Creator. Not the other way round.

EIGHT

Metaphysical and Baroque

Efforts to define the phases of late Renaissance or post-Renaissance styles have usually been as unsatisfactory as attempts to isolate their causes and origins. Literary scholars are still debating the meaning, extension and validity of the term "metaphysical,"[1] and art historians have experienced similar difficulties in defining "mannerism" and "baroque" and in accounting for their origins and development. Critics of the arts of design have found this nomenclature embarrassingly imprecise, and exactly how far either "baroque" or "mannerist" categories are valid for the criticism of poetic and prose styles remains controversial. Though most literary scholars are aware of the possible irrelevance of art historical terminology, they have been reluctant to discard it.

Criticism of baroque and mannerist styles has made frequent and ingenious use of sophistic proofs — circular arguments, arguments from analogy, and arguments based on equivoques or on a literal interpretation of metaphors. On the assumption that a period style is the expression or projection of sociopsychological complexes — reflections of conscious or unconscious tensions within a particular culture — historians frequently exaggerate the correlation between society and art, employing the literature or the art of a period as a gloss on society or a commentary on its worldview — and vice versa. Changes in cosmology or epistemology or social structure are regarded as the root conditions of changes in artistic and literary modes. Asymmetrical or loosely organized compositions are (they assume) projections of psychological disturbances, symptoms of a disintegrating social structure or *Weltanschauung*. Visual representations of movement and conflict are signs of spiritual restlessness; the dynamic tensions within a work of art or literature reflect unresolved emotional and social tensions; distorted images mirror distorted souls. The verbal or visual icon thus becomes emblematic of far more than the particular subject or the universal idea that the artist has consciously chosen to portray or exemplify. It is the hieroglyph of a worldview, the embodiment of the spirit of the age.

Within limitations this approach is justifiable. We can no more dissociate the literature or art of an age from its intellectual and social developments, than we can regard them as interchangeable and interconvertible. The primary difficulties in this approach are methodological. Not only are its assumptions unproven and its terminology either vague or extrinsic, but it tends to subordinate the role of conscious technique in literary invention, composition and elocution to factors that are largely unconscious and must, on the whole, remain so. The mixture of conscious and unconscious elements in the production of a work of art or literature makes it virtually impossible to apply the techniques of depth psychology with precision (aside from the critic's amateur status as psychoanalyst); and the unconscious intent — whether collective or individual — underlying a Cinquecento or Seicento poem remains virtually as elusive for the modern interpreter as for the poet and his immediate audience. Though we shall never achieve absolute precision (for neither literary nor art historical criticism is an exact art or science), we can reduce the element of imprecision, conjecture and semantic ambiguity by endeavoring to reconstruct the composition of a poem or painting of the period in terms of contemporary principles of construction and the aesthetic assumptions shared in common by the artists and their contemporaries.

If historians are to make effective use of twentieth century theories of symbolic or significant form and unconscious expression, they must clearly recognize the points where these theories agree with — or diverge most profoundly from — Cinquecento and Seicento principles of composition. The consciously composed structures of Renaissance or baroque art and literature cannot be reduced simply to Gestaltist configurations, nor are they strictly susceptible to the structuralist approaches current in linguistic and anthropological scholarship. The Crocean theory of artistic expression, with its sharp distinction between "structure" and "poetry" inverts the conventional relationship between expression and structure in Renaissance (as well as in classical and medieval) theory. In literary and art theory, "expression" itself tends to become something of an equivoque; and discussions of the expressional content of art and literature, a variant of the controversy over conscious and unconscious intent.

Just as earlier criticism of the baroque was strongly conditioned by the concept of the *Zeitgeist,* more recent studies have been influenced by concepts of expression and structure essentially alien to the sixteenth and seventeenth centuries. There has been a tendency to understress the principles of structure defined in Renaissance treatises on literary or artistic composition and to interpret Renaissance art instead in the light of twentieth century psychological or philosophical conceptions of structure and form. Critics have sometimes mistaken the deliberate imitation of action and movement for the spontaneous expression of psychological tensions, the conscious representation of passion for unconscious rendition of the artist's own emotion, the labored effort to depict or arouse the tragic affections of pity and fear for symptoms of deep-seated psychoses, and the play of wit for signs of neurosis. Others have confused the imitation of nature[2] with the expression of a worldview, and studied attempts to suggest the surface appearance of things with the conviction that the world is no more than appearance, insubstantial and unreal.

1.

"Baroque" and "metaphysical" are no longer terms of opprobium. Few scholars are still inclined (like neoclassical critics) to dismiss them as "corrupt" styles, a reflection of the corruption of aesthetic judgment and taste. Literary historians now are more skeptical of notions of artistic decadence, more objective in their appraisal of the Counter-Reformation, and more cautious in their assessment of the alleged decadence of Seicento society. Nevertheless, many of the concepts associated with the older stereotypes persist (often unconsciously) in contemporary criticism. Structural tensions in a work of art — instances of *stilistische Spannung* — are interpreted as instinctive expressions of social or spiritual tensions in the culture of the age, projections of a crisis in the conscience of Europe. The deliberate appeal to the senses in religious art and the conscious parallel between secular and sacred love become a pathological symptom, the perverted eroticism of "religious melancholy." The clever manipulation of rhetorical schemes and tropes in poetry — paradox and irony, metaphor and paranomasia, hyperboles and witty ambiguities — or *trompe l'oeil* effects in painting and sculpture are regarded as characteristic signs of the "baroque mentality," and "baroque illusionism" seems virtually indistinguishable from casuistry and equivocation.

If the stereotype of a corrupt and decadent age endures even in sympathetic criticism of its art, this is, in large part, the result of a tendency on the part of earlier cultural historians to overstress the unity of a historical epoch, and to regard artistic and social developments as manifestations of the same "spirit of the times." For the exponent of *Geistesgeschichte*, for the neo-Hegelian who conceives historical process as dialectic, it would be logical to interpret the characteristics of the literary and artistic styles of a period as expressions of its social and spiritual tensions, to use aesthetic developments as a gloss on social developments and vice versa, and to treat both as complementary and mutually coherent statements of the same "inner" history — the autobiography, so to speak, of the spirit of the age.

The "tensions" within seventeenth century European society were, on the whole, not altogether different from, nor significantly greater than, those of the preceding century. Moreover, they varied in intensity (and sometimes in character) in different countries and social classes, and in different branches of learning. When these tensions do appear in art or literature, they are usually there for a definite purpose — consciously introduced and deliberately developed. The critic should not, for instance, mistake conscious stylistic devices such as *contrapposto* (which was common to literary and artistic theory alike) for instinctive expressions of psychological or social conflict. The use of antithesis was not only a rhetorical ornament, but a logical device for defining a concept more clearly through juxtaposing it to its contrary. A cliché like "baroque tension" is, in fact, an equivoque; it probably owes its currency to a combination of associations — psychological and social as well as literary. In confusing these senses, students of the seventeenth century have sometimes tended to take a convenient critical term that has proved especially useful in analysis of "metaphysical" poetry and invest it with historical and psychological associations. The result is to exaggerate the pathological stereotype of the "baroque age," and, on occasion, to mistake jest for earnestness. Ornaments that were originally intended to delight — *scherzi* and *arguzie*, sophisms and witticisms, that were designed to amuse; hyperboles and paradoxes, ingenious metaphors and conceits, that aimed at surprise — are interpreted as the expression of a morbid sensibility.

Generalizations about baroque art and metaphysical poetry are necessary and inevitable, but also dangerous. The historian must necessarily recognize differences and variations not only in national styles, but even in the style of the same writer or artist at different stages and in different genres and subjects. In much of the religious art and literature of the Seicento, one must also recognize the influence of older and traditional theories — the dual emphasis on sensuous presentation and intellectual or spiritual reference, the twofold ends of utility and delight combined with the rhetorical end of persuasion by moving the will through the affections and the imagination; the poetic objectives of imitating thought and passion as well as action and character; the distinction between design and ornament, and the association of ornament, particularly, with delight. Though the Counter-Reformation (and, to a certain extent, the Reformation itself) attempted to subordinate literature to the requirements of the faith, this meant rather an intensification of emphasis, a fixing of direction, than a new orientation. (The Protestants — not surprisingly, in view of their opinion concerning images — were, on the whole, more concerned with "divine poetry" than with sacred art. This bias did not prevent them, however, from compiling emblem-books, which frequently contained sacred themes, nor did it deter painters like Rembrandt from portraying sacred persons and subjects.)

The paradoxical appeal to the senses as a means of leading the mind beyond the sensuous and "aesthetic" to the intelligible and "noetic" — from the realm of opinion to the realm of truth — had been implicit in Platonic and Ciceronian theories of rhetoric. The paradoxical exploitation of illusion as an instrument of truth had been implicit in medieval theories of allegory. The paradoxical use of the imagery of carnal love in order to persuade to divine love was likewise traditional — and in the opinion of many Christian exegetes, this possessed divine sanction in the Song of Songs. Attempts to arouse devotion through direct visual appeal — representations of the Passion of Christ, the agonies and triumphs of martyrs, the joys or terrors of the Four Last Things — or through meditation on the paradoxes and *mirabilia* of the faith had been made by medieval and Renaissance artists and writers; these complemented the disciplines of the cloister and the exhortations of the pulpit. Though this emphasis may (as both literary and art historians have justly argued) have been heightened by Ignatian meditative formulae, it was not new. It represents, rather, an adaptation and continuation of an older and well-established tradition.

For many Seicento theorists, *concetti* were (among other things) a source of delight, a means of entertaining and amusing an audience while instructing them in the deeper mysteries of the faith. Clergy employed them in the pulpit, as witty *scherzi* or jests: *concetti predicabili*. This mixture of jest and earnest, the sport of the limited human intellect confronted by the suprarational doctrines of the faith, could be (and often was) condemned as a violation of decorum. On occasion the metaphysical manner might seem close to becoming "high camp." Crashaw's extravagant but ingenious imagery (as critics have convincingly argued) is at times only half-serious; it is meant to amuse as well as to astonish. Moreover, at least one of his *concetti* — explicitly condemned by William Empson as morbid and perverse — is little more than an elaboration of a conceit already conventional in the Christian tradition. Crashaw's epigram on *"Blessed be the Paps"* combines the material of Luke 11:27 with eucharistic imagery, and it is scarcely more extravagant or shocking than Cyprian's image in *De Coenâ Domini*, "Cruci haeremus, sanguinem sugimus & inter ipsa redemptoris nostri vulnera figimus linguam."[3] The metaphysical conceit can be shocking or just, amusing or tragic, mere extrinsic ornament or an essential part of a poem's argument and structure — the nucleus for the development and transformation of the theme. It cannot be reduced to a single formula any more than the baroque style itself — alternately or simultaneously flaunting and concealing art — can be confined within a single definition.

Perhaps we have accepted too readily the cultural historian's concept of a "baroque age," and the facile antitheses between Renaissance optimism and baroque pessimism, world-affirmation and world-denial, serenity and tension, certitude and doubt. Perhaps we have taken too literally the analogies that Mario Praz and Morris Croll and others have drawn between baroque art and Seicento literature; they are useful as conceits rather than as statements of fact, and like most metaphorical correspondences they are apt to break down if one endeavors to elaborate them in detail. Perhaps we have overemphasized the "metaphysical shudder"[4] at the expense of the *play* of wit, the sport of fancy. And perhaps we have exaggerated the unity of the metaphysical tradition, both in England and on the Continent, seeking a common denominator for writers as diverse as Marino and Quevedo, Góngora and Herbert, Crashaw and Donne, instead of stressing the differences between them.

2.

Most critics of metaphysical poetry have tended to concentrate on limited aspects of the tradition. Some have stressed the search for novelty and marvel, especially in examining Crashaw's debts to

Strada and Marino and other Continental poets and in analyzing his own innovations in his borrowings. Some have explored the influence of Donne and the cross-influences among later metaphysical poets. Others have discussed the influence of Ovid and Anacreon, the epigrams of Martial and the Greek Anthology, Renaissance sacred epigrams and emblem-books, the Italian burlesque tradition and the conceited sonnet and madrigal. Rosemond Tuve examined the logical and rhetorical tradition shared by Elizabethan and metaphysical poets but (in the opinion of other scholars) did not explain their differences in style. Louis Martz has analyzed the tradition of meditative poetry, which sometimes overlaps (but does not coincide with) the metaphysical tradition; meditative poetry also frequently employs the methods of logical demonstration and rhetorical persuasion, but primarily and ostensibly to move the will and affections of the meditator rather than an external audience. Alfred Alvarez has stressed the dramatic quality and the dialectical process of Donne's poetry rather than the farfetched metaphor or conceit. Morris Croll argued that the theory of *concettismo* was primarily influenced by Aristotle's discussion of metaphor, and Joseph Mazzeo has emphasized the theory of universal analogy or cosmic correspondence.[5]

Most critics have noted the conjunction of comparatively simple diction and complexity of thought, plain language often obscured by the "difficult ornament" of tropes and *figurae sententiae*, figures of thought. In style they have recognized the diversity of these poets, contrasting Donne's roughness with Herbert's understatement and restraint, Donne's dialectical structure and Herbert's control of form with Crashaw's "rosary" of epigrams. Some have detected variations in courtly, academic and ecclesiastical adaptations of the metaphysical style, and emphasized its points of similarity as well as dissimilarity with the Jonsonian and Spenserian traditions.

Most of the English metaphysicals were university men and had received a thorough grounding in logic and rhetoric. They had participated in scholastic disputations; they had learned to distinguish between real and sophistic proofs; they were quite aware of the logical dangers as well as the rhetorical advantages of arguments from analogy or resemblance. Like Milton, in his academic prolusions, they had learned to season philosophical arguments with jest and to exploit scholastic terminology as a source of wit on festive occasions. In their use of metaphorical conceits as in their exploitation of dialectic arguments, one might expect to find both game-playing and earnestness, an ironic manipulation of deliberate sophisms as well as solid logic. The invention of dialectical arguments as well as the invention of metaphors (which could easily be classified under the conventional headings of invention) belonged to *ingenium*, and in both of these, poets might demonstrate their natural — though tutored — wit.

Though Crashaw translated the first book of Marino's brief epic on the massacre of the innocents, though Marino himself composed an extended epic on Adonis, and though Cowley employed a conceited style in his incomplete *Davideis*, the metaphysical style was, on the whole, better adapted to shorter poems — the love-lyric, the hymn, the epicedium, the verse-epistle, the elegy, the satire. One also encounters this style frequently in the pastoral eclogue and the Ovidian idyll. In contrast to epic and tragedy — where the primary invention or argument was a story, where any "thesis" or logical argument that the poet desired to develop had to be presented in terms of the plot, and where structure or design consisted of an arrangement of narrative incidents — many of these briefer genres permitted the poets to organize their works in terms of the logical or quasi-logical development of a thesis, to elaborate their arguments in and through their conceits, or (in some instances) to construct an entire poem around a central and controlling conceit, as an extended metaphor or verbal emblem. Much of this poetry is occasional verse, written for births and marriages and funerals, for times of illness or the presentation of gifts, for partings and reunions of friends or lovers, or for the fasts and festivals of the liturgical year. Much of it (as Louis Martz has observed) is meditative poetry, designed to stimulate devotion through contemplating the mysteries of the Christian faith. In some instances, as in the epigram, the epitaph, the love-lyric and (to some extent) the Ovidian idyll itself, where *concetti* and *arguzie* were already conventional, the innovation consists in manner rather than in substance, a heightening of the dramatic element and the element of paradox, a more closely argued exhortation or dehortation, the introduction of more ingenious and startling comparisons and conceits.

To call the metaphysical style "anticlassical" (as has sometimes been done) is probably a misnomer, especially in view of the strong influence of the classical epigram and (as Croll has argued) of Aristotelian rhetoric. Like mannerist painting, this style takes its departure from a classical style but its line of development tends to diverge from the classical manner and from antique models. The student of the Renaissance should, moreover, recognize the embarrassing ambiguity of terms like "classical" and "anticlassical" in

both literary and art history.[6] In different contexts, the same critic
may be referring alternately to Greek and Roman literature (or art)
in general, or to the styles and authors of a particular period of
Greco-Roman civilization, to later styles consciously modelled on
those of classical antiquity, or (more loosely) to "classicism" as a
constant in the art and literature of both Western and oriental
civilizations and the antithesis of "mannerism," and "romanticism" and similar concepts.

Though the doctrine of signatures and universal analogy undoubtedly influenced the Hermeticists, Henry and Thomas
Vaughan — and partly conditioned the imagery of other poets,
metaphysical and nonmetaphysical alike (as in the widespread
exploitation of the macrocosm-microcosm ratio) — it was merely
one of many sources of conceits. Biblical typology, the tropological
interpretation of natural history (already elaborated by Berchorius
in his commentary on Bartholomew's *De Proprietatibus Rerum*), the
symbolism of the liturgy, the imagery of proverbs and emblem-
books, and — perhaps most important of all — the poet's own free
imagination, were contributing sources. Aristotle had defined metaphor (and Gracián would subsequently define the conceit) in
terms of analogy or correspondence. Poets might communicate
greater authority (and probability) to their arguments by basing
their metaphors or similes on traditional correspondences, but
they could best display their wit and ingenuity by embellishing
and elaborating these correspondences or by inventing new and
fresh ones of their own.

3.

In analyzing the devotional literature and art of the late Renaissance, it may be worthwhile to distinguish between those poems
or pictures which were conceived primarily as *aids* to meditation —
instruments of contemplation designed to stimulate religious
thought and feeling and to assist the observer (and perhaps the
author) in concentrating mind and will — and those which were
composed primarily as *imitations* of meditation, representations of
devotional thought or passion, *dianoia* or *pathos*. These two categories may sometimes overlap, but they are not necessarily identical
nor do they always coincide. In certain contexts, characteristic features of metaphysical or "baroque" writing styles — hyperboles and
extravagant metaphors, paradoxes and apostrophes, exclamations
and interrogations, pious "ejaculations" and "expostulations,"

mixtures of ratiocination and irrationality, logic and sophistry, passion and faith — may indeed be designed to stimulate the author's devotion and to persuade the audience. On other occasions, such features may be primarily dramatic rather than strictly meditative aids — mimetic devices for portraying an act of contemplation and a variety of ethical or emotional states ranging from doubt to resolution, from rebellion to acceptance, and from contrition to ecstasy.

In painting, these affections could be represented only through sign or symbol, through the language of facial expression and gesture, or indirectly through allegory. In poetry, they might be presented allegorically and metaphorically, or imitated directly through depicting the movement of thought and the progression of emotions. In this case, imagery could perform a mimetic as well as a metaphoric function, insofar as it served to characterize the passion and disposition of the speaker as a *dramatis persona*. In such instances, where the primary object of mimesis was the process of internal discourse, the instruments of the interior dialogue — logical and rhetorical arguments, impassioned words and images — might serve the ends of dramatic imitation. Not infrequently, the extravagant images in Seicento poetry — the farfetched tropes and figures of thought — which seem at first glance to violate decorum, actually maintain the decorum of devotional experience. These images reflect the excitement of religious passion and the dilemma of the human soul compelled by its very nature to approach *invisibilia* through *visibilia*,[7] to use reason in contemplating objects above reason, and to love what it cannot comprehend by sense or rational discourse and can know only through pure intellectual intuition and through faith conjoined with charity. On occasion, then, the apparent excesses of the metaphysical mode may paradoxically serve the ends of decorum and verisimilitude in the imitation of religious experience, just as in other instances they may serve the ends of personal meditation.

Though the distinction between the literary genres remained intact in seventeenth century theory and usually in practice, the charge that the metaphysicals sometimes tended to blur this distinction is partly justified. In the case of divine poetry this is understandable. Charity was not only a theological virtue and an infused virtue; it was also, for Catholic theologians, the supreme heroic virtue; saints had merited canonization primarily for charity *in gradu heroico*. Traditionally, love had been associated with "irregular" genres like the romance or with minor genres like the elegy, or with the epithalamium, the comedy and the pastoral. In tragedy and heroic poetry, love had frequently been presented in a pejorative context, though Tasso had defended the representation of "heroic love" in the epic. In the religious poetry of the so-called "baroque era," the representation of charity as *amor erga Deum*, or love toward God, tends to transcend generic limitations without directly or explicitly challenging them. The same devout passion can be treated heroically in tragedy and epic, elegy and epithalamium, epicedium and epigram. Moreover, as in the illustration of other emotions, both painter and poet face analogous problems in attempting to represent through a sensuous medium, visual or verbal, a passion for an object beyond images and words and a mode of knowledge — mystical experience — that transcends sensuous apprehension and abstract concept. The charity of the saint and even the devotion of the repentant sinner could be expressed and comprehended not *per se* but only through analogies, just as the *arcana Dei* experienced by the mystic could be suggested only through similitudes, correspondences and enigmas.

4.

The degree to which the "metaphysical" style involved a deliberate variation on earlier stylistic fashions is apparent not only in its departures from conventional decorum and in its rejection of the apparatus of Ovidian mythology, but (perhaps more significantly) in its contrast with the smooth cadences and metrical regularity sought by many of the humanists. In *The Reason of Church Government*, Milton had extolled the poet's power to "paint out and describe" the matter of religion and moral philosophy, the changes of fortune, and the processes of thought "with a solid and treatable smoothness. . . ."[8] Following Horace, Ben Jonson had insisted on painstaking polish and had condemned Donne for not keeping just accent. But the complaint of roughness and harshness went far beyond issues of metrical regulariy or irregularity and harmonious or discordant cadences. Asperity, roughness and obscurity could be justified on the grounds of satiric decorum — and Tasso had approved *asprezza* as an element of the magnificent style. In the eyes of their own near-contemporaries, the metaphysicals were culpable for applying these qualities to lyric poetry, where grace and beauty (*vaghezza*), smoothness and harmony were normally to be expected. In using terms and methods adapted from scholastic philosophy, they were challenging the common presuppositions cherished by Renaissance humanists and by many poets of the period. To adapt Santayana's phrase, this seemed a "poetry of barbarism."

Erasmus and many of his fellow humanists had ridiculed the language and style of the schoolmen, and Milton's own remarks on the subject belong to the humanist tradition. In his academic prolusions, Milton deplored "those enormous and near monstrous volumes of the so-called subtle doctors" and "warty disputes of the sophists." "No flowers of rhetoric relieve this lifeless, flaccid, crawling stuff, but the jejune, juiceless style matches its thin substance. . . ." Milton asserted that the schoolmen had "filled men's breasts with thorns and briars and have brought endless discord into the schools. . . ." Later, in his treatise on education, he complained that the universities had not yet recovered from "the scholastic grossness of barbarous ages," presenting their young novices at the very first with the "most intellective abstractions of logic and metaphysics. . . ."[9]

For the most part, Renaissance poetic theory had advised the poet to avoid excessive subtlety and the matter and terminology of the sciences; but these views had been partly conditioned by the question of whether the poet should address a popular or a learned audience. Arguing that poetry had been invented "to delight and recreate the common people," Castelvetro maintained that, because "the matter of the sciences and the arts is not understood by the people," the poet should not only eschew it as a subject for poetry, but should also avoid using any "part of these arts and sciences" in "any part of the poem."[10] Tasso similarly believed that the poet "should not become fascinated with material too subtle, and fitted for the schools of the theologians and the philosophers rather than the palaces of princes and the theaters, and [that] he should not show himself ambitious in the questions of nature and theology."[11] Mazzoni maintained, against Castelvetro, that the poet might legitimately "treat things pertaining to the sciences and to the speculative intellect, if only he treats them in a credible manner, making idols and poetic images. . . ."[12]

The *affected* scholasticism of the metaphysicals was, for the most part, intended to be taken lightly, in the spirit of the academic burlesque; it would be alien to their spirit, or *esprit*, to take them too seriously, either as the funeral knell of the unified sensibility that T.S. Eliot perceived or of the schizoid sensibility posited by theorists of mannerism. In a sense, their poetry is comparable to the burlesque element in the *Parnassus* plays or (to come to more recent times) in the techniques of an undergraduate review or *The Pooh Perplex*. Pedantry itself becomes a source of wit, and techniques of disputation acquired at Oxbridge or the Inns of Court are no less the objects of parody and ridicule than the stances and conceits of the Petrarchan lover. This is an elitist poetry — and also a poetic of revolt — deliberately flouting rhetorical techniques intended to move and delight a popular audience and consciously eschewing rhetorical conventions fashionable not only among humanists but among an older generation of lettered amateurs at Renaissance courts. Through its scholastic methods and its affectation of mystery and obscurity, metaphysical poetry dissociates itself not only from the common herd but from the poetic affectations of an older generation of courtiers; but in doing so, it also subjects the techniques of the legalists and the schoolmen to parody and burlesque. It is unfortunate that, in attempting to analyze this poetry, twentieth century critics must make use of the pedantries of literary history, adducing analogues to elucidate jests and making earnest of game.

5.

The poetic modes of both Donne and Jonson, in their own day, were regarded as variants from the "aureate" and embroidered tradition of Elizabethan poetry: Donne through his deliberate cultivation of metaphysical quiddities and metrical irregularities, Jonson through his radical simplicity, his exploitation of classical authors and his meticulous craftsmanship. The style of neither could be described as "sugared" or (despite the emphasis on Donne's originality) as the product of a "fine frenzy" or heroic furor. Despite their influence on early seventeenth century poetry, they remained in a sense *sui generis*. Donne's immediate successors were, for the most part, far less adroit in their manipulation of scholastic logic; the wit of George Herbert was usually tamed by a stricter judgment, and the facetious pedantries of Cleveland were often brilliant accidentals, without functional significance for either theme or structure. The "Jonsonian tradition" in turn, was generally lighter, less labored and less dependent on classical models, less redolent of the lamp, than that of the master himself. The ideals of Jonson, if not his poetry, found their true posterity in neoclassicism. Donne, despite his resurrection in the twentieth century, never found a real descendant, even among those who aspired to imitate him; the scholastic conventions which he so skillfully parodied were no longer significant, and at best one could merely emulate his example in subverting an outmoded poetic tradition, with its hackneyed vocabulary of mythological allusion, its stereotyped diction and its limited range of metaphors. The neo-Spenserians, for their part, extended the ornamental Elizabethan tradition beyond its natural lifetime, largely through retaining its emphasis on verbal copiousness and through heightening and elaborating its repertory of conceits.

If the term "metaphysical" can be misleading when applied to a wide variety of "individualists" and *concettisti* in both poetry and prose, the mannerist label, borrowed from art history, can be even more unsatisfactory. Detached from its historical context and interpreted in terms of a phenomenology of style, it can be applied to virtually any writer endowed with a "double vision," with a sense of paradox and incongruity, or with a preoccupation for the tension between opinion and reality. Yet even in the context of literary history, the mannerist label may be as ambiguous as the mannerist mode itself is alleged to be. In the criticism of the visual arts, this term usually denotes a historical style which deliberately disintegrated and recombined classical motifs (yet how vague are our conceptions of Renaissance "classicism" in art and literature alike!). Though mannerism is found to coexist with the Renaissance "classical" tradition, it was nevertheless historically consequent to the latter, dependent on the latter for many of its essential elements and taking the Renaissance tradition as its points of departure. One could legitimately find a literary analogy in the works of Donne and other poets of the late Renaissance; Donne's renunciation of the resources of classical myth and other traditional ornaments of poetry, and the bizarre variations on conventional Renaissance images and *topoi* achieved by Góngora and Marino and other Continental authors, presuppose the Renaissance tradition as their point of departure.

Yet this is scarcely the case with such allegedly "mannerist" poets as Ariosto and Spenser. In both instances, the supposedly mannerist features result not so much from a deliberate (or even an unconsidered) reaction against an established "classical" mode as from the survival (or in some respects, the revival) of a medieval tradition and a concession to contemporary taste. In varying degrees, both of these poets were continuing the tradition of medieval romance in the milieus of Renaissance courts, where the trappings of the chivalric age still possessed a sentimental and a literary value long after its social, political and military structures had begun to disintegrate. In a sense, both authors — despite their humanist education, their knowledge of classical authors, and their exploitation of classical motifs and allusions — were *pre-*

neoclassical, adapting and revaluing a tradition springing from sources anterior to the Renaissance and still fashionable among their own contemporaries. They were not, on the whole, reacting positively *against* the Renaissance modes as "mannerist" artists are supposed to have done.

In his sequel to Boiardo's romance-epic, Ariosto treats the chivalric tradition ironically, undercutting the code of the *cavalieri antichi* and their wandering ladies while apparently extolling it, and occasionally intermixing transparent allegory. Spenser, in turn, moralizes the romance tradition, loading it with a heavier freight of moral and historical and theological allegory than it was accustomed to supporting, outside the commentaries of Harington, Bononome and Fornari. Ariosto introduces a few of the conventions of classical epic, while retaining intact the structural principles of the romance: *entrelacement*, the episodic plot, a variety of subplots and heroes. Spenser, on the other hand, endeavors to achieve a greater degree of unity through centering the separate books of his poem on different protagonists as patterns of distinct virtues, and linking them through the figure of Prince Arthur and the court of the Faerie Queene. Despite their obvious difference from classical models of the heroic poem, neither work can be regarded as a deliberate reaction against the epics of Homer and Virgil or the "rules" of Aristotle. Instead, they represent (more demonstrably in Spenser's case) a partial accommodation of the long-lived tradition of medieval romance to the conventions of classical epic.

Tasso's epic of the Crusades was likewise a compromise, attempting to preserve the variety of the romance while achieving the unity of action demanded by Aristotle and theoretically observed by both Homer and Virgil. Because of this uneasy tension between the two traditions, the poem has been called "baroque"; yet again the work is essentially *pre*-neoclassical — unless one chooses to define the Renaissance epic in terms of Vida and Trissino. Artistically, it is a concession both to the contemporary taste for romantic variety and to neo-Aristotelian theories of epic structure. Attempting to satisfy critics and courtiers alike, this poem endeavored (apparently to the satisfaction of neither the author nor his critics) to reconcile the principles of a newly revived classicism with those of a medieval genre still fashionable at the height of the Renaissance.

In the literary theory of the Italian Renaissance, the predominant tone is indeed classical — however diversely the theorists themselves may have interpreted the *artes poeticae* of the ancients

— and those speaking for the moderns are generally on the defensive. In practice, however, the poetry of the age, in the West and even in Italy, is often a compromise between classical standards and contemporary tastes. In vernacular literature, Renaissance "classicism" is in a sense a halfway stage on the road to the neoclassicism of the late seventeenth and early eighteenth centuries; and from the perspective of these latter critics it frequently appeared insufficiently classical, sometimes powerful in its imaginative force but deficient in polish, decorum and structure.

The situation is comparable to that of the relation of late neoclassical "wit" to the literature of *ingenio* of the earlier Seicento. Though they were in fact ultimately indebted to it, the later poets and critics tended to dismiss the earlier tradition as barbarous and fantastic, ingenious but wanting in taste and judgment. Because of the continuity of the "line of wit," in spite of the refinements and restrictions imposed by later poets — and, more significantly, through the attempt to correlate art historical categories with those of literary history — these neoclassical poets are sometimes classified as "late baroque." Yet they could also be regarded as the product of cultural lag: the belated acceptance of the classicizing tendencies of the Renaissance critical tradition by vernacular poets and their lay audiences. The taste of the moderns had, at length — but in a significant degree — caught up with theorists, committed as these poets were to reimposing the "standards" of the ancient.

In such instances — and in literature if not in the visual arts — the distinctions between a "classical" Renaissance phase, a "mannerist" phase, the "high baroque," and the "neoclassical" or "late baroque" are usually inadequate as historical and stylistic categories. In certain cases, such distinctions may help to illuminate certain aspects, thematic or stylistic, in a particular work by a particular author, but they will not of themselves enable the reader to pinpoint the work historically or to assign it a fixed and determinate place in literary tradition.

Afterword

Many of the features commonly regarded as characteristic of mannerist or baroque style in literature — the exploitation of antithesis and counterpoint and *contrapposto*; the heightened use of metaphor and conceit, oxymoron and paradox; distortions of syntax and normal word order; exuberant diffusion of ornament; striving for magnificence and energy, ingenuity and marvel — would appear to represent a deliberate, and in some instances highly academic, application of recognized rhetorical and poetic principles rather than a spontaneous expression of emotional attitudes or metaphysical and epistemological viewpoints. This emphasis on deliberate art does not, however, undercut the expressive qualities of style. Writers of the period may have *consciously* chosen a style capable of expressing and dramatizing the spiritual and secular tensions of their age. As Arnold Hauser has suggested, both poets and painters may have "singled out the contradictory quality of things" and "cultivated it as artists. . . ."[1]

The stylistic *differentiae* of literary mannerism and baroque are often commonplaces of the European rhetorical tradition and may, accordingly, prove unreliable criteria for defining, delimiting or explaining these modes. Moreover, the relationships of these styles to the intellectual and historical developments of the sixteenth and seventeenth centuries are still controversial. Both René Wellek and Lowry Nelson have emphasized the inadequacy of attempts to explain the baroque primarily in terms of Counter-Reformation (or, more specifically, Jesuit) spirituality or in terms of a "courtly" milieu. They have also pointed out the inherent weaknesses involved in efforts to interpret it largely in terms of synaesthesia, of correspondences between microcosm and macrocosm, or of paradoxical tensions between "content and form," "word and thing," "sensualism and spirituality," or "naturalism and illusionism."[2]

In endeavoring to explain changes in literary style through the hypothetical schemas of the art historian or of *Kulturgeschichte*, literary historians have often understressed the rhetorical and poetic schemas that belong properly to their own field and for which they possess ample evidence in the numerous treatises and manuals of the sixteenth and seventeenth centuries. Though these usually reflect the continuity of theoretical principles underlying the vicissitudes of period styles, they also may show marked variations in their interpretation of these principles and may throw significant light on the conscious aims and methods of the writers of the age. These rhetorical and poetic theories tended to perpetuate the classical and humanistic conception of eloquence as the concrete and senuous vehicle of abstract universals — "ideal" or spiritual truths — and as an instrument of emotional as well as logical persuasion. These theories have an impressive parallel, moreover, in the "humanistic theory of painting" whose development from the fifteenth to the eighteenth century has been explored by Erwin Panofsky, Rensselaer Lee and other art historians. Many of the basic concepts of this theory of pictorial art, and much of its technical vocabulary, were borrowed or adapted from rhetorical and poetic theory; and it may, on the whole, provide a valid though limited basis for evaluating parallels and analogies between the verbal and visual arts.[3]

Analogies between the verbal and visual arts of the Renaissance provide a valid but tentative frame of reference for literary history. These parallels between diverse representational media may sometimes yield genuine insights, but they may easily degenerate into a game of wit — a search for analogies not altogether dissimilar to the farfetched correspondences of Seicento *concettisti*. Like two unequally matched horses harnessed to the same chariot, these analogies cannot be pressed too hard or driven too far.

The chief (and most reliable) basis for such comparisons is the common theoretical and social background of Renaissance art and literature. Poets and painters frequently addressed the same audience and sought patronage from the same individuals or institutions. Most of them held similar views on the analogy between poetry and painting and on the relationship between art and ethics, image and idea. From a common rhetorical and poetic tradition, the sister arts had derived similar technical vocabularies, principles of genre and levels of style, and theories of composition and imitation. Both acknowledged the distinction between ornament and design. Both emphasized natural genius and original invention, as well as adherence to the rules of art and the example of the ancients or eminent moderns and the methods and principles of nature. Both, on occasion, advised selective imitation, through combining the principal merits of several models or through studying the idealized nature of major poets or artists, as a means of improving on nature's works and approximating more closely the ideal forms that nature herself had attempted, albeit imperfectly, to imitate. Both, on occasion, aimed at harmony or asymmetry, at repose or movement, at clarity and obscurity, at *energeia* and *enargeia*. Both exploited the resources of emblem-books and mythographies, proverbs and conceits, and conventional topics of invention. Both attempted, at times, to arouse marvel, or to evoke other passions and appetites: pity and fear, love or hate. Both usually professed to persuade and instruct as well as delight.

In both arts, nevertheless, there were frequent gaps between theory and practice. The concepts of rhetoric and classical poetics were hand-me-downs, not tailor-fashioned garments, and in many instances they fitted very awkwardly. In recognizing the frequent inadequacies of Cinquecento and Seicento theories as a guide, the student of Renaissance styles must, in particular, make due allowance for the limitations of the *ut pictura poesis* concept. In Horace, and perhaps in Simonides, this classical commonplace may have functioned largely as a conceit; for many Renaissance theorists, however, it had become a point of doctrine. Finally, while acknowledging the cross-influences between the visual and verbal arts, the literary historian should exercise restraint in appropriating the categories of art history. Many of the characteristic features of late Cinquecento and Seicento styles in painting developed as solutions to compositional problems peculiar to the visual arts, and must be explained primarily in art historical terms.[4] Similarly, the literary styles of the period frequently reflect solutions to problems peculiar to the verbal arts and must be approached, on the whole, through the methods of literary history and criticism. To mix one's methodologies, imposing the stages and substages of mannerist and baroque painting on poetry and prose, is apt to adulterate the history of literature and art alike.

The objections that René Wellek and Rosemond Tuve[5] have raised concerning the ambiguity of art historical categories like "mannerist" and "baroque," the vague and sometimes contradictory criteria that commonly serve as *differentiae* of both concepts, and the methodological difficulties inherent in attempts to explain stylistic characteristics in terms of a worldview or "state of mind" undoubtedly undermine the reliability of these categories for literary history. Nevertheless, as both critics were aware, these drawbacks do not altogether destroy the value of these terms. They may still encourage fresh and suggestive insights, as they have done in the past, provided one is content to treat them metaphorically rather than literally. One should, for the most part, regard these formal analogies between mannerist or baroque art and the literature of the late or post-Renaissance as suggestions only — as conceits and ingenious correspondences — rather than as scientific evidence. Like other metaphorical analogies, they may serve as inventions to clarify a concept or adorn discourse; but they may prove treacherous in logical demonstrations.

Whatever the value of these abstract categories for the cultural historian and the philosopher of civilization, they are usually less effective as instruments of literary criticism. One's conceptions of a period style tend all too easily to petrify into rigid and inflexible stereotypes, prejudicing and distorting the analysis of a particular work. In practical criticism, these categories frequently seem superfluous. As long as their definition and extension remain uncertain and variable, critics will be compelled to break the categories down into more intelligible and manageable units — defining and illustrating the specific qualities that (in their opinion) are essential to the various poets of the period. If the critic's methodology is sound, it will be these particular qualities — rather than large-scale abstractions like "mannerism" and "baroque" — that will serve as the most effective points of departure and comparison for an analysis of the style and method of a given poem. Like other precision tools, the criteria of the critic will normally be more useful in proportion to their subtlety, their refinement, their limited scope, and their ability to isolate and distinguish the finer shades of meaning and expression in the concrete details of a text, the more elusive nuances of style in a specific passage in a specific work. For these functions, stereotypes of *the* baroque or *the* mannerist sensibility may be unnecessary, if not misleading.

In the case of a poet like Milton, these art historical categories may serve as convenient labels for differentiating facets or phases of his style, but their utility is vitiated by their uncertain denotation. The same poems that one critic regards as mannerist, another classifies as baroque; the poems that one categorizes as baroque, another regards as neoclassical or Renaissance. In several instances, moreover, the controversial poems are heavily indebted to the tradition of Spenser (whom Heinrich Wölfflin had regarded as an exemplar of Renaissance style — in contrast to the "baroque" Tasso — but whom Harold B. Segel and John Shearman would identify as "mannerist"), to the tradition of Ben Jonson (usually regarded as neoclassical), to the English metaphysical tradition, or to the tradition of the Italian *canzone*. If these labels possessed a fixed denotation and if they could be dissociated from the controversial art historical and sociohistorical stereotypes they usually evoke, they might be more effective in practical criticism.

Conversely, though the concepts usually associated with mannerism or baroque may sometimes yield fresh insights into the structure, the ideological or thematic tensions , and the techniques of Milton's poetry, their value is diminished by the rigid historical and stylistic schemas with which they are usually linked, as well as by their dubious reliability as *differentiae* of style. When applied as criteria of mannerism or baroque, they may result in arbitrary classifications, blurring and distorting aspects of Milton's poetics that are constants in much of his earlier and later work. Such criteria, for instance, as unresolved or resolved tension, disintegrated or reintegrated structure, and doubt or assurance do not effectively differentiate the stages of Milton's poetic development. In his allegedly "baroque" and "late baroque" works, as in his allegedly "mannerist" poems, Milton consciously develops tensions between doubt and faith, uncertainty and assurance; and in early and late works alike he deliberately heightens and resolves them. In certain of his earlier poems, he shows less restraint in his exploitation of conceits and in his use of allegory and personification (a license frequently indulged by mannerist painters), but this is partly contingent on genre.

Though these categories have enriched our critical vocabulary — most notably through the emphasis on *Spannung*, or "tension" — they have also confused it; and we should regard them with no less caution than gratitude. Yet one would be reluctant to banish them altogether from the republic of letters, however honorable the exile they would share with Plato's Homer.

APPENDIX A

Studies of Mannerism

Among discussions of mannerism in literature and art, see John Shearman, *Mannerism: Style and Civilization* (Harmondsworth and Baltimore, 1967); Arnold Hauser, *Mannerism, The Crisis of the Renaissance and the Origin of Modern Art*, tr. Eric Mosbacher (New York, 1965); Hauser, *The Social History of Art*, tr. Stanley Godman, Vol. 2, *Renaissance, Mannerism, Baroque* (New York, n.d. [1951]); Alastair Smart, *The Renaissance and Mannerism Outside Italy* (London, 1972); Wylie Sypher, *Four Stages of Renaissance Style: Transformations in Art and Literature, 1400–1700* (Garden City, N.Y., 1955); Roy Daniells, *Milton, Mannerism and Baroque* (Toronto, 1963); *The Meaning of Mannerism*, ed. Franklin W. Robinson and Stephen C. Nichols, Jr. (Hanover, N.H., 1972); M. Treves, "Maniera, The History of a Word," *Marsyas*, Vol. 1 (1941), pp. 69–88; Riccardo Scribano, *Manierismo, barocco, rococo: concetti e termini* (Rome, 1962); Paola Barocchi, *Trattati d'arte del cinquecento fra manierismo e controriforma*, Vols. 1 and 2 (Bari, 1960–1962); Giulio Briganti, *Il Manierismo e Pellegrino Tibaldi* (1945); Gustav René Hocke, *Die Welt als Labyrinth. Manier und Manie in der europäischen Kunst* (Hamburg, 1957); Hocke, *Manierismus in der Literatur, Sprachalchemie und esoterische Kombinationskunst* (Hamburg, 1959); Marco Ariani, *Tra classicismo e manierismo: Il teatro tragico del Cinquecento* (Florence, 1974); Marcel Raymond, *La poésie française et le maniérisme 1546–1610?* (Geneva, 1971); Nikolaus Pevsner, *Academies of Art, Past and Present* (1940); James V. Mirollo, *Mannerism and Renaissance Poetry* (New Haven, 1985); Milton Kirchman, *Mannerism and Imagination: A Reexamination of Sixteenth-Century Italian Aesthetic*, ed. James Hogg, Salzburg Studies [Longwood (originally published 1979)]; James V. Mirollo, *Mannerism and Renaissance Poetry: Concept, Mode and Inner Design* (New Haven, 1985); Richard Studing and Elizabeth Kruz, *Mannerism in Art, Literature and Music: A Bibliography* (San Antonio, Texas, 1979); John Greenwood, *Shifting Perspectives and the Stylist Style: Mannerism in Shakespeare and His Jacobean Contemporaries* (Toronto, 1988); Klaus Peter Lange, *Theoretiker des literarischen Manierismus; Tesauros und Pellegrinis Lehre von der "acutezza" oder von der Macht der Sprache* (Munich, 1968).

For further references, see the bibliographies in Sypher, Shearman, Hauser; Harold B. Segel, *The Baroque Poem: A Comparative Survey* (New York, 1974); Frank J. Warnke, *Versions of Baroque: European Literature in the Seventeenth Century* (New Haven, 1972).

Sydney Joseph Freedberg, *Painting in Italy, 1500 to 1600* (Harmonds-worth, Middlesex, 1971), distinguished "counter-maniera" from "anti-maniera" and provided a detailed analysis of regional styles. For fantasy and *concettismo* in painting, see pp. 167, 209–310, 325, 335; for allegory in painting, see pp. 289, 299, 307, 310, 314, 411. There is an extensive bibliography on pp. 482, 515–527.

Eric Cochrane observed that Ettore Bonora, *Critica e letteratura nel Cinquecento* (Turin, 1964), and other recent historians of Italian literature had distinguished two separate, consecutive movements: "one led by Ariosto and Pietro Bembo, which they called the Renaissance proper, and another, which they called 'mannerism' rather than 'late Renaissance' or 'pre-Baroque' to emphasize its autonomy, beginning with Giovanni Della Casa, culminating with Tasso and giving way to still another phase with Marino"; Eric Cochrane (ed.), *The Late Italian Renaissance, 1525–1630* (New York and Evanston, 1970), p. 17. Ettore Mazzali (Cochrane, pp. 134–148) regarded Tasso's "cultural formation" as a "typical product of the late Renaissance," a period in which "the concepts and style of the Cin-quecento were being codified in treatises on aesthetics and in manuals of polite conduct" and whose principal institutions were the court and the academy. Fritz Strich (Cochrane, p. 832 n.) stressed "the preoccupation with the present, with the particular moment, with immediacy, and with the theme of vanity" in the seventeenth century lyric.

See also my discussion of "Milton and Mannerism," in *A Milton Encyclopedia*, ed. William B. Hunter Jr. et al., Vol. 5 (1979), pp. 62–66. In *Idea: A Concept in Art Theory*, tr. Joseph H.S. Peake (Columbia, S.C., 1968; first published in German in 1924). Erwin Panofsky defined mannerism as an attempt to "outdo the classic style . . . by modifying the regrouping of plastic forms as such." Rebelling against "all rigid rules, especially mathe-matical ones," it "distorted and twisted the balanced and universally valid form of the classic style in order to achieve a more intense expres-sivity. . . ." Stressing the Neoplatonic element in mannerist art theory, he argued that the chief distinction between "Renaissance" and "mannerist" attitudes toward art lay in the mannerist conviction that "the visible world is only a 'likeness' of invisible, 'spiritual' entities. . . ."

In *Art and Illusion*, Ernst H. Gombrich observed that in the "context of Renaissance theories and prejudices, insistence on inspiration and imagi-nation goes hand in hand with emphasis on art as the high intellectual activity and the rejection of mere menial skill." In Giorgio Vasari's praise of the sudden "frenzy of art that expresses the idea in a few strokes" in contrast to "labored effect and too much industry," Gombrich found a parallel with Castiglione's doctrine of *sprezzatura*. In 1660, Marco Boschini similarly contrasted "the *diligente* with the *manieroso*. . . ." See E.H. Gom-brich, *Art and Illusion: A Study in the Psychology of Pictorial Representation*. Second Edition, Revised (Princeton, 1969), pp. 193–199.

In *Shifting Perspectives and the Stylist Style: Mannerism in Shakespeare and His Jacobean Contemporaries* (Toronto, 1988), John Greenwood discusses "possibilities concerning Shakespeare's exposure to mannerist art" (p. 12), emphasizing "Shakespeare's enormous interest in the power of illusion" (p. 19). In Greenwood's opinion, "The effect of the commentator device in Jacobean drama is analogous to a similar device" in painting. "In painting, the narrator, or *Sprecher*, is the figure in the composition who arrests our glance by looking directly at us, thereby diverting our attention away from the rest of the work" (p. 53).

Harold B. Segel observed (p. 17) that "much of what Wölfflin called Baroque is often recognized now as Mannerist." Frank J. Warnke denied that mannerism as a literary concept actually distinguished a clearly discernible literary period between Renaissance and Baroque. He employed the term *baroque* to denote "not a precisely definable style but a period complex made up of a whole cluster of more or less related styles. . . ." In a review of Warnke's book (*MLR*, Vol. 71, 1976), Alan M. Boase disagreed with this judgment of mannerism, citing Marcel Raymond's study *La poésie française et le maniérisme*. Raymond had maintained that mannerism was essentially a "cluster of extremes" and that in recent years the simple Wölfflinian opposition between Renaissance and Baroque had given way to the "notion of varieties of both, and that the earliest of these is Mannerism. . . ." Boase called attention to Borgerhoff's opinion that whereas mannerism tended to embody "expressive deviation from the norm," the baroque tended toward a "return to the norm with some elements of compromise."

Though Segel agreed with Warnke in applying the term baroque to the period between the Renaissance and classicism, he disagreed on the existence of a mannerist period between Renaissance and baroque. In his opinion, mannerism "manifested itself earlier than the crystallization of the Baroque," though to a "greater extent in the visual arts than in literature. . . ." It was a "development in the arts coterminous with the dissolution of the Renaissance and the early formation of the Baroque." Nevertheless "the energies of the Baroque did not spell the end of mannerism." Instead, the mannerist style was "absorbed by the Baroque and modified by it," becoming yet "another component of the Baroque aesthetic"; Segel, pp. 21–22.

Noting that Vida's *De Arte Poetica* (1527) had emphasized the value of variety, Segel stressed the "greater variety and inventiveness" in mannerist art and sixteenth century Italian literature. In his opinion, Ciceronianism in Latin and Petrarchism in the vernacular were mannerist developments. Segel considered Bernardo Tasso's *L'Amadigi* (1942–1960), Ariosto's *Orlando Furioso*, and the dramatic pastorals of Torquato Tasso, G.B. Guarini and Agostino Beccari to be mannerist poems. Sacrificing unity of plot for "variety, inventiveness and technical virtuosity," the *Orlando* was an essentially mannerist poem in its variety, its *meraviglie* and its "proliferation of character and incident." Bernardo Tasso had recognized the pleasure that variety conferred, and Ariosto appealed to the contemporary taste for the romance. Even though Camillo Pellegrino, in his treatise on the epic *Il Caraffa* (1584), had preferred the more unified *Gerusalemme Liberata* of Torquato Tasso to Ariosto's *Orlando*, the "style" of Tasso's epic (as distinct from its structure) exhibited, (Segel suggested) the "Mannerist enthusiasm for novelty, cultivated artificiality, obscurity," and *meraviglie*." In the discussions of style in Tasso's *Dell'Arte Poetica* (1570) and *Del Poema Eroico* (1594), Segel observed the "desire to provoke wonderment of the Mannerist style"; Segel, pp. 23–27.

Segel believed Spenser's poetry to have been based on the "same Mannerist aesthetic as his Italian sixteenth century counterparts. . . ." He also regarded as manneristic Harington's translation from Ariosto's *Orlando Furioso* (1591), Fairfax's translation of Tasso's *Jerusalem Delivered* (1600), the poems of Wyatt and Surrey in *Tottel's Miscellany* (1557) and George Gascoigne's *The Supposes* (1566), translated from Ariosto. Lyly's *Euphues* (1579, 1580) and Sidney's *Arcadia* (published in 1590) also fell within the pale of Mannerist aesthetics." Stressing the element of surprise in the mannerist aesthetic, Segel observed that "the search for novelty and richer texture led the mannerists to embrace ornamentalism and deliberate distortion." He approved Shearman's belief that the intermezzo was "the most comprehensive manifestation of the Mannerist style in literature"; Segel, pp. 27, 29, 38–39.

For Wylie Sypher, mannerism represented the "formal dissolution of a style," the disintegration of the Renaissance style based on "proportion and harmony and unity." Emphasizing the "disturbed balance" of mannerist style, its "dramatic artifice" and "revolving view," its "shifting planes of reality" and "shifting levels of statement," its "uncertain intervals" — and, above all, its "unresolved tensions," tensions that were "accommodated" through technical skill and ingenuity rather than truly resolved — Sypher found mannerism to be a "constant" principle in the arts of western Europe. In "whatever period, ancient, medieval or modern," it was essentially a "reaction against the norms of 'classicism'. . . ."

Moreover, according to Sypher, "mannerism in style accompanies mannerism in thought and feeling. Mannerist art is 'troubled' and 'obscure,' if not 'illogical.' It treats its themes from unexpected points of view and eccentric angles. . . ." Its "images and metaphors seem perverse and equivocal." The period in which it flourished was a time when European society was "inwardly shaken by some tremor of malaise and distrust," a time when "renaissance optimism is shaken, when proportion breaks down and experiment takes the form of morbid ingenuity or scalding wit; art and thought curve away unpredictably along private tangents; approximation, equivocation and accommodation are accepted as working principles. . . ."

In the art of mannerism, Sypher recognized a "disturbing disrelationship of mind and body. . . . Sometimes the mannerist world has the appearance of delirium, as if the too-too solid flesh had really melted . . . and resolved itself." Hamlet, then, exists "in a mannerist world." "Donne's double personality, like the double personality of Hamlet, Gratiana, or Vendice, operates within a moral framework of extreme values: pure and impure, vicious and virtuous, profane and saintly." The "drama of Tridentine faith is a conflict between sense and soul — another half-medieval crisis in the mannerist situation" — and this tension is as great in Saint Teresa of Avila and St. Ignatius Loyola as in John Donne. (Wylie Sypher, *Four Stages of Renaissance Style*, pp. 100–102, 106–107, 147–151, 165, 171, 184.)

As literary exemplars of mannerism, Sypher included the plays of John Ford, Middleton and Rowley, Webster and Tourneur, the poetry of John Donne, several plays by Shakespeare (notably *Hamlet, Troilus and Cressida, Measure for Measure* and *Timon of Athens*), Marvell's "To His Coy Mistress," Milton's Nativity Ode and *Lycidas*, and such literary traditions as Gongorism, Marinism, preciosity. Unlike Segel and Shearman, he placed Spenser with Botticelli in "the renaissance style of decorative isolation of 'fractional seeing' . . ." rather than among the mannerists. In his opinion, the "conceited" style of Elizabethan prose and verse was not truly mannerist since "the techniques of renaissance wit are only a kind of verbal affectation or complexity, not a mark of malaise, double vision and tormented sensibility." Yet he also recognized elements of mannerist affectations in "the fantastic grace and conscious elegance of Botticelli and Spenser"; Sypher, pp. 89–94, 102–104, 107.

APPENDIX B

Studies of the Baroque

Among recent studies of the baroque in the verbal and visual arts, see Carl J. Friedrich, *The Age of the Baroque, 1610–1660* (New York, 1952); Marian Szyrocki, *Die deutsche Literatur des Barock, eine Einführung* (Rowohlt, Reinbek bei Hamburg, 1968); Jean Rousset, *La littérature de L'âge baroque en France: Circé et le paon* (Paris, 1953); Riccardo Scribano, *Manierismo, barocco, rococo: concetti e termini* (Rome, 1962); Marcel Raymond, *Baroque et Renaissance poétique* (Paris, 1955); Giovanni Getto, *Barocco in prosa e in poesia* (Milano, 1969); *Rettorica e Barocco*, ed. Enrico Castello (Rome, 1955); Luciano Ancheschi, *Le poetiche del Barocco* (Bologna, 1963); Imbrie Buffum, *Agrippa d'Aubigné's Les Tragiques: A Study of the Baroque Style in Poetry* (New Haven, 1951); Buffum, *Studies in the Baroque from Montaigne to Rotrou* (New Haven, 1957); Gerald Gillespie, *German Baroque Poetry* (New York, 1971); Helmut Hatzfeld, *Der Gegenwartige Stand der romanistischen Barockforschung* (München, 1961); Hatzfeld, *Estudio sobre el barocco* (Madrid, 1966); Rudolf Stamm (ed.), *Die Kunstform des Barockzeitalters* (Bern, 1956); Manfred Windfuhr, *Die barocke Bildlichkeit und die Kritiker. Stilhaltung in der deutschen Literatur des 17. und 18. Jahrhunderts* (Stuttgart, 1966); Emilio Carilla, *El barocco literario hispanico* (Buenos Aires, 1969); Dymtro Chzhevs'kyĭ, *Slavische Barockliteratur* (München, 1970); Paul Hankamer, *Deutsche Gegenreformation und deutsches Barock* (Stuttgart, 1935); Darnell H. Roaten and F. Sanchez y Escribano, *Wölfflin's Principles in Spanish Drama, 1500–1700* (New York, 1952); Miguel Matllori, *Gracián y el barocco* (Roma, 1958); Joachim Dyck, *Ticht-kunst. Deutsche Barockpoetik und rhetorische Tradition* (Bad Homburg, 1966); Benedetto Croce, *Storia della età barocca in Italia* (Bari, 1929); Wilfried Barner, *Barockrhetorik: Untersuchungen zu ihrem geschichtlichen Grundlagen* (Tübingen, 1970); Pierre Charentrat, *Le Mirage baroque* (Paris, 1967); Julius Schlosser-Magnino, *La Letteratura artistica*, tr. Filippo Rossi (Firenze, 1935); Karl Borinski, *Die Antike in Poetik und Kunsttheorie, von Ausgang der klassischen Altertums bis auf Goethe und Wilhelm von Humboldt* (Leipzig, 1914); Ruth C. Wallerstein, *Studies in Seventeenth-Century Poetic* (Madison, 1950); Joseph Mazzeo, *Renaissance and Seventeenth-Century Studies* (New York, 1974); Rudolph Wittkower, *Art and Architecture in Italy, 1600–1700* (London, 1958); Paul Meissner, *Die geistesgeschichtlichen Grundlagen des englischen Literaturbarocks* (München, 1934); Mario Praz, *Studies in Seventeenth-Century Imagery*, 2 vols. (London, 1939); Praz, "Richard Crashaw and the Baroque," *The Flaming Heart* (New York, 1958); Praz,

Secentismo e Marinismo in Inghilterra (Florence, 1925); Guido Morpurgo Tagliabue, "Aristotelismo e barocco," *Retorica e barocco* (Roma, 1955), pp. 119–195.

Murray Roston, *Milton and the Baroque* (Macmillan, 1980); Mark F. Bertonasco, *Crashaw and the Baroque* (University, Alabama, 1971); Roy Daniells, *Milton, Mannerism and Baroque* (Toronto, 1963); Daniells in *John Milton: Introductions*, ed. John Broadbent (Cambridge, 1973); Oskar Walzel, "Shakespeares dramatische Baukunst," *Jahrbuch der Deutschen Shakespeare-Gesellschaft*, Vol. 52 (1916); L.L. Schücking, *The Baroque Character of the Elizabethan Hero* (1938); Wilhelm Michels, "Barockstil in Shakespeare und Calderon," *Revue Hispanique*, Vol. 75 (1929), pp. 370–458; Alois Riegl, *Die Entstehung der Barockkunst in Rom* (1908); Eugenio d'Ors y Rovira, *Du Baroque* (1935); Werner Weisbach, *Der Barock als Kunst der Gegenreformation* (1924); T.H. Fokker, *Roman Baroque Art: The History of a Style* (Oxford, 1938); Manfred F. Bukofzer, *Music in the Baroque Era* (1947); Robert Haas, *Die Musik des Barock* (1934); Frank J. Warnke, *Versions of Baroque* (New Haven and London, 1972); M.M. Mahood, *Poetry and Humanism* (New York, 1970); J.M. Cohen, *The Baroque Lyric* (London, 1963); Karl Viëtor, *Probleme der deutschen Barockliteratur* (Leipzig, 1928); Karl Scheffler, *Verwandlungen des Barocks in der Kunst des Neunzehnten Jahrhunderts* (1947); Andor Pigler, *Barockthemen, Eine Auswahl von Verzeichnissen zu Ikonographie des 17. und 18. Jahrhunderts* (Budapest, 1956); Albrecht Schöne, *Emblematik und Drama im Zeitalter des Barock* (München, 1964); Victor L. Tapié, *Baroque et Classicsme* (Paris, 1957); H. Härten, *Vondel und der deutsche Barock* (1934); Walter Jockisch, *Andreas Gryphius und der literarische Barock* (1930); Wilhelm Hausenstein, *Vom Geist des Barock* (1921); Eugen Friedell, *Baroque and Rococo* (1931); W. Stammler, *Von der Mystik zum Barock, 1400–1600* (1927); the bibliographical references and discussions in Harold B. Segel, *The Baroque Poem: A Comparative Survey* (New York, 1974); Wylie Sypher, *Four Stages of Renaissance Style: Transformations in Art and Literature 1400–1700* (Garden City, N.Y., 1955); Arnold Hauser, *The Social History of Art*, tr. Stanley Godman, Vol. 2, *Renaissance, Mannerism, Baroque* [New York, n.d. (1951)]. See also my "Milton and the Baroque," in *A Milton Encyclopedia*, ed. William B. Hunter Jr., et al., Vol. 1 (1978), pp. 127–131; Giuliano Pellegrini, *Barocco inglese* (Messina, 1953); Pellegrini, *Dal manierismo al barocco: studi sul teatro inglese del XVII secolo* (Firenze, 1985).

John H. Mueller, in *JAAC*, Vol. 12, pp. 421–437, observed that eighteenth century critics condemned the music of Rameau as "bizarre, baroque, et dépourvu de mélodie" and that of Durante as "baroque, coarse and uncouth." Wölfflin compared Tasso's poetry to baroque art, contrasting it with the "Renaissance" style of Ariosto. In varying contexts (as René Wellek has noted) Shakespeare, Vondel, Dryden, Molière and Racine have also been ranked among baroque poets.

Though Walter Schirmer and others have refused to include John Milton in this category, several critics — Meissner, Reynold, Cerny, Hatzfeld, Lebègue, Buffum, Raymond, Rousset, M.M. Mahood, Carl J. Friedrich — have regarded him as a baroque artist. Hatzfeld termed him "the most hispanized poet of the age, who to the foreigner appears the most baroque"; see Wellek, "Definitions." Margaret Bottrall saw him as "the one major poet whose work exemplifies the full grandeur of the baroque style." Though she accepted Crashaw as baroque, she placed

Donne, Quarles, Herbert and Benlowes among the mannerists instead; it was "precisely their mannerisms which so worried Dr. Johnson." E.I. Watkin excluded Milton from the category of baroque poets on the grounds that he was "too classical and too Hebraic" to be called such. In the third temptation of *Paradise Regained*, Hanford recognized "an English masterpiece of the baroque," analogous to Italian painting. Lowry Nelson Jr. stressed the baroque element in Milton's treatment of time and space. Frank Kermode also saw Milton as baroque. Mario Praz denied this label to Donne, but applied it to Milton and Crashaw. Joseph Frank saw Milton as a baroque artist who deliberately distorted "traditional materials in order to make his creative acts more difficult, his productions more sensational, his talents more conspicuous." René Wellek has also stressed the significance of "unmistakable Protestant baroque" in several countries.

Basil Willey regarded Thomas Browne's "use of a classical image to enforce a Christian moral" as "a piece of hybridization which has its obvious analogies in baroque architecture and much else that is typical of the age. . . ." See Basil Willey, *The Seventeenth Century Background: Studies in the Thought of the Age in Relation to Poetry and Religion* (London, 1949), p. 51. Nevertheless, this kind of hybridization had occurred throughout the Middle Ages and the Renaissance. Dante's *Commedia* offers numerous such instances. One also encounters it in late classical Christianity — Christ represented as Orpheus or Apollo, pagan motifs employed symbolically on Christian sarcophagi, Virgilian centos relating a Biblical story.

APPENDIX C

Studies of the Metaphysical Style

Historically, the term *metaphysical* referred not to the philosophical *content* of a poem but to its philosophical *style* — to the poet's method rather than to the matter of the verse. William Drummond of Hawthornden deplored the attempt to denude poetry of its traditional habits and ornaments and to "abstract" it to "Metaphysical Ideas and Scholastical Quiddities. . . ." Dryden in turn censured Donne for affecting "the metaphysics, not only in his satires, but in his amorous verse, where nature only should reign," for perplexing "the minds of the fair sex with nice speculations of philosophy, when he should engage their hearts" and entertain them with "the softnesses of love." In the present age (Dryden continued), we are "not so great wits as Donne," but we are indubitably "better poets" than he.

In both of these instances, the term "metaphysical" referred to the manner rather than to the subject of the poem. Both critics were blaming the poet for exploiting the method of philosophy rather than the proper method of poetry.

Samuel Johnson emphasized the novel but artificial wit of the conceit as a principal characteristic of the metaphysicals. In his life of Cowley, Johnson echoed Dryden's reference to Donne's metaphysical affectation and extended it to "the *metaphysical poets*," who appeared at the beginning of the seventeenth century. To "show their learning was their whole endeavor. . . ." They "cannot be said to have imitated anything; they neither copied nature nor life, neither painted the forms of matter, nor represented the operations of intellect." They "endeavoured to be singular in their thoughts, and were careless of their diction." Although their "thoughts are often new," they are seldom natural; "they are not obvious, but neither are they just." Such poets "were not successful in representing or moving the affections. . . ."

Johnson's strictures against these poets, like the objections raised earlier by Drummond and Dryden, were strongly conditioned not only by personal taste but by their conceptions of what poetry traditionally had been and ought still to be: by their views of the decorum of "amorous verse," of the conventional ornaments of poetry, and of the nature and ends of poetic imitation. Thus poetry ought to imitate nature or the movements of the mind. It ought to represent and move the passions. Thoughts (or *concetti*) ought to be both natural and just, in accordance with propriety, verisimilitude and decorum.

172

Nevertheless, despite his distaste for their poetry, Johnson effectively isolated one of the essential aspects of their poetic method. Their wit, he observed, is "a kind of *discordia concors*; a combination of dissimilar images, or discovery of occult resemblances in things apparently unlike. . . . The most heterogeneous ideas are yoked by violence together; nature and art are ransacked for illustrations, comparisons and allusions. . . ."

He also recognized their preoccupation with the novel and the marvellous. These poets were "wholly employed on something unexpected and surprising"; their only wish was to "say what they hoped had never been said before," and in their search for novelty, they descended to minute details and subtle distinctions. Their methods were "always analytic," breaking "every image into fragments," and resulted in "slender conceits and labored particularities. . . ." Lacking true sublimity, they relied on hyperbole, leaving reason and fancy behind them and producing incredible and unimaginable "combinations of confused magnificence. . . ."

Nevertheless, Johnson admitted, despite their false or farfetched conceits, these metaphysical poets managed to stimulate the "powers of reflection and comparison" and sometimes "struck out unexpected truth." Their "acuteness often surprises," and "genuine wit and useful knowledge" may sometimes be found in the mass of assorted materials that "ingenious absurdity" had brought together.

See John Donne, *Selected Poetry*, ed. Marius Bewley (New York and Toronto, 1966), pp. ix–xiii; John Donne, *Poetry and Prose*, ed. Frank J. Warnke (New York, 1967), pp. xxiv–xxvi; *The Metaphysical Poets*, ed. Helen Gardner, Second Edition (London, 1967), pp. xix–xx; *The Metaphysical Poets*, ed. Frank Kermode (Greenwich, Conn., 1969), pp. 121–125.

Johnson suggested that the metaphysicals had derived this "fashionable style" of writing from Marino and his followers, as well as from the example of Donne and Ben Jonson. Earlier in the century, Alexander Pope had similarly noted the influence of Marinism on Richard Crashaw, emphasizing several of the qualities that Johnson would regard as characteristic of the metaphysicals. In Pope's opinion, Crashaw's "thoughts" (i.e. *concetti*) were

> oftentimes farfetch'd, and often too strained and stiffened to make them appear the greater: For men are never so apt to think a thing great, as when it is odd or wonderful; and inconsiderate authors would rather be admir'd than understood. This ambition of surprising a reader, is the true natural cause of all fustian, or bombast in poetry.

In Pope's opinion, "The Weeper" was a strange "mixture of tender gentle thoughts and suitable expressions, of forc'd and inextricable conceits, and of needless fillers-up to the rest." See *The Verse in English of Richard Crashaw* (New York, 1949), pp. 13–15. Although Pope did not apply the term "metaphysical" specifically to Crashaw, on another occasion he allegedly referred to the "metaphysical style" of Cowley, Davenant and Donne; see Helen Gardner, p. xix.

Notes

NOTES TO INTRODUCTION

1. Axiomatic in both logic and rhetoric was the principle that any concept could be understood most clearly through juxtaposition with its contrary. Cf. Milton's observations on efficacy of contraries in logic and in ethics; *Works*, 4 (New York, 1931), p. 311; 6 pp. 167, 178 (New York, 1932); John M. Steadman, *Milton's Epic Characters: Image and Idol* (Chapel Hill, 1968), p. 40 and passim. For the prominence of classification according to dichotomies in Ramist logic, see Leon Howard, "'The Invention' of Milton's Great 'Argument': A Study of the Logic of 'God's Ways to Men,'" *Huntington Library Quarterly*, Vol. 9 (1945–1946), pp. 149–173.

2. Yet cf. Max Dvořák, *Kunstgeschichte als Geistesgeschichte* (1928). In *A Defence of Poetry*, Shelley had redefined the epic in terms of the poet's relation not only to the mind of the poet's own era but to the succeeding age: "Homer was the first and Dante the second epic poet: that is, the second poet, the series of whose creations bore a defined and intelligible relation to the knowledge and sentiment and religion and political conditions of the age in which he lived, and of the age which followed it: developing itself in correspondence with their development. . . . Milton was the third epic poet." See *Shelley's Critical Prose*, ed. Bruce R. McElderry, Jr. (Lincoln, Nebraska, 1967), p. 25.

In *The Breaking of the Circle* (New York, 1962), Marjorie Nicolson associated the poetics of the seventeenth century with the worldview of the time — the "magical universe" of the Renaissance, and its world-system of cosmic correspondences and universal analogies. In *Touches of Sweet Harmony: Pythagorean Cosmology and Renaissance Poetics* (San Marino, California, 1974), S.K. Heninger Jr. has investigated analogies between Renaissance views of the macrocosm and the poem as a miniature cosmos.

In *The Baroque Poem: A Comparative Survey* (New York, 1974), Harold B. Segel expressed his belief "that a period term and concept such as Renaissance, Classicist, Romantic, Symbolist or Baroque considers not only a time segment but a way of looking at the world (*Weltanschauung*) and an aesthetic proclivity characteristic of the period and distinguishable in important respects from those of the preceding and following periods." Nevertheless, he acknowledged that "this world and stylistic preference . . . cannot always be reduced to what Warnke speaks of as a 'single, unified and simply definable style' . . ."; Segel, *The Baroque Poem*, pp. 21–22.

3. Roy Strong, *Holbein and Henry VIII* (London and New York, 1967), p. 26.

4. On problems of periodization, see Roger Murray, "A Case for the Study of Period Styles," *College English*, Vol. 33 (1971), pp. 139–148. On the differentiation of medieval and Renaissance styles, see Dagobert Frey, *Gotik und Renaissance* (1929).

NOTES TO CHAPTER ONE

1. The imagery of rebirth in the Renaissance may refer to a variety of recoveries or rediscoveries: a) the recovery of the language and style of classical antiquity; b) the restoration of the classical genres, and the reformation of popular forms like romance and satire according to classical models; c) the revival of the visual arts of antiquity and the imitation of classical sculpture and architecture; d) the recovery of the erudition of the ancients; e) the rebirth and restoration of religion and the doctrine and discipline of the early church; f) the retrieval of the *prisca theologia* and *prima philosophia* of the ancients, concealed under a veil of myth and fable; g) the revival of Hermetic wisdom. The Renaissance schema of the decline and revival of learning and eloquence is paralleled by the pattern of decadence and renovation in the classical schema of the cycle of the four world ages, and by the pattern of fall and renovation in Christian theology. Cf. *Paradise Lost*, Book 11, on the pattern of world history: "good with bad/ Expect to hear, supernal Grace contending/ With sinfulness of Men"; Book 12, "so shall the World goe on,/ To good malignant, to bad men benigne,/ Under her own waight groaning, till the day/ Appear of respiration to the just. . . ."

2. *Selected Writings of Francis Bacon*, ed. Hugh G. Dick (New York, 1955), pp. 180–182.

3. Milton, *Of Reformation*, in *Prose Works* (Bohn), Vol. 2, pp. 366–367.

4. *The Metaphysical Poets*, ed. Helen Gardner, Second Edition (Oxford Univ. Press, 1967), p. 202.

5. Gardner, pp. 116–117.

6. For the concept of *pietas literata* in the northern Renaissance, see recent discussions of "Christian humanism." In *Die Theologie des Erasmus* (Basel, 1966), Ernst-Wilhelm Kohls discusses the relationship between *pietas* and *eruditio*, *pietas* and *litterae*, the ideal of a "sapiens et eloquens pietas" (pp. 47, 64, 66, 68, 207), and the "philosopia christiana" (p. 74 and passim). In "Dévotion Moderne et Chrétien," W. Lourdeaux considers the ideal of a "docta pietas"; see *The Late Middle Ages and the Dawn of Humanism Outside Italy*, ed. Mag. G. Verbeke and J. Ijsewijn (Leuven and the Hague, 1972), *Mediaevalia Lovaniensia*, Series 1, Studia 1, pp. 57–77.

Among other studies of "Christian humanism," see Douglas Bush, *The Renaissance and English Humanism* (Toronto, 1939); Wallace K. Ferguson, *The Renaissance* (New York, 1940), pp. 120–123; Ferguson, *The Renaissance in Historical Thought* (Boston, 1948), p. 256 and passim; Ida Walz Blayney, *The Age of Luther . . .* (New York, 1957), pp. 62–66; Emil Lucki, *History of the Renaissance, 1350–1550* (Salt Lake City, 1963), Book 3, p. 104; Ray C. Petry, "Christian Humanism and Reform in the Erasmian Critique of Tradition," *Medieval and Renaissance Studies*, No. 1, ed. O.B. Hardison, Jr. (Chapel Hill, 1966), pp. 138–170; Albert Rabil, *Erasmus and the New*

Testament: The Mind of a Christian Humanist (San Antonio, 1972); John C. Olin, *Six Essays on Erasmus* . . . (New York, 1979).

7. The character of humanist education in stressing the close study of classical authors, partly for their own intrinsic value but also in order to master the principles of grammar and rhetoric, was to a considerable degree responsible for some of the principal features of Renaissance styles in literature and in the visual arts (for example, its "secular," "classical," "paganizing" qualities). These were, in part, mannerisms resulting not only from personal taste but more significantly from the imitation of the ancients. Their importance has been, in many respects, exaggerated — especially when one treats them less as literary and artistic conventions than as spontaneous reflections of the inner sensibility and convictions of the age. Because the poet and artist had learned to use classical myth as a vocabulary of symbols, a source of ornamentation, and as a means of structuring and organizing a poem or painting, critics of the last century often overstressed its allegedly "pagan" aspects. Again, the emphasis on the aristocratic, courtly, princely facets of Renaissance civilization has been partly based on the social contexts of early humanist schools. The analogous emphasis on the personality of the individual, so often regarded as an essential characteristic of Renaissance society, is also in part a result of the humanist pedagogical scheme, which had stressed *natura* and *ingenium* (as well as art, imitation and exercise) and which had emphasized the individual and concrete as well as the universal.

8. See Cicero, *De Inventione*, tr. H.M. Hubbell (Loeb: London and Cambridge, Mass., 1949), p. 18.

9. On the ambiguous relationship between the Renaissance and antiquity, see Erwin Panofsky, *Renaissance and Renascences in Western Art* (New York, Evanston, San Francisco, London, 1972); Panofsky, *Idea, A Concept in Art Theory*, tr. Joseph J.S. Peake (Columbia, S.C., 1968); and the studies cited in John M. Steadman, *The Lamb and the Elephant: Ideal Imitation and the Context of Renaissance Allegory* (San Marino, 1974), pp. 18–24, 51–52, 69–70, 165–179, 200–212, 229–231.

10. For medieval and Renaissance conceptions of poetry as fiction and of the poet as "maker" or "creator" (interpretations partly based on the etymological sense of *poiētes* and *poēma*), see Charles G. Osgood (tr.), *Boccaccio on Poetry* (Indianapolis and New York, 1956); Allan H. Gilbert (ed.), *Literary Criticism, Plato to Dryden* (Detroit, 1962); O.B. Hardison, Jr. (ed.), *English Literary Criticism: The Renaissance* (New York, 1963); S.K. Heninger, *Touches of Sweet Harmony: Pythagorean Cosmology and Renaissance Poetics* (San Marino, California, 1974); Sir Philip Sidney, *An Apologie for Poetrie*, in *Elizabethan Critical Essays*, ed. G. Gregory Smith (London, 1904), Vol. 1, pp. 148–207; Torquato Tasso, *Discourses on the Heroic Poem*, tr. Mariella Cavalchini and Irene Samuel (Oxford, 1973). See also Stanley E. Fish, *Self-Consuming Artifacts: The Experience of Seventeenth-Century Literature* (Berkeley, Los Angeles, London, 1972).

NOTES TO CHAPTER TWO

1. See A.C. Howell, "'Res et Verba': Words and Things," *ELH*, Vol. 13 (1946), pp. 131–142.

2. For a discussion of the metaphor of style as garment, see Josephine Miles, *Style and Proportion, The Language of Prose and Poetry* (Boston, 1967), pp. 38–46. George Downame described dialectic as the body of oratory and rhetoric as the clothing. He compared invention, disposition and memory to Hercules; elocution (i.e. style) and delivery to "merely the Hydra and skin of eloquence." See Madeleine Doran, *Endeavors of Art: A Study of Form in Elizabethan Drama* (Madison, Wisconsin, 1964), p. 402.

3. For the three traditional levels of style or *genera dicendi* (high, middle, low), see J.W.H. Atkins, *Literary Criticism in Antiquity* (Cambridge, 1934), Vol. 2, pp. 121–123, 197–198, 284; Bernard Weinberg, *A History of Literary Criticism in the Italian Renaissance* (Chicago, 1961), pp. 83–84 and passim; Ruth Wallerstein, *Studies in Seventeenth Century Poetic* (Madison, Wisconsin, 1950), pp. 28–29.

4. See Annabel M. Patterson, *Hermogenes and the Renaissance, Seven Ideas of Style* (Princeton, 1970). For alternative classifications of style, see George Williamson, *The Senecan Amble, A Study in Prose Form from Bacon to Collier* (Chicago, 1966), pp. 41–43. Dionysius of Halicarnassus distinguished the "austere or severe" style of Thucydides from the "smooth, polished, or florid" style of Isocrates; in Herodotus and Demosthenes, he found a "harmoniously blended" style midway between these extremes. Demetrius associated the elevated style with periodic construction and component members (colons, semicolons, commas, etc.) of extended length, the elegant style with symmetry and pointing, the forcible style with brevity and abruptness, and the plain style with detached clauses. Cicero assigned the rhetorical ornament of the sophists to the middle style, while Quintilian contrasted the "vehement and copious" grand style and the "simple and concise" plain style with the "florid" middle style. In his *Discorsi del arte poetica*, Tasso retained the traditional fourfold division of Demetrius. See Torquato Tasso, *Discourse on the Heroic Poem*, tr. with notes by Mariella Cavalchini and Irene Samuel (Oxford, 1973).

5. See W.S. Howell, *Logic and Rhetoric in England, 1500–1700* (Princeton, 1956). The *Rhetorica ad Herennium* defined style (*elocutio*) as the "adaptation of suitable words and sentences to the matter devised"; it is one of the five traditional parts of rhetoric, along with invention, disposition, memory and delivery; tr. Harry Caplan (Cambridge, Mass., and London, 1954), pp. 6–7. Quintilian observed that "what the Greeks call *phrasis*," the Latins call *elocutio* or style, and that this is revealed "both in individual words and in groups of words. As regards the former, we must see that they are Latin, clear, elegant, and well-adapted to produce the desired effect. As regards the latter, they must be correct, aptly placed, and adorned with suitable figures"; *The Institutio Oratoria of Quintilian*, tr. H.E. Butler (Cambridge, Mass. and London), Vol. 3 (1966), p. 195. J.W.H. Atkins (Vol. 2, pp. 265–277) observed that for Quintilian, "style is, broadly speaking, a matter of words, of words singly, and words in combination" and that he expounds his views on style in terms of "choice of words, then the use of appropriate ornament, and lastly the effects of artistic structure or arrangement."

In his observations on letter writing, John Hoskins distinguished between "the invention and the fashion." The latter consists in four qualities of your style: brevity, perspicuity (which includes plainness), vitality ("the very strength and sinews . . . of your penning, made up by pithy sayings, similitudes, conceits, allusions to some known history, or other commonplace") and respect (i.e. decorum) — "to discern what fits yourself, him to whom you write, and that which you handle"; John Hoskins, *Directions for Speech and Style*, ed. Hoyt H. Hudson (Princeton, 1935), pp. 4–8.

According to Bernard Weinberg (pp. 169–171), Sperone Speroni "places the whole essence of poetry in ornament." From the "process of applying a method of invention, disposition and elocution there results a fairly consistent poetic. The plot, from invention, must be single and simple . . . so that a proper amount of ornamentation may be added. . . . If the poet strikes a proper balance between invention and elocution, . . . he is . . . worthy of the highest praise. . . ."

Cf. Cicero, *Orator* on invention, disposition and elocution; style or manner of presentation; the correlation of the three functions of the orator (*probare, delectare, flectere*) with the three *genera dicendi* (subtle or plain style, middle style, vigorous or vehement style); and the distinction between the style of the orator and the styles of philosophers, poets, historians and sophists; tr. H.M. Hubbell, Loeb Classical Library (Cambridge, Mass. and London, 1939), pp. 319–357. For discussion of Aristotle's *Rhetoric* and sixteenth and seventeenth century conceptions of wit, for the topics of invention and contemporary commonplace books, for rhetorical instruction in the sixteenth century, and for the theory of imitation, see William G. Crane, *Wit and Rhetoric in the Renaissance* (New York, 1937), pp. 9–112.

6. In an essay on "Style," in *Anthropology Today*, ed. A.L. Kroeber (Chicago, 1953), pp. 287–312, Meyer Schapiro has provided a valuable critique of the cyclical theory of the evolution of styles (in which "archaic, classic, baroque, impressionist and archaistic are types of style that follow an irreversible course") and of the views of Heinrich Wölfflin, Paul Frankl, Emanuel Löwy and Alois Riegl. For a reference to this essay, I am indebted to Dr. Robert Wark.

7. Schapiro (see above) has stressed the inadequacies of attempts to explain style as "a concrete embodiment or projection of emotional dispositions and habits of thought common to the whole culture," the product of a particular worldview or way of thinking and feeling. Such "attempts to derive style from thought are often too vague to yield more than suggestive *aperçus*; the method breeds analogical speculations which do not hold up under detailed critical study." Erwin Panofsky, *Renaissance and Renascences in Western Art* (New York, Evanston, San Francisco, London, 1972), p. 1, observed that modern scholarship "has become increasingly skeptical of periodization," citing George Boas's opinion that "What we call 'periods' are simply the names of the influential innovations which have occurred constantly in history. . . ." In Boas's view, "periodization . . . does the most harm" in the history of the arts; George Boas, "Historical Periods," *Journal of Aesthetics and Art Criticism*, Vol. 11 (1953), pp. 248–254.

8. Williamson, pp. 41–43.

9. Patterson, pp. 44–68.

10. Schapiro, in "Style," has defined style as "the constant form — and sometimes the constant elements, qualities and expression — in the art of an individual or a group." Noting its different significance for various disciplines — archaeology, art history, and the history of culture — he observed that for the art historian, style was essentially "a system of forms with a quality and a meaningful expression through which the personality of the artist and the broad outlook of a group are visible." For the cultural historian or philosophy of history, style was "a manifestation of the culture as a whole, the visible sign of its unity," reflecting or projecting the "inner form" of "collective thinking and feeling."

11. For the various meaning of *style* in the Renaissance, during the seventeenth and eighteenth centuries, and in our own time, see the studies cited in John M. Steadman, *The Lamb and the Elephant: Ideal Imitation and the Context of Renaissance Allegory* (San Marino, California, 1974), pp. 165–166.

12. Williamson, p. 60.

13. In *Art and Illusion, A Study in the Psychology of Pictorial Representation*, Second Edition, Revised (Princeton, 1961), E.H. Gombrich discusses the reciprocal influences of the terminology for visual and verbal styles. In "analyzing the psychological effects of various stylistic devices and traditions," classical rhetoricians sometimes brought in "comparisons with painting and sculpture" in order to describe the various "characters" of style. Although these rhetoricians rarely disentangled "the problems of expressive modes . . . from that of varying skills," they nevertheless provided "perhaps the most careful analysis of any expressive medium ever undertaken."

According to Gombrich, art criticism subsequently borrowed the notion of style "from the ancient teachers of rhetoric," and the application of this term to "painting and sculpture dates precisely from Poussin's period." The main distinction which the classical orator would observe "was really a social one, the gamut between noble and lowly," and when Winckelmann "in the eighteenth century first applied the categories of style systematically to the history of art, he projected these shifting categories onto the development of representation"; pp. 10–11; 374–375. For the relative significance of skill and vision in artistic imitations of reality and the question whether "changes in style" result not only from improved skill but also from "different modes of seeing the world," see Gombrich, pp. 10–30. In his opinion, "The history of taste and fashion is the history of preferences, of various acts of choice between given alternatives"; p. 21. In Gombrich's view, it is "because art operates with a structured style governed by technique and the schemata of tradition that representation could become the instrument not only of information but also of expression"; p. 376.

14. See Schapiro, "Style," on the views of Riegl and Löwy.

15. For the correlation of subject matter and level of style in painting, see E.H. Gombrich, "The Renaissance Theory of Art and the Rise of Landscape," in *Norm and Form: Studies in the Art of the Renaissance* (London, 1966), pp. 107–121; Elizabeth Wheeler Manwaring, *Italian Landscape in Eighteenth-Century England* (New York and London, 1925); Henry V.S. Ogden and Margaret S. Ogden, *English Taste in Landscape in the Seventeenth Century* (Ann Arbor, Michigan, 1955); and Jean H. Hagstrum, *The Sister*

Arts: The Tradition of Literary Pictorialism in English Poetry from Dryden to Gray (Chicago, 1958). Historical pictures were often associated with the high style (just as the medieval and Renaissance category of "historical" poetry was frequently associated with epic and tragedy and demanded the *stilus altus* or *genus grande*). Though landscape was frequently associated with pastoral and rural subjects, which in literature normally demanded the low (or alternatively the middle) style, critics of the seventeenth and eighteenth century recognized a category of "heroic" landscape. Often characterized by rugged and savage grandeur and associated with the sublime and with emotions or sentiments of terror and awe, such scenes of untamed nature provided a striking contrast to milder landscapes and exhibited the *asprezza* often associated with the grand or magnificent style in literature.

The paintings of Salvator Rosa were especially admired for their savage fury, and contrasted with the milder moods of nature portrayed in landscapes by Poussin and Claude Lorrain. In Gilpin's opinion, Claude "admired the tamer beauties of Nature," whereas Salvator "caught fire and rose to the sublime" (Manwaring, p. 54). John Scott contrasted the "sweet quiescence" of Claude's groves and lawns and the calmness of his grazing herds and gazing peasants with "bold" Salvator's "turbid skies," his "scath'd hills" and "blasted trees," his "wild rocks" and "wild stream" and "vast cliffs" (Manwaring, p. 228). Thomson's couplet:

> Whate'er *Lorrain* light-touch'd with softening Hue,
> Or savage *Rosa* dash'd, or learned *Poussin* drew

was frequently quoted during the eighteenth century; as Manwaring observes (p. 107), "If for sixty or seventy years to come Claude is *soft*, Salvator *dashes*, and Poussin is *learned*, the responsibility is Thomson's." In a eulogy of the lake-district written near the middle of the eighteenth century (Manwaring, p. 175), Keswick is praised for uniting "beauty, horror and immensity" — perfections associated respectively with Claude, Salvator and Poussin. "The first should throw his delicate sunshine over the cultivated vales . . ., the lakes and wooded islands. The second should dash out the horrors of the rugged cliffs, the steeps, the hanging rocks and foaming waterfalls, while the grand pencil of Poussin should crown the whole with the majesty of an impending mountain."

Gombrich argues (*Norm and Form*, pp. 107–121) that the emergence of landscape as a new genre resulted primarily from the interaction of northern European practice and southern theory. The development of landscape painting in northern Europe followed "a demand that existed in Southern Europe." Italian theorists approached northern landscape paintings with preconceptions derived from Pliny's account of the Roman landscape painter Studius and from Vitruvius's emphasis on "naturalistic prospects" in wall decorations and on the differences between tragic, comic and satiric scene. See also Otto Benesch, *The Art of the Renaissance in Northern Europe: Its Relation to the Contemporary Spiritual and Intellectual Movements* (Cambridge, Mass., 1945).

16. See F.T. Prince, *The Italian Element in Milton's Verse* (Oxford, 1954).

17. The late Renaissance "grand style" has sometimes been labelled "mannerist" or "baroque" or "proto-baroque." For certain critics, the

writings of both Bembo and Della Casa are mannerist, while the poetry of Torquato Tasso is regarded as "baroque" or "proto-baroque." To turn to other stylistic modes or levels, Ariosto, Spenser and Bernardo Tasso are sometimes described as mannerist because of their catering to the contemporary taste for romance — as Torquato Tasso's *Aminta* and Giambattista Guarini's *Pastor Fido* and other Cinquecento dramas appealed to the contemporary taste for pastoral and/or tragicomedy — and thus appear either anticlassical or nonclassical in the eyes of various critics. One finds it difficult, however, to accept this accommodation to contemporary taste as essentially post-Renaissance or mannerist. It is to some extent a survival of a medieval heritage — though one should also note the medieval and early Renaissance elements cultivated by certain of the mannerist painters.

18. Allan H. Gilbert (ed.), *Literary Criticism: Plato to Dryden* (Detroit, 1962), pp. 144–198.

19. Gilbert, pp. 162–165.

20. Cf. A.C. Howell, "'Res et Verba' . . ."; *Style, Rhetoric, and Rhythm: Essays by Morris W. Croll*, ed. J. Max Patrick et al. (Princeton, 1966); W.S. Howell, *Logic and Rhetoric in England, 1500–1700* (Princeton, 1956).

21. Helen Gardner (ed.), *The Metaphysical Poets*, Second Edition (London, 1967), pp. 115–117, 121–122. Sir John Denham applied similar terms of praise to Cowley. Ben Jonson had made bold "To plunder all the *Roman* stores/ Of Poets, and of Oratours. . . ." Abraham Cowley, on the other hand, showed greater originality and independence in his use of learning. "To him no Author was unknown,/ Yet what he wrote was all his own. . . ." Emulating Horace's wit and Virgil's state instead of plundering them, Cowley successfully reached the altitude of "Old *Pindar's* flights. . . ." See *Seventeenth-Century Verse and Prose*, ed. Helen C. White, Ruth C. Wallerstein, Ricardo Quintana, Vol. 1 (New York, 1951), pp. 413–414.

22. Noting Scaliger's view that Virgil's *umiltá* in the sublime style (i.e. in the *Aeneid*) differed from the *umiltá* of the *Bucolics* in species, but that the *altezza* and *umiltá* of the *Aeneid* differed not in species but in mode, Torquato Tasso asserted that the tempered and sublime and low styles of the heroic poem were not the same as those of other poems. If heroic poets descend to the low style, Tasso said, they should not sink to the baseness proper to comedy, as Ludovico Ariosto had done. There is greater conformity between the lyric and the epic, however, and Ariosto did not violate decorum in employing "la mediocrità lirica," following Catullus in his stanza "La verginella è simile a la rosa. . . ." The heroic style is "not far from the gravity of the tragic and the *vaghezza* of the lyric," but surpasses both in "the splendor of a marvellous majesty"; see Torquato Tasso, *Prose*, ed. Francesco Flora (Milano-Roma, 1935), pp. 472–474. In Tasso's view, the style of the lyric is less grand than that of heroic poetry, abounds in *vaghezza* and *leggiadria*, and is much more florid, since the "flowers" of rhetoric and exquisite ornaments are proper to the middle style according to Cicero (p. 475). In the "ornate and graceful" style, there are certain *piacevolezze* and *scherzi* and *giuochi* that are greater and nobler and appropriate for lyric poets, others that are humbler and suitable for comedy. The graces particularly fitting for lyric and heroic poetry are *Imenei* and *Amori*, joyful woods and gardens. Nevertheless, the lyric and heroic poets do not possess the same license in employing this style, and even in treating the

same things (*cose*) they do not always use the same *concetti*. Their diversity of style derives more from variety of *concetti* than of things (*cose*). Lyric poetry derives its form (i.e. essential style) primarily from the *piacevolezza*, grace and beauty of its *concetti*. To illustrate this point, Tasso contrasted the simplicity, gravity and acuteness of Virgil's *concetti* with the greater ornament and *vaghezza* of Petrarch's (Flora, pp. 498–504).

23. See the note in Alexander Pope's *Dunciad Variorum*, 2, line 71.

NOTES TO CHAPTER THREE

1. Erwin Panofsky, *Meaning in the Visual Arts* (Garden City, N.Y., 1955), pp. 40–54. Cf. Panofsky, *Renaissance and Renascences in Western Art* (New York, Evanston, San Francisco, London, 1972), pp. 1–113. Panofsky suggested (*Renaissance*, p. 84) that this "principle of disjunction" apparently operated not only in medieval art but also in medieval literature; "epics classical in language and meter as well as in content are in a minority as compared to treatments of classical myth and fable in very mediaeval Latin or one of the vernacular languages. . . ."

2. For defense of the vernacular languages and for the influence of classical studies on vernacular style, see William Harrison Woodward, *Studies in Education During the Age of the Renaissance 1400–1600*, ed. Lawrence Stone (New York, 1967), pp. 50, 64, 75, 134, 311–312. The majority of "humanist teachers in France or England, hardly less than in Italy (excepting the purists, like Erasmus), were concerned with rhetoric not as training in Latin only, but as an essential instrument for the acquisition of a sound and cultivated vernacular style." In urging the study of Roman oratory in "preparation for civil eloquence," Francesco Patrizi had in mind the "command of the vernacular"; Guillaume Budé's *L'Institution du Prince*, composed in French, was "evidence of the relation of training in classical composition to skill in vernacular speech." In James Cleland's discussion of prose composition, involving conversion of an English translation from Cicero into both Latin and French, Woodward found further evidence that "the humanists, however much stress they laid upon Latin writing, recognized that the outcome of the logical training therein involved was the formation of a coherent and lucid vernacular style."

The humanist emphasis on purity of Latin style (one of the reasons for studying Cicero's *Epistles* and the comedies of Terence) was paralleled in the Renaissance insistence on purity in the vernacular tongues: appeals for "pure" English, Tuscan or French.

3. Renaissance theories of beauty are often dense with classical *topoi*, in accordance with the conventional rhetorical procedures of the age, and they were sometimes in open conflict with practice and taste. Committed to defining the perfect "idea" of comedy, tragedy or epic and the rules that ought ideally to govern composition, these theories were frequently more likely to state what the various species of poetry ought to be, or had been, than what they actually were. The defenders of the moderns were likewise compelled to resort to theory, asserting the independence of imagination from the rules of antiquity and insisting that beauty was to be found in

variety and even in irregularity rather than in strict unity and severe harmony. Thus Jacopo Mazzoni, while defending the art of Dante's *Commedia* as consonant with Aristotelian canons, nevertheless maintained that "even when the laws of the Lyceum have been broken and destroyed, it is still possible to write poetry legitimately in another fashion" and that "the beautiful and attractive variety of our epic poets . . . is much more to be commended than the severe and rigid simplicity of the ancients." See Allan H. Gilbert, *Literary Criticism, Plato to Dryden* (Detroit, 1962), p. 359.

In *The Anniversaries*, Donne associated beauty with color and proportion, and Torquato Tasso held similar views: "Beauty is a work of nature, and since it consists in a certain proportion of limb with a fitting size and beautiful and pleasing coloring, these conditions that once were beautiful in themselves will ever be beautiful, nor can custom bring about that they will appear otherwise. . . . But if such in themselves are the works of nature, such must needs be the works of that art which without any intermediary is an imitator of nature. . . . And . . . if the proportion of the members in itself is beautiful, it will be in itself beautiful when imitated by the painter and the sculptor. . . ."; Gilbert, p. 497. Tasso's views, in turn, were partly influenced by Aristotle's discussion of the "well-constructed Plot": " . . . to be beautiful, a living creature, and every whole made up of parts, must not only present a certain order in its arrangement of parts, but also be of a certain definite magnitude. Beauty is a matter of size and order. . . ." In a very minute creature, "our perception becomes indistinct," and in a creature of vast size, its "unity and wholeness . . . is lost to the beholder." *Aristotle on the Art of Poetry*, tr. Ingram Bywater (Oxford, 1945), p. 40. In the *Metaphysics*, Aristotle also included *symmetria* in his definition of beauty, along with *taxis* (arrangement) and *to horismenon* ("defined," "delimited"). Gerald F. Else, *Aristotle's Poetics: The Argument* (Cambridge, Mass., 1967), pp. 284, 351. For variety as a source of beauty, see Gilbert, p. 544 and passim. Milton regarded decorum as the "grand masterpiece to observe" in poetic composition; John Milton, *Complete Poems and Major Prose*, ed. Merritt Y. Hughes (New York, 1957), p. 637.

4. The methods of study and composition, the choice of authors and the manner of imitating or adapting them would leave their imprint on students' later work: on their literary tastes, their command of learning, and their style. In *Smalle Latin and Lesse Greeke* (Urbana, 1944), Thomas W. Baldwin examined the curriculum at the King's New School at Stratford-on-Avon and at other English schools; and in *Shakespeare's Use of Learning* (San Marino, 1953), pp. 21–42, Virgil K. Whitaker emphasized the importance of this education, with its "intensive study of rhetoric and Latin composition" for Shakespeare's "method of writing his plays. . . ." With Baldwin, he believed that Shakespeare had progressed from elementary works like the *Sententiae Pueriles* of Leonhardus Culmannus and the *Disticha Moralia* of Cato, through Aesop's fables, the comedies of Terence, Mantuan's *Eclogues*, and the *Zodiacus Vitae* of Palingenius. Other authors studied would have been Ovid, Virgil and Horace. In composition, it was customary "to begin with epistles in prose or verse and then to go on to themes of set types and finally to orations." In rhetoric, the basic text was the *Rhetorica ad Herennium*, supplemented (Whitaker believed) by Cicero's *Topics* and Quintilian's discussion of the oration. Letter writing was probably based on Erasmus's *De Conscribendis Epistolis*, with the same

author's *Copia* as an aid for language and matter. Aphthonius's *Progymnasmata* was a fundamental text for themes, and Susenbrotus's *Epitome troporum ac schematum* was "often used in English schools" as a manual of rhetorical and grammatical ornaments.

5. See William Harrison Woodward, *Desiderius Erasmus Concerning the Aim and Method of Education* (Cambridge, 1904) and *Studies in Education*, pp. 18–19, 41, 114, 312.

6. For the imitation of Cicero as a model of pure Latinity, see Woodward, *Studies in Education*, pp. 174, 199–201, 311–312, 326. Cardinal Sadoleto, a close friend of Cardinal Bembo and, like Bembo, an ardent Ciceronian, nevertheless believed that in taking Cicero as a model for imitation one ought to "place him side by side with Demosthenes and Isocrates." Juan Luis Vives "ridiculed excessive veneration for Cicero, as on other grounds for Plato or Aristotle," denying that the ancients had "attained final truth in all subjects of enquiry" and recommending that the classics be studied so that "they might be if possible surpassed." James Cleland maintained that in correcting a student's compositions (based on Ciceronian models) "the tutor should value the feeling for Latin sentence structure more than Ciceronian precedent for word or phrase. . . ." See also *Style, Rhetoric, and Rhythm: Essays by Morris W. Croll*, ed. J. Max Patrick et al. (Princeton, 1966); Izora Scott, *Controversies over the Imitation of Cicero as a Model for Style and Some Phases of their Influence on the Schools of the Renaissance* (New York, 1910); W.H. Woodward, *Vittorino da Feltre and Other Humanist Educators* (Cambridge, 1897).

Morris Croll observed (p. 248) that "in the educational scheme of the later humanists literary culture . . . came to consist chiefly in rhetorical excellence, to be attained through the study of the ancients; and the exclusive theory of Ciceronian imitation, which had been so effectively ridiculed by Erasmus, resumed its sway, though in a somewhat less rigorous form, in the teaching of Melanchthon, Sturm and Ascham."

John M. Wallace (Croll, *Style, Rhetoric, and Rhythm*, pp. 51–52) noted several objections to the term "Anti-Ciceronian." It indicated "only revolt . . . in a movement that had a definite rhetorical program." It suggested "hostility to Cicero himself . . . instead of to his sixteenth century 'apes,' whereas in fact the supreme *rhetorical* excellence of Cicero was constantly affirmed by them, as it was by the ancient Anti-Ciceronians whom they imitated." It was "not the term usually employed in contemporary controversy, and was never used except by enemies of the new movement." The leaders and friends of the new style referred to it as "Attic."

7. See Woodward, *Studies in Education*, pp. 8–10, 15, 31, 72–73, 150, 173, 323. The complete text of Cicero's *De Oratore* was rediscovered in 1422, and that of Quintilian's *Institutio Oratoria* in 1416. As "the prime authority upon the Roman educational ideal," Quintilian's book soon became "the textbook of every humanist in the matter of classical instruction." It appealed to the contemporary interest in rhetoric and the command of eloquence, in education, and in an idealized image of Roman antiquity. "When we remember," Woodward continued, "the anxiety of the man of education in the Revival to recognize the ideal of his social and intellectual life in that of ancient Rome, we do not wonder that the humanists, whether professed students or just cultivated men of affairs,

seized upon the one systematic manual of Roman education as the authoritative guide for an age in which the virtues and glory of the ancient civilisation were to be reborn." For the study of Cicero and Quintilian as "guides to systematic prose composition" at the school of Guarino da Verona and other humanist educators, see Woodward, *Studies in Education*, p. 45 and passim. At Ferrara, the *Rhetorica ad Herennium*, wrongly attributed to Cicero, was "the starting point and standing authority." On Cicero's epistles and Terence's comedies as guides to purity of style, see Woodward, pp. 42–43, 121, 311–312.

Woodward observed (p. 18) that in general "the study of Greek in humanist schools was literary rather than linguistic, and in its later stages has for its chief end 'eruditio,' or subject matter." One motive for the reading of classical, "and particularly of Greek, authors lay in the fact that every student of antiquity, and of the ethical and scientific lore enshrined in ancient literature, was compelled to have recourse to original sources." The "antique civilization had not yet been systematized, and the only avenue to genuine knowledge lay in the ancient books." Battista Guarini asserted that "without a knowledge of Greek, Latin scholarship is in the true sense impossible." Erasmus declared that without a knowledge of Greek literature all learning is blind ("caeca est omnis eruditio"), maintaining that "Within the two literatures of Greece and Rome are contained all the knowledge that we recognize as vital to mankind." In James Cleland's opinion, Greek learning was "as profitable for the understanding as the Latin tongue for speaking"; Woodward, *Studies in Education*, pp. 18–19, 41, 114, 312. On the imitation of models in school, see pp. 86, 121, 174, 284. The humanist emphasis on the study of the Greek language and literature was partly influenced by the testimony of Latin authors like Cicero and Quintilian, Horace and Cato; the humanists echoed Roman statements that a person must know Greek to be called educated. See also Woodward, *Erasmus*, and idem, *Vittorino da Feltre*. Woodward (*Erasmus*, pp. 111–115) observed that Erasmus's *De Ratione Studii* reproduced, on the whole, Quintilian's choice of writers for study and imitation; it was essentially a method for the teaching of language, with additional concern for interest and edification.

8. See R.R. Bolgar, *The Classical Heritage and Its Beneficiaries* (New York, 1964), on the notebook-and-heading method in Renaissance schools.

9. Hughes, *Complete Poems*, p. 632.

10. See Woodward, *Vittorino da Feltre*.

11. Hughes, *Complete Poems*, p. 668.

12. See the Foreword by Lawrence Stone in Woodward, *Studies in Education*, pp. xi–xii.

13. For the political and social implications of Ciceronianism and Anticiceronianism — the former associated with conservative orthodoxy; the latter with heterodoxy, libertinism and Stoicism — see Croll, pp. 110–125, 245. In the intellectual history of the sixteenth century, Croll distinguished two tendencies. The first was "the growth of scientific and positive rationalism," which gave free play to "the spirit of skeptical enquiry. . . ." The second was "the tendency to summarize and systematize the gained knowledge of the world" through "formulistic methods or abstracts which would serve the practical purposes of general education." Conservative and often reactionary, it was nevertheless "eminently literary and

classical, . . . the friend of the beauties and symmetries of Renaissance art, Ciceronian imitation was . . . the representative of all that was best and worst in it." Merely "because it was a *rhetorical* doctrine, Ciceronianism ideally represented the aims and interests of the conservative orthodoxies." The preeminence of Ciceronianism reflected "the love of authority and a single standard of reference which still flourished in the medieval mind of the sixteenth century." Thus an essentially "rhetorical doctrine made common cause with philosophical and religious orthodoxies"; in the indictments drawn up against Peter Ramus, "the rhetorical doctrine of his *Ciceronianus* marches *pari passu* with his anti-Aristotelian logic and his ecclesiastical heresy."

Conversely, in Croll's opinion, anti-Ciceronianism was "associated with the radical and rationalistic tendency in whatever fields of controversy it manifested itself. . . ."

14. Croll, p. 290.

15. Cf. Jean Seznec, *The Survival of the Pagan Gods*, tr. Barbara F. Sessions (New York, 1953); Gustave E. von Grunebaum, *Medieval Islam*, Second Edition (Chicago, 1961); George Sarton, *Appreciation of Ancient and Medieval Science During the Renaissance* (New York, 1961).

16. See F.T. Prince, *The Italian Element in Milton's Verse* (Oxford, 1954).

17. Hughes, *Complete Poems*, p. 201. Like his syntax and blank verse, Milton's vocabulary may consciously evoke the image of antiquity. Even though the Latin element in his poetry is less prominent than earlier critics believed it to be, his frequent use of words in their original Latin sense as well as in their contemporary English meaning enhances the impression that he is deliberately fostering the continuity of the epic tradition.

18. Hughes, *Complete Poems*, p. 550.

NOTES TO CHAPTER FOUR

1. Thomas Carew praised Ben Jonson for his judicious use of other authors. He extolled John Donne for his originality and "fresh invention," his strict rules of poetry, and his rejection of the paraphernalia of classical mythology. William Drummond of Hawthornden, on the other hand, deplored the contemporary habit of discarding the traditional ornaments of poetry for metaphysical subtleties. An apparently "unclassical" or "anticlassical" writer like Donne also turned to several of the classical genres in which Ben Jonson excelled: the elegy, the verse epistle, the satire. Abraham Cowley — whose poetry served as a point of departure for Samuel Johnson's discussion of the "metaphysical" school of poetry — endeavored to imitate or adapt the conventions of the Pindaric ode and the odes of Anacreon; his epics utilized classical conventions, though they were, by classical standards, too heavily seasoned with conceits.

2. E.H. Gombrich, "Norm and Form," in *Norm and Form: Studies in the Art of the Renaissance* (London, 1966), pp. 81–98.

3. Walter Friedlaender, *Mannerism and Anti-Mannerism in Italian Painting* (New York, 1965); Anthony Blunt, *Artistic Theory in Italy, 1450–1600* (London, Oxford, New York, 1962).

4. George Williamson, *The Senecan Amble: A Study in Prose Form from Bacon to Collier* (Chicago, 1951), p. 65.

5. *Style, Rhetoric, and Rhythm: Essays by Morris W. Croll*, ed. J. Max Patrick et al. (Princeton, 1966), pp. 98, 130, 177.

6. E.H. Gombrich, "Norm and Form," pp. 81–98.

7. One of the difficulties of the "classical-anticlassical" schema in literary criticism (whatever its merits or demerits in the history of the visual arts) has been the problem of fitting the neoclassical movements of late seventeenth century and eighteenth century Europe into this pattern. Are they a reaction against "baroque" or merely against an earlier phase of "baroque?"

In *The Social History of Art*, tr. Stanley Godman, Vol. 2, *Renaissance, Mannerism, Baroque* (New York, n.d. [1951]), p. 202, Arnold Hauser discussed the change from the "sensualistic to the classicistic baroque" in France. For Wylie Sypher, *Four Stages of Renaissance Style: Transformations in Art and Literature, 1400–1700* (Garden City, N.Y., 1955), pp. 253–257, "Late-Baroque" included the "neoclassical" tradition in France, where the "French Academicians" reimposed the "rules of decorum, propriety, unity and *vraisemblance*" on art and literature. Associating the late baroque with a "Franco-Roman-Augustan tradition heavily indebted to baroque, but usually called 'neoclassicism' or 'academism,'" Sypher traced this tradition in the art of Bernini and Poussin and Sir Christopher Wren, in Milton's brief epic *Paradise Regained*, in the heroic plays of Corneille and Dryden and the tragedies of Otway and Racine, in Samuel Johnson's *Irene* and the *Discourses* of Sir Joshua Reynolds, and other works. "In spite of their strong individuality, Corneille, Boileau, Du Fresnoy, Dryden, Johnson and Reynolds are kindred in their notions of style." The "academic-neoclassic tradition" retained "much of the baroque 'augment,'" along with the baroque emphasis on "ideals of 'elevation' and the 'grand style'; but at the same time it has a strengthened sense of 'decorum' regularity, unity, and whatever is tectonic."

In particular, Sypher stressed the "late-baroque mode of inwardness," apparent in Descartes, Racine, Madame de Lafayette, Pascal, and the "final Milton." In these writers he perceived the "conflict of a divided will, a discourse of the mind existing under the shadow of doubt," an "examination of the self according to a logic of contradictions." With its "Protestant self-consciousness and its debate between Christ and Satan, *Paradise Regained* illustrates the "late-baroque encounter of opposing spiritual forces. . . ." Refusing to be "seduced by any magnificent high-baroque spectacles," both Milton and Racine "reduce life to its essential inner debate. . . ."

8. See Richard Foster Jones, *Ancients and Moderns*, Second Edition (Berkeley, 1965).

9. See Erwin Panofsky, *Renaissance and Renascences in Western Art* (New York, Evanston, San Francisco, London, 1972).

10. John Dryden, *Of Dramatic Poesy and Other Critical Essays*, ed. George Watson (London, 1968), Vol. 1, pp. 66–68, 178, 231, 239.

11. *Selected Writings of Francis Bacon*, ed. Hugh G. Dick (New York, 1955), pp. 180–182.

12. See J.W.H. Atkins, *Literary Criticism in Antiquity* (Cambridge, 1934),

Vol. 2, pp. 257–290 for a discussion of Quintilian's views on imitation. Basing his theory primarily on nature, reason and experience rather than on the authority and practice of the classical Greeks, as Cicero and Horace, Dionysius and Longinus had done, Quintilian regarded art as essentially a "methodizing" of nature's processes, a means of rendering natural effort more effective. Skill in speaking or writing was perfected by nature, art and exercise; and a correctness based on the speech of ordinary life was the first essential for eloquence in expression. Insisting on the necessity for judgment in imitation, and the selection of the "best" authors as models, Quintilian warned his readers against slavish copying and against taking any single writer or style as an exclusive model.

13. See Donald L. Guss, John Donne, *Petrarchist: Italianate Conceits and Love Theory in the Songs and Sonets* (Detroit, 1966); Arturo Graf, "Petrarchismo e antipetrarchismo," *Attraverso il cinquecento* (Turin, 1888).

14. William Harrison Woodward, *Desiderius Erasmus Concerning the Aim and Method of Education* (Cambridge, 1904).

15. Woodward, *Erasmus*, pp. 53–57.

16. Woodward, *Erasmus*, pp. 54–57.

17. On the *maniera antica* and efforts to imitate the style and form (as distinguished from the subject matter) of antiquity, see Erwin Panofsky, *Meaning in the Visual Arts* (Garden City, (Garden City, N.Y., 1955); Panofsky, *Idea, A Concept in Art Theory*, tr. Joseph J.S. Peake (Columbia, S.C., 1968); Panofsky, *Renaissance and Renascences in Western Art*; Panofsky, *Studies in Iconology, Humanistic Themes in the Art of the Renaissance* (New York, 1939).

18. As Panofsky has observed, Renaissance artists reacting against the prevailing styles sometimes attempted to lend the sanction of authority and antiquity to their own views by citing analogous developments in classical painting as reported by Pliny and other ancient historians.

19. See Rensselaer Lee, *Ut Pictura Poesis: The Humanistic Theory of Painting* (New York, 1967).

20. Aristotle, *On the Art of Poetry*, tr. Ingram Bywater (Oxford, 1945), p. 38. Paolo Beni, comparing painting and poetry, includes fable and action (i.e. disposition or plot) under the heading of *design*; character, sentences and style under *coloring*; Madeleine Doran, *Endeavors of Art: A Study of Form in Elizabethan Drama* (Madison, Wisconsin, 1964), p. 402. Among other relationships between verbal and visual modes in the sixteenth and seventeenth centuries were the common concern among theorists for reconciling unity and variety, the principle of rendering the "idea" in concrete, sensuous form, and the imitation of classical exemplars as a means to imitating an idealized nature. In recommending an eclectic approach to the literature or art of antiquity in pursuit of an ideal beauty in form or in style, theorists of both the visual and the verbal arts appealed to the examples of Phidias and Zeuxis. In the literature and art of the late Renaissance and the "age of the baroque," critics have stressed the element of impressionism, the attempt to render the changing and phenomenal, relative and transient, and the interest in passing moods, changes wrought by age and time, and other "accidents." These concerns appear in Rembrandt's self-portraits, in the essays of Montaigne, and to a lesser extent in the *Religio Medici* of Thomas Browne. Critics have also called attention to the common interest in the representation of personal-

ity: in the drama, in the character literature of the period, in the literary self-portraits by Burton and Montaigne, and in such paintings as Franz Hals's portrait of Descartes. The interest in change and variety in landscape is reflected in both art and literature: the variety depicted in *L'Allegro* and *Il Penseroso*, in *Cooper's Hill*, in *To Penshurst*, and in *Upon Appleton House* — and in Dutch landscapes: in the variety of scenery, the effects of light and shadow, cloud-effects, and reflections in water.

21. For the relationship between universals and particulars in medieval and Renaissance art, see E.H. Gombrich, *Art and Illusion: A Study in the Psychology of Pictorial Representation*, Second Edition revised (Princeton, 1961), pp. 152, 155–156. The Neoplatonic doctrine that the painter possessed the "gift of perceiving, not the imperfect and shifting world of individuals, but the eternal patterns themselves," that the painter must "purify the world of matter, erase its flaws, and approximate it to the idea" — aided by knowledge of the laws of beauty ("harmonious, simple geometrical relationships") and by study of those antiques which represent an "idealized" reality — held "sway in the academies for at least three hundred years, from 1550 to 1850," but in Gombrich's opinion it "rests on self-deception."

NOTES TO CHAPTER FIVE

1. See Appendix A: Studies of Mannerism for recent discussions of mannerism in literature and art.

2. See Appendix A: Studies of Mannerism for the views of Harold B. Segel, Frank J. Warnke and others on mannerism.

3. Wylie Sypher, *Four Stages of Renaissance Style* (Garden City, N.Y. 1955), p. 16. See Appendix A: Studies of Mannerism for further discussion of Sypher's views on mannerism.

4. Donald Posner in Walter Friedlaender, *Mannerism and Anti-Mannerism in Italian Painting* (New York, 1965), p. xii.

5. Sypher, pp. 18, 100.

6. Sypher, pp. 137–138, 147, 153.

7. Friedlaender, pp. 80–81.

8. Friedlaender, pp. 41–43.

9. Friedlaender, p. 6.

10. Friedlaender, pp. 50–51. Cf. Rensselaer Lee, *Ut Pictura Poesis: The Humanistic Theory of Painting* (New York, 1967), pp. 39, 44, 57) on Gilio da Fabriano's condemnation of Michelangelo's "capriccio," Lomazzo's assertion of the right of poet and painter to "feign and invent," and Leonardo's insistence on the superiority of the painter's sight to the poet's imagination and to the sense of hearing.

11. Ernst Robert Curtius, *European Literature and the Latin Middle Ages* (New York and Evanston, 1953). For Gracián, the conceit or *concepto* was "a mental act which expresses the correspondence between two things," though it can be "employed in every genre and style" of poetry and prose (Curtius, p. 298).

12. Cf. the similar opinions advanced earlier by Alberti. In the exercise of the painter's art, Alberti warned against the appearance of excessive

care. The painter must "have diligence joined with quickness"; Leon
Battista Alberti, *On Painting*, tr. John R. Spencer, rev. ed. (New Haven and
London, 1966), p. 95. In "making the *istoria* we should have speed of
execution joined with diligence; this ought to obviate fastidiousness or
tediousness of execution in us" (pp. 96–97). Before executing a particular
work, the painter should "have every part well thought out in [the] mind
from the beginning, so that in the work [the painter] will know how each
thing ought to be done and where located" (p. 96). "Never take the pencil
or brush in hand if you have not first constituted with your mind all that
you have to do and how you have to do it. . . . When you acquire the
habit of doing nothing without first having ordered it, you will become a
much faster painter than Aesclepiodorus . . ." (p. 95). For mannerism and
the ideals of *sprezzatura* and inspired "frenzy," see Gombrich, *Art and
Illusion, A Study in the Psychology of Pictorial Representation*, 2d ed. rev.
(Princeton, 1961), pp. 191–199.

13. Anthony Blunt, *Artistic Theory in Italy, 1450–1600* (London, Oxford,
New York, 1962), pp. 88–98.

14. Blunt, pp. 105–159.

15. Rensselaer Lee, pp. 14–15, 73; cf. pp. 38–40, 61. Erwin Panofsky,
Idea, A Concept in Art Theory, tr. Joseph J.S. Peake (Columbia, S.C., 1968).

16. Cf. Lee, pp. 60–61n.

17. Arnold Hauser, *Mannerism, The Crisis of the Renaissance and the Origin
of Modern Art*, tr. Eric Mosbacher (New York, 1965), pp. xviii–xix. Hauser
attempted to relate mannerist art to the intellectual tensions of the Renaissance and to the economic and social revolution. He explored its connections with the scientific thought of Copernicus and Kepler, with
Montaigne's image of the "fluid self," with Machiavelli's political thought,
and with the paradoxes of the Reformation and its theory of predestina-
tion. He also stressed the "antimannerist tendency of the Counter-
Reformation." Hauser, pp. 3–143.

In Hauser's view (pp. 4–6), periods of classical art were "characterized
by the absolute discipline of form, the complete permeation of reality by
the principles of order, and the total subjection of self-expression to
harmony and beauty," but such periods were of comparatively brief
duration. During the Renaissance, the classical style — characteristic of a
generation of artists who "were at one with themselves and apparently in
complete harmony with the outside world" — lasted "for barely more
than twenty years"; hence it was "only in a limited sense that the
Renaissance can be said to have been classical. . . ." In the later work of
Raphael and Michelangelo, Hauser perceived baroque or mannerist
trends, and he noted that even Titian "went through a mannerist
phase, . . ." Even though the "classical tradition for a long time survived
side by side with the new trends . . ., the breach with the past is unmistakable." "Something terrible," he inferred, "must have happened to that
generation, something which shook it to its core and made it doubt its
highest values."

18. Hauser, *Mannerism*, pp. 3–143; see especially pp. 1–12, 15, 111.
Hauser associated the birth of modern tragedy and the discovery of humor
(pp. 137–143) with mannerism and traced the history of mannerist style in
art and literature within and outside Italy (pp. 147, 352). In most of the
leading Cinquecento artists, he found mannerist, baroque and classical

strains. In his opinion, the early rivalry between mannerist and baroque trends concluded "to the advantage of the former with the establishment of mannerism as a sharply defined and unmistakable style that dominated artistic output in Italy practically until the end of the century . . ." (pp. 150–151). Both mannerism and baroque were "anticlassical and were the product of the same spiritual crisis" and reflected the "open split between the spiritual and physical values on the harmony between which the survival of the Renaissance principally depended." Nevertheless, the parallels between mannerism and the baroque ("the dynamic representation of space, asymmetry as a compositional principle," the "obscuration and complication of forms," the trend toward "the forced, the strained and the surprising") were, for Hauser, less significant than the affinities between the Renaissance and the baroque. These resulted primarily from the fact "that the baroque returned to the Renaissance naturalism and rationalism that mannerism dropped" (pp. 151–152).

19. Hauser, *Mannerism*, pp. 272–277. In *Social History* (Vol. 2, p. 106), Hauser explained mannerism as "the artistic expression of the crisis which convulses the whole of Western Europe in the sixteenth century and which extends to all fields of political, economic and cultural life." He noted that the pejorative conception of mannerist art as "a rigid routine slavishly imitating the great masters" was first developed by Bellori in his biography of Annibale Caracci. The classicists of the seventeenth century — Bellori and Malvasia — were "the first to connect with the concept of the *maniera* the idea of an affected, hackneyed style of art reducible to a series of formulae; they are the first to be aware of the breach that mannerism introduces into the development of art, and the first to be conscious of the estrangement from classicism which makes itself felt in art after 1520." (Hauser, *Social History*, pp. 97–98). For Hauser, mannerism was "the first movement to raise the epistemological question: for the first time the agreement of art with nature is felt to constitute a problem." In contrast to Renaissance art, mannerism "drops the theory of art as a copying of nature; in accordance with the new doctrine, art creates not merely from nature but *like* nature. Both Lomazzo and Federigo Zuccari think that art has a spontaneous origin in the mind of the artist." For the former, "the artistic genius works in art as the divine genius works in nature"; for the latter "the artistic idea — the *disegno interno* — is the manifestation of the divine in the artist's soul." Zuccari was "the first to ask explicitly whence art derives its inner substance of truth, whence comes the agreement between the forms of the mind and the forms of reality, if the 'idea' of art is not acquired from nature." The "true forms of things arise in the artist's soul as a result of his direct participation in the divine mind." (Hauser, *Social History*, p. 128.)

20. Hauser, *Social History*, Vol. 2, p. 171.

21. Hauser, *Social History*, Vol. 2, pp. 147–148. Hauser further noted the phenomenon of "conscious self-deception" in Cervantes's various allusions to the "fact that the world of his narrative is a fictitious one, the constant transgression of the frontiers dividing the reality immanent in the work and reality outside the work. . . . The grotesque and capricious style of the presentation, the arbitrary, formless and extravagant nature of the structure, is manneristic. . . ." Also characteristic of mannerism were the frequent introduction of "new episodes, commentaries and excursions,"

the "digressions and 'dissolves,'" the "mixture of the realistic and imaginative elements in the style," the incongruity between "the naturalism of the details and the unreality of the total conception. . . ." The "lack of uniformity in the execution, the mixture of virtuosity and delicacy with the negligence and crudity" belonged to mannerism. In uniting the "characteristics of the idealistic novel of chivalry and the vulgar picaresque novel" and in combining "dialogue based on everyday conversation . . . with the artificial rhythms and affected figures of speech of *conceptism*," Cervantes was again exhibiting the traits of the mannerist artist.

22. See John Shearman, *Mannerism: Style and Civilization* (Harmondsworth and Baltimore, 1967).

23. Sypher, pp. 6–19.

24. Blunt, pp. 1–2.

25. Curtius, p. 298, "a mental act which expresses the correspondence between two things."

26. Cf. Joseph Anthony Mazzeo, "A Critique of Some Modern Theories of Metaphysical Poetry," in *Seventeenth-Century English Poetry: Modern Essays in Criticism*, ed. William R. Keast, Revised Edition (London, Oxford, New York, 1971), pp. 77–88.

27. For criticism of the poetry of Góngora, see Jorge Guillén, *Language and Poetry: Some Poets of Spain* (Cambridge, Mass., 1961), pp. 27–75; Gerald Brenan, *The Literature of the Spanish People*, Second Edition (Cleveland and New York, 1957), pp. 222–274; *Poems of Góngora*, ed. R.O. Jones (Cambridge, 1966); Dámaso Alonso, *La Lengua poetica de Góngora*, Second Edition (Madrid, 1950); Dámaso, *Estudios y ensayos gongorinos* (Madrid, 1955).

28. See Robert L. Montgomery Jr., "Allegory and the Incredible Fable: The Italian View from Dante to Tasso," *PMLA*, Vol. 81 (1966), pp. 44–55; and John M. Steadman, "Allegory and Verisimilitude in *Paradise Lost*: The Problem of the 'Impossible Credible,'" *PMLA*, Vol. 78 (1963), pp. 36–39.

29. Friedlaender, Plate 15.

30. Cf. Curtius, pp. 247–272 on the classical, medieval and Renaissance canon of authors. Curtius observed (p. 264) that "at the height of French Classicism" (*circa* 1680), "the literary world still adhered to a canon of authors" (as examples of pure Latinity) "which on the whole coincides with that of Hugh of Trimberg (1280)."

31. In contrasting the "unambiguous, constructed space" of the "normative" and "classic" art of the High Renaissance, "in which equally unambiguous fixed figures move and act," with the "figures of the rhythmic anticlassical painter," Friedlaender observed that for the latter "the problem of three-dimensional space vanishes, or can do so. The volumes of the bodies more or less displace the space, that is, they themselves create the space." Even "where a strong effect of depth is desired or is inevitable, the space is not constructed in the Renaissance sense as a necessity for the bodies, but often is only an incongruous accompaniment for the bunches of figures, which one must read together 'by jumps' in order to reach the depth." In contrast to Quattrocento art (where the landscape exhibits "effects of depth" through perspective, while the bodies "often remain unreal and relatively flat") and High Renaissance painting (where the contradiction is "resolved in favor of a common harmony of figures and space"), the figures in "anticlassic Mannerism . . . remain plastic and have volume . . ., while space . . . is

not pushed to the point where it produces an effect of reality" (pp. 8–9). Nevertheless, in its "plastic, anatomical treatment of the body," and its "desire for a strongly tied composition," mannerism is "linked with the preceding Renaissance," in contrast to "the loosening of organization that occurs in the outspoken Baroque" (p. 11). Moreover, several of the characteristic features of mannerist style — "the elongation of the figures and distortions of proportions," the method of "narrowing the space and compressing the bodies," and the "emphasis" on "the anatomical at the expense of the normal and the proportional" — had already appeared in Michelangelo's late work (pp. 13–18). In Florentine mannerism particularly, Friedlaender perceived a triumph of the "art of inward and outward design" over the "spatial ideal of the Renaissance" (p. 10).

In his opinion, the manneristic technique of achieving a "certain effect of depth . . . through adding up layers of volumes . . ., along with an evasion of perspective," represented a special solution to a constant artistic problem — "the struggle between picture surface and presentation of depth in space. . . . A peculiarly unstable situation is created: the stress on the surfaces, on the picture planes, set behind each other in relief layers, does not permit any plastic or three-dimensional volumes of the bodies to come through in full force, while at the same time it hinders the three-dimensional bodies from giving any very flat impression" (pp. 8–9).

In Pontormo's late religious paintings (Figs. 5–7), Friedlaender recognized a "consciously retrospective" style, "anticlassical" and "rhythmical," conditioned by Gothic art and the designs of Dürer, and deliberately discarding the "formal achievements of Renaissance art in spatial organization and exact placement of figures" for the sake of greater spirituality (pp. 24–28). In Rosso Fiorentino's picture *Moses Defending the Daughters of Jethro* (Fig. 11), he emphasized the "unstable tension between the picture surface and the effect of depth" created by the succession of "parallel layers" moving with the surface of the painting. "Apart from the bodies, each of which builds its own spatial volume, there is no indication of depth through perspective," and the "extreme plasticity of the single figures" tends to be "absorbed into the two-dimensional quality of the picture surface. . . ." (pp. 32–33).

NOTES TO CHAPTER SIX

1. See Appendix B: Studies of the Baroque for recent discussion of the baroque in literature and art.

2. Donald Posner in Walter Friedlaender, *Mannerism and Anti-Mannerism in Italian Painting* (New York, 1965), pp. xi–xii.

3. Heinrich Wölfflin, *Renaissance and Baroque*, tr. Kathrin Simon (Ithaca, N.Y., 1964), pp. 15–17, 23, 73–74, 84–85.

4. Wölfflin reduced the development from the "classic" art of the High Renaissance to baroque representational forms to "five pairs of concepts": the development "from the linear to the painterly" and from "plane to recession," the development from "closed to open form" and from "multiplicity to unity," and the "absolute and relative clarity of the subject," pp. 14–15. These have become standard frames of reference for many literary

scholars. Nevertheless, despite attempts to correlate them with contemporary literary developments, their relevance for the history of literary styles has not been satisfactorily demonstrated. Although applicable in large part to a particular stage in the development of European art, they cannot be transferred to the prose and poetry of the period without introducing concepts alien to the literary criticism and theory of the sixteenth and seventeenth centuries. There would appear, however, to be several areas in which the application of these concepts to literature could be significant. The conflicting, though by no means contradictory, demands for unity and variety engaged literary theorists as well as critics of the visual arts during the Cinquecento and Seicento. Clarity and obscurity were traditional principles of literary style; the merits of the plain style and (conversely) the value of tropes (allegory, metaphor, irony, etc.), syntactical distortions, unusual words, and various figures of thought or speech often hinged on this antithesis. In the prose of this age, the contrast between loose syntax and tightly knit syntactical structure in the composition of periods and paragraphs is scarcely less pronounced than the opposition between closed and open form in pictorial composition. Though these parallels result primarily from technical problems intrinsic to each art, in at least a few instances they may reflect the influence of poetic theory on art theory or the joint legacy of rhetorical concepts inherited by both visual and verbal arts.

Commenting on the inherent weaknesses in Wölfflin's system, Meyer Schapiro noted that it was difficult to fit mannerism into this scheme. Moreover, Schapiro asserted, Wölfflin treated the preclassical art of the fifteenth century as an "immature, unintegrated style because of its inaptness for his terms." His assumption that the "classic phase" in art must necessarily lead to a baroque style is not true of all epochs, and it was a mystery "how this process could have been repeated after the seventeenth century in Europe . . ., since that required . . . a reverse development from the Baroque to the Neo-Classic." See Meyer Schapiro, "Style," *Anthropology Today*, ed. A.L. Kroeber (Chicago, 1953), p. 298. For a further critique of Wölfflin's views, see E.H. Gombrich, *Norm and Form: Studies in the Art of the Renaissance* (London, 1966), pp. 90–98.

5. Heinrich Wölfflin, *Principles of Art History*, tr. M.D. Hottinger (New York, 1950), pp. 9–10, 226–229, 237.

6. Wölfflin, *Principles*, pp. 18, 22, 27, 135, 198. Wölfflin's categories tend to reduce Renaissance and baroque styles to the categories of art favored or condemned by Plato, representative of reality and of mere appearance, the realm of being and the realm of becoming.

7. Wölfflin, *Principles*, pp. 10–13.

8. Benedetto Croce, *Storia della età barocca in Italia* (Bari, 1967), pp. 22–25, 33.

9. René Wellek, "The Concept of Baroque in Literary Scholarship," *JAAC*, Vol. 5 (1946), pp. 77–109.

10. Benedetto Croce, pp. 22–25, 33. For Croce, the baroque was "an esthetic sin, but also a universal and perpetual one like all human sins"; "a sort of artistic ugliness" responsive to the law "of desire, of convenience, of caprice, and therefore utilitarian or hedonistic. . . ."

11. Austin Warren, *Richard Crashaw, A Study in Baroque Sensibility* (University, Louisiana, 1939), pp. 63–76.

12. *Style, Rhetoric, and Rhythm: Essays by Morris W. Croll*, ed. J. Max Patrick et al. (Princeton, 1966), pp. 207–208, 221–229.

13. Erich Auerbach, *Mimesis: The Representation of Reality in Western Literature*, tr. Willard R. Trask (Garden City, N.Y., 1957), pp. 250–251. Taking this passage as a point of departure for discussing the method of the *Essays*, Auerbach reduced Montaigne's train of reasoning to syllogistic form: "I describe myself; I am a creature which constantly changes; ergo, the description too must conform to this and constantly change." The *Essays*, Auerbach noted, are "based on no artfully contrived plan and do not follow chronological order . . . Strictly speaking, it is 'things' after all which direct him," but he "follows his own inner rhythm, which, though constantly induced and maintained by things, is not bound to them, but freely skips from one thing to another." Even though the "form of the *Essays* stems from the collections of exempla, quotations and aphorisms" — a popular genre from antiquity through the Middle Ages and the Renaissance — Montaigne soon abandoned this pattern, retaining "the principle of clinging to concrete things," but maintaining his own "freedom not to tie himself to a fact-finding method or to the course of events in time"; Auerbach, pp. 252, 258.

14. Arnold Hauser, *Social History*, Vol. 2, pp. 180–182. Hauser maintains that "Even behind the calm of the Dutch painters of daily life one feels the impelling force of infinity, the constantly imperilled harmony of the finite."

15. Hauser, Vol. 2, pp. 174–180.

16. Hauser, Vol. 2, p. 182.

17. See the study by Franco Croce in Eric Cochrane (ed.), *The Late Italian Renaissance, 1525–1630* (New York and Evanston, 1970), pp. 377–400.

18. Roy Daniells, "English Baroque and Deliberate Obscurity," *JAAC*, Vol. 5 (1946), pp. 115–121.

19. Roy Daniells, "Baroque Form in English Literature," *UTQ*, Vol. 14 (1945), pp. 393–408. In a more extensive study *Milton, Mannerism and Baroque* (Toronto, 1963), Daniells recognized a heavy reliance on mannerist method in *Lycidas* (p. 49); in *Samson Agonistes*, *Paradise Lost* and *Paradise Regained*, on the other hand, he found cogent "reasons for regarding Milton as a great exponent of the Baroque style" (p. 219).

20. William Fleming, "The Element of Motion in Baroque Art and Music," *JAAC*, Vol. 5 (1946), pp. 121–128.

21. Wylie Sypher, *Four Stages of Renaissance Style*, pp. 180–185, 189, 216–227.

22. Frank J. Warnke, *European Metaphysical Poetry* (New Haven and London, 1961), pp. 2–4; Warnke, *Versions of Baroque* (New Haven and London, 1972); Harold B. Segel, *The Baroque Poem*, pp. 21–22. In Warnke's view, the mannerist currents in baroque literature could be observed in the writings of Donne, Herbert, Marvell, Quevedo, Huygens, Fleming and Jean de Sponde; the High Baroque was exemplified by Crashaw, Gryphius, Marino, Vondel, d'Aubigné and Góngora.

23. Segel, pp. 29–30, 62.

24. Segel, pp. 62–65.

25. Segel, pp. 97, 116.

26. Wolfgang Stechow, "Definitions of the Baroque in the Visual Arts," *JAAC*, Vol. 5 (1946), pp. 109–115.

27. R.A. Sayce, "The Use of the Term Baroque in French Literary History," *Comparative Literature*, Vol. 10 (1958), pp. 246–253. In an essay "Baroque and Mannerist Milton?" Rosemond Tuve emphasized the "intimate relation in literature between poetic subject and the decorum of the piece," censuring the neglect of this factor in attempts to differentiate specific writers and particular compositions as either "mannerist" or "baroque"; *Milton Studies in Honor of Harris Francis Fletcher* (Urbana, 1961), pp. 209–225. In *Baroque Lyric Poetry* (New Haven and London, 1961), pp. 3–17, 80–82, Lowry Nelson Jr. reexamined alternative theories of the baroque and concluded that no explanation seemed able to "take into account all phases of life during the period" and that no "characterization of style" seemed "adequate to all the arts."

28. René Wellek, "The Concept of Baroque in Literary Scholarship," *JAAC*, Vol. 5 (1946), pp. 77–109.

29. René Wellek, "Postscript 1962," in *Concepts of Criticism*, ed. Stephen G. Nichols Jr. (New Haven and London, 1963), pp. 115–127.

30. Wölfflin, *Principles*, pp. 23, 27.

31. Milton, *The Reason of Church Government*; see my *Epic and Tragic Structure in Paradise Lost* (Chicago and London, 1976), p. 16.

32. Wölfflin, *Principles*, p. 23.

33. Wölfflin, *Principles*, p. 126.

34. Wölfflin, *Principles*, p. 126.

NOTES TO CHAPTER SEVEN

1. See Helen Gardner, *The Metaphysical Poets*, Second Edition (London, 1967).

2. See Barbard K. Lewalski, *Protestant Poetics and the Seventeenth Century Religious Lyric* (Princeton, 1979), Louis L. Martz, *The Poetry of Meditation* (New Haven and London, 1954).

3. See Appendix C: Studies of the Metaphysical Style for discussion of Samuel Johnson's observations on metaphysical poetry.

4. Cf. Milton's judgment of scholastic learning, as harsh and rough, full of thorns and brambles, in his Prolusions; see John Milton, *Complete Poems and Major Prose*, ed. Merritt Y. Hughes (New York, 1957), p. 605, "Against Scholastic Philosophy." In *Ecclesiastes, or a Discourse Concerning the Gift of Preaching*, John Wilkins insisted that the style of preaching should be "plain and naturall, not being darkened with the affectation of Scholasticall harshnesse, or Rhetoricall flourishes." In his view, "Obscurity in the discourse" was "an argument of ignorance in the minde"; R.F. Jones, "Science and English Prose Style in the Third Quarter of the Seventeenth Century," in *Seventeenth-Century Prose: Modern Essays in Criticism* (New York, 1971), pp. 55–56. Seneca himself had disparaged *obscura brevitas*; George Williamson, "Senecan Style in the Seventeenth Century," in *Seventeenth Century Prose*, p. 127.

5. See H.J.C. Grierson, "Metaphysical Poetry" in *Seventeenth-Century English Poetry: Modern Essays in Criticism*, ed. William R. Keast, Revised Edition (London, Oxford, New York, 1961), pp. 3–5, 14.

6. See Frank Kermode (ed.), *The Metaphysical Poets: Key Essays on*

Metaphysical Poetry and the Major Metaphysical Poets (Greenwich, Conn., 1969), p. 97; Frank J. Warnke, *European Metaphysical Poetry* (New Haven and London, 1961).

7. On "strong lines," see George Williamson, "Strong Lines," *English Studies*, Vol. 18 (1936), pp. 152–159; see also Williamson, "Senecan Style in the Seventeenth Century," in *Seventeenth Century Prose*, p. 127, on the views of Robert South. In South's opinion, "Wit in divinity is nothing else, but sacred truths suitably expressed."

8. For wit in English religious prose during the seventeenth century, see R.F. Jones, *The Seventeenth Century*, pp. 137–138, on Glanvill's remarks concerning the use of wit in preaching. In Glanvill's opinion, "Wit in the understanding is a sagacity to find out the nature, relations and consequences of things: Wit in the imagination, is a quickness in the phancy to give things proper Images . . . .: and without Wit of these kinds, Preaching is dull and unedifying." Cf. Douglas Bush, *English Literature in the Earlier Seventeenth Century, 1600–1660* (Oxford, 1945), pp. 309–310, on the metaphysical style: "In prose as in verse wit involved not merely verbal tricks and surprises but the linking together of dissimilar objects, symbols, and ideas philosophized and fused by intellectual and spiritual perceptions and emotions, weighted by frequently abstruse or scientific learning, and made arresting by pointed expression. Along with the general and philosophic causes behind this mode of thought and feeling, there were the general stylistic influences represented by Euphuism and Senecanism and, for preachers, the example of some of the Fathers and their scholastic and schematic successors." For a fuller discussion of pulpit wit, see Horton Davies, *Like Angels from a Cloud: The English Metaphysical Preachers 1588–1645* (San Marino, 1986).

9. In *Posterior Analytics* (McKeon, p. 158), Aristotle defined quick wit as "a faculty of hitting upon the middle term instantaneously."

10. See Louis L. Martz, *The Wit of Love* (Notre Dame and London, 1969).

11. Though one would not include Chapman among the metaphysicals, he nevertheless offers a basis for comparison and contrast on both of these points. Though he does not, like Donne, treat love's mysteries or love's philosophy jocularly, Donne does not always do so himself, and may on occasion appear as serious as Chapman in his handling of this theme and in his exploitation of neo-Platonic philosophy.

12. *Seventeenth-Century Verse and Prose*, eds. Helen C. White, Ruth C. Wallerstein, Ricardo Quintana (New York, 1951), Vol. 1, pp. 423–425. A well-known variant of this line reads "a tall *Metaphor* in the *Oxford* way."

13. *The Poems of John Donne*, ed. H.J.C. Grierson (London, 1929), p. 134. Cf. J. Max Patrick et al. (eds.), *Style, Rhetoric, and Rhythm, Essays by Morris W. Croll* (Princeton, 1966), on the style of the Bartholists, legalists and antiquarians in France.

14. See Martz, *The Poetry of Meditation*; Lewalski, *Protestant Poetics and the Seventeenth Century Religious Lyric*; Frank J. Warnke, *European Metaphysical Poetry*; Walter J. Ong, S.J., "Wit and Mystery: A Revaluation in Mediaeval Latin Hymnody," *Speculum*, Vol. 22 (1947), pp. 310–341. Father Ong identifies wit poetry as "that poetry which characteristically employs conceit, that is, paradoxical or curious and striking comparison and analogy, and which favors the development of word-play."

15. Joseph Anthony Mazzeo, "A Critique of Some Modern Theories of

Metaphysical Poetry," *Modern Philology*, Vol. 50 (1952), pp. 88–96; Mazzeo, "A Seventeenth-Century Theory of Metaphysical Poetry," *Romanic Review*, Vol. 42 (1951), pp. 245–255; "Metaphysical Poetry and the Poetic of Correspondence," *Journal of the History of Ideas*, Vol. 14 (1953), pp. 221–234; Ruth Wallerstein, *Studies in Seventeenth Century Poetic* (Madison, Wisconsin, 1950); Martz, *The Wit of Love*.

16. Martz, *The Poetry of Meditation*.

17. See my *The Lamb and the Elephant: Ideal Imitation and the Context of Renaissance Allegory* (San Marino, California, 1974), pp. 144–145.

18. Rosemond Tuve, *Elizabethan and Metaphysical Imagery* (Chicago, 1946).

NOTES TO CHAPTER EIGHT

1. Among recent studies of metaphysical poetry and its relationships to mannerism and baroque, see Boris Ford (ed.), *From Donne to Marvell*, The Pelican Guide to English Literature, Vol. 3 (Harmondsworth, Middlesex and Baltimore, Maryland, 1970); Malcolm Bradbury and David Palmer (eds.), *Metaphysical Poetry* (Bloomington and London, 1971); Frank Kermode (ed.), *The Metaphysical Poets: Key Essays on Metaphysical Poetry and The Major Metaphysical Poets* (Greenwich, Conn., 1969); Earl Miner, *The Metaphysical Mode from Donne to Cowley* (Princeton, 1969); Louis L. Martz, *The Poetry of Meditation* (New Haven and London, 1954); Martz, *The Wit of Love: Donne, Carew, Crashaw, Marvell* (Notre Dame, 1969); Frank J. Warnke, *European Metaphysical Poetry* (New Haven and London, 1961); George Williamson, *Six Metaphysical Poets: A Reader's Guide* (New York, 1967); Lloyd E. Berry, *A Bibliography of Studies in Metaphysical Poetry, 1939–1960* (Madison, Wisconsin, 1964); H.B. Leishman, *The Metaphysical Poets* (Oxford, 1934); Helen Gardner, *The Metaphysical Poets* (Oxford, 1961); Joan Bennett, *Five Metaphysical Poets*, 3rd edition (Cambridge, 1964); Arno Esch, *Englische religiöse Lyrik des 17. Jahrhunderts* (Tübingen, 1955); Barbara K. Lewalski, *Protestant Poetics and the Seventeenth Century Religious Lyric* (Princeton, 1979); Joseph H. Summers, *The Heirs of Donne and Jonson* (London, 1970); Robert Ellrodt, *L'Inspiration personelle et l'esprit du temps chez les poètes metaphysiques anglais* (Paris, 1960); Alfred Alvarez, *The School of Donne* (New York, 1961); Geoffrey Walton, *Metaphysical to Augustan: Studies in Tone and Sensibility in the Seventeenth Century* (London, 1955); Joseph E. Duncan, *The Revival of Metaphysical Poetry: The History of A Style* (Minneapolis, 1959); Barbara K. Lewalski and Andrew J. Sabol (eds.), *Major Poets of the Earlier Seventeenth Century.* . . . (New York, 1973), pp. xix–xxxv; R.L. Sharp, *From Donne to Dryden: The Revolt against Metaphysical Poetry* (Chapel Hill, 1940); Helen C. White, *The Metaphysical Poets: A Study in Religious Experience* (New York, 1936); Stanley Stewart, *The Enclosed Garden: The Tradition and the Image in Seventeenth-Century Poetry* (Madison, Wisconsin, 1966).

2. Wölfflin justly observed that it was "a mistake for art history to work with the clumsy notion of the imitation of nature, as though it were merely a homogeneous process of increasing perfection." The "decisive point" in comparing landscapes of figures of different periods was "that

the conception in each case is based on a different visual schema — a schema which . . . is far more deeply rooted than in mere questions of the progress of imitation"; Heinrich Wölfflin, *Principles of Art History*, tr. M.D. Hottinger (New York, 1950), p. 13.

3. *The Works of Henry Vaughan*, ed. L.C. Martin, Second Edition (Oxford, 1957), p. 163. Literally translated, Cyprian's image reads: "We cleave to the cross, we suck blood, and we thrust our tongue into the very wounds of our Redeemer."

4. This term has frequently been transferred to "metaphysical" poetry from discussions of another and different facet of Secentismo: the emotional as well as the intellectual impact of the new cosmology on Pascal and his contemporaries. To associate the *frisson metaphysique* with "metaphysical" poetry is to depend too uncritically on the equivocal senses of a term notoriously fraught with ambiguities.

5. Rosemond Tuve, *Elizabethan and Metaphysical Imagery* (Chicago, 1947); Louis L. Martz, *The Poetry of Meditation* (New Haven and London, 1954); Alfred Alvarez, *The School of Donne* (New York, 1961); *Style, Rhetoric, and Rhythm: Essays by Morris W. Croll*, ed. J. Max Patrick et al. (Princeton, 1966); Joseph Anthony Mazzeo, *Renaissance and Seventeenth-Century Studies* (New York and London, 1964).

6. Cf. the variety of meanings attributed to the terms "classical" and "anticlassical" in the writings of Ernst Curtius, Heinrich Wölfflin and Sydney Joseph Freedberg. Though Carew praised Donne for banishing the classical divinities from his poetry — and William Drummond of Hawthornden deplored the efforts of his contemporaries to strip poetry of its customary ornaments — Donne exercised his talents in several of the same classical genres in which his "classical" contemporary Ben Jonson excelled. A later metaphysical, Abraham Cowley, endeavored to revive the Pindaric ode.

7. On this point see Erwin Panofsky, *Idea: A Concept in Art Theory*, tr. Joseph J.S. Peake (Columbia, S.C., 1968); D.W. Robertson Jr., *A Preface to Chaucer* (Princeton, 1962); John M. Steadman, *The Lamb and the Elephant: Ideal Imitation and the Context of Renaissance Allegory* (San Marino, 1974).

8. John Milton, *Complete Poems and Major Prose*, ed. Merritt Y. Hughes (New York, 1957), p. 670.

9. Hughes, *Complete Poems*, pp. 605–606, 632.

10. Allan H. Gilbert (ed.), *Literary Criticism, Plato to Dryden* (New York, 1940), p. 308.

11. Gilbert, p. 489.

12. Gilbert, p. 366.

NOTES TO AFTERWORD

1. Arnold Hauser, *Mannerism, The Crisis of the Renaissance and the Origin of Modern Art*, tr. Eric Mosbacher (New York, 1965), pp. 15, 111.

2. René Wellek, "The Concept of Baroque in Literary Scholarship," *JAAC*, Vol. 5 (1946), pp. 77–109; Lowry Nelson Jr., *Baroque Lyric Poetry* (New Haven and London, 1961), pp. 3–17, 80–82.

3. On this point, see Rensselaer Lee, *Ut Pictura Poesis: The Humanistic*

Theory of Painting (New York, 1967); Erwin Panofsky, *Idea: A Concept in Art Theory*, tr. Joseph J.S. Peake (Columbia, S.C., 1968); Roland Mushat Frye, *Milton's Imagery and the Visual Arts: Iconographic Tradition in the Epic Poems* (Princeton, 1978); John Doebler, *Shakespeare's Speaking Pictures: Studies in Iconographic Imagery* (Albuquerque, 1974); Doebler, "Bibliography for the Study of Iconography in Renaissance English Literature," *Research Opportunities in Renaissance Drama*, 22, 1971 (University of Kansas, 1980), pp. 45–55; E.H. Gombrich, "Icones Symbolicae: The Visual Image in Neo-Platonic Thought," *Journal of the Warburg and Courtauld Institutes*, Vol. 11 (1948), pp. 163–192; Peter M. Daly, "Trends and Problems in the Study of Emblematic Literature," *Mosaic*, Vol. 5, No. 4 (Summer, 1972), pp. 53–68; Henry Green, *Shakespeare and the Emblem Writers* (London, 1870); Arthur Henkel and Albrecht Schöne (eds.), *Emblemata, Handbuch zur Sinnbildkunst des XVI. und XVII. Jahrhunderts* (Stuttgart, 1967); and reviews by Henri Stegemeier, *JEGP*, Vol. 67 (1968), pp. 656–672, and by William S. Heckscher and Cameron F. Bunker, *RQ*, Vol. 23 (1970), pp. 59–80; Arthur H.R. Fairchild, *Shakespeare and the Arts of Design*, The University of Missouri Studies 12, No. 1 (Columbia, Mo., 1937); Arthur O. Lewis, Jr., *Emblem Books and English Drama: A Preliminary Survey, 1581–1600* (Pennsylvania State College diss., 1951); Dieter Mehl, *The Elizabethan Dumb Show, the History of a Dramatic Convention* (Cambridge, Mass., 1966); Roy Strong, *Festival Designs by Inigo Jones . . .* (International Exhibitions Foundation, 1967–68); Jean H. Hagstrum, *The Sister Arts: The Tradition of Literary Pictorialism and English Poetry from Dryden to Gray* (Chicago, 1958); Jane Aptekar, *Icons of Justice: Iconography and Thematic Imagery in Book V of "The Faerie Queene"* (New York, 1969); *Research Opportunities in Renaissance Drama*, 13–14, 1970–71, ed. S. Schoenbaum (Evanston, 1972); Peter Daly, *Literature in the Light of the Emblem* (Toronto, 1979).

4. In another context — the contrast between the "geometrism" of early Irish art and the naturalness of early Irish poetry — Arnold Hauser observed "that here, as so often, evolution does not run parallel in all the different forms of art, and that here too we have one of those historical periods the artistic manifestations of which cannot be reduced to the common denominator of a single style. The degree of naturalism in the different arts and genres of a period depends not only on the general cultural level of the period, not even if its sociological structure is uniform, but also on the nature, age, and special tradition of each individual art and genre. . . . Absolute parallelism of stylistic approach in the different arts and genres presupposes a level of development on which art no longer has to wrestle for the means of expression but is able, to a certain extent, to choose freely among the different possibilities of formal treatment." Arnold Hauser, *The Social History of Art*, tr. Stanley Godman, Vol. 1, *Renaissance, Mannerism, Baroque* (New York, 1951), pp. 144–146.

5. Wellek, "The Concept of Baroque in Literary Scholarship"; Rosemond Tuve, "Baroque and Mannerist Milton?" in *Milton Studies in Honor of Harris Francis Fletcher* (Urbana, 1961), pp. 209–225.

Index

About the Author

JOHN M. STEADMAN is senior research associate for The Huntington Library in San Marino, California. Dr. Steadman is also the author of *Milton's Biblical and Classical Imagery* (Duquesne University Press, 1984), *Epic and Tragic Structure in "Paradise Lost"* (University of Chicago Press, 1976) and *The Lamb and the Elephant: The Context of Renaissance Allegory* (Huntington Library, 1974).